MARKET SEGMENTATION

A step-by-step approach to creating profitable market segments

Malcolm McDonald
and
Ian Dunbar

Foreword by Sir Colin Marshall

MACMILLAN
Business

1140 0315

First published 1995 by
MACMILLAN PRESS LTD
Houndmills, Basingstoke, Hampshire RG21 2XS
and London
Companies and representatives
throughout the world

ISBN 0–333–63722–4 hardcover
ISBN 0–333–63723–2 paperback

A catalogue record for this book is available
from the British Library.

10   9   8   7   6   5   4   3   2   1
04   03   02   01   00   99   98   97   96   95

Learning Resources
Centre

Copy-edited and typeset by Povey–Edmondson
Okehampton and Rochdale, England

Printed in Great Britain by The Bath Press, Avon

Contents

List of Tables   ix

List of Figures   x

Foreword by Sir Colin Marshall   xv

Preface   xvii

1 **Preparing for Segmentation**   1
   Summary   1
   Defining Markets   1
   Segmentation Case Histories   4
   Objective of this Book   9
   Definition of Market Segmentation   10
   Segmentation Archetypes in Companies   11
   Segmentation Team   14
   Rules for Segmentation   15
   The Advantages of Segmentation   15
   The Segmentation Process   16
   Useful Definitions   17

PART I   THE SEGMENTATION PROCESS

2 **Market Mapping (Step 1)**   27
   Summary   27
   Constructing your Market Map   27
   Identifying the Junction(s) where Segmentation should occur (Market Leverage Points)   38

3 **Who Buys (Step 2)**   44
   Summary   44
   The Preliminary List of Who Buys   44
   Adding Further Profile Information to the List of Who Buys   48
   Standard Approaches to Business Market Segmentation   49
   Standard Approaches to Consumer Market Segmentation   54

4   **What, Where, When and How (Step 3)**   60
    Summary   60
    What is Bought   60
    Where it is Bought   62
    When it is Bought   63
    How it is Bought   63
    Reducing the Complexity of the 'What', 'Where', 'When' and 'How'
    Lists   63
    A Brief Comment about Price   65

5   **Who Buys What, Where, When and How (Step 4)**   66
    Summary   66
    Developing Micro-Segments in your Market   66
    Screening within a Preliminary Segment through Prioritising   69
    Screening across the Preliminary Segments by Eliminating Repeated
    Items   70
    Further Screening by Removing Superfluous Items   71
    Removing 'Unattractive' Micro-Segments   72
    Attaching Volumes or Values to each Micro-Segment   73
    Completing the Profile for each Micro-Segment   75

6   **Why is it Bought (Step 5)**   76
    Summary   76
    Understanding the Real Needs, the Real Benefits   76
    Attributes   85
    The Key CPIs   85
    Attaching the CPIs and their Values to the Micro-Segments   88
    Features, Advantages and Benefits   90

7   **Segmentation: Stage 1 (Step 6)**   94
    Summary   94
    Size and Number of Market Segments   94
    Clustering Micro-Segments into Market Segments   95
    Progressively Building your Market Segments (Option A)   96

8   **Segmentation: Stage 2 (Step 7)**   100
    Summary   100
    The Segmentation Checklist   100

9   **Segment Attractiveness (Steps 8–11)**   103
    Summary   103
    Portfolio Analysis   103
    Time Horizon   108
    Segmentation Team   108
    Definition   109

Segment Attractiveness Factors (Step 8)   109
Weighting the Factors (Step 9)   112
Defining the Parameters for each Attractiveness Factor (Step 10)   113
Scoring Segments (Step 11)   113
Plotting the Position of Segments on the Portfolio Matrix   114
When the Final Result is not what you Expected   118

10   **Company Competitiveness and the Portfolio Matrix (Step 12)   119**
Summary   119
Definition   119
Competitiveness Factors   119
Weighting the Factors   121
Scoring your Company and your Competitors   121
Producing the Portfolio Matrix   123
The DPM   125

11   **Setting Marketing Objectives and Strategies for Identified Segments   127**
Summary   127
Marketing Objectives: What they are and How they Relate to Corporate Objectives   127
How to set Marketing Objectives   130
Competitive Strategies   137
Where to Start (Gap Analysis)   145
Marketing Strategies   150

PART II   SEGMENTATION AND ORGANISATIONS

12   **Organisational Issues in Market Segmentation   157**
Summary   157
Segmentation as a Company Exercise   157
Successful Implementation of Segmented Marketing   167
The Human Face in Segmentation   170

PART III   THE EPILOGUE

13   **The Contribution of Segmentation to Business Planning: A Case Study of the Rise, Fall and Recovery of ICI Fertilizers   175**
Summary   175
Background   175
1917–87   177
1987–89   189
1990   200
And then . . .   210
Postscript   211

Appendix 1: Customer classification systems   212

    Social Grading   212
    Classification of Occupations   229
    Life Cycle (An Over-view)   231
    Registrar-General's Social Class   233

Appendix 2: Standard Industrial Classifications   235

    UK   235
    USA   250

Appendix 3: Postcode Areas of the United Kingdom   266

Index   268

List of Tables

1.1 Segments in the toothpaste market   7
2.1 Market map in tabular form   36
2.2 A completed market map for a UK manufacturing company   37
2.3 Brand specification by final users from the market map for a UK manufacturing company   42
5.1 A 'what, where, when and how' list for a preliminary segment   67
5.2 Scoring the purchase categories   70
5.3 Allocating volume (or value) in the 'who buys what' cascade   74
6.1 Determining the CPIs   86
6.2 Benefit analysis sheet   93
7.1 Age profiles of segments in a market   99
7.2 Segment demographics of the historical romance novel market   99
9.1 Porter's Five Forces model   110
9.2 Profit potential sub-factors in the pharmaceutical market   111
9.3 Weighting segment attractiveness factors   113
9.4 Parameters and their scores for the segment attractiveness factors   114
9.5 Segment attractiveness evaluation (for Year 0)   114
9.6 Segment attractiveness evaluation (for Year 3)   115
9.7 The range of weighted attractiveness scores in a market with nine segments   117
10.1 Weighting CSFs   121
10.2 Business strength evaluation   122
11.1 Other functional guidelines suggested by portfolio matrix analysis   139
13.1 A brief summary of the segments in the UK fertiliser market   193
13.2 ICIF's segment strategy, 1990–93   208

List of Figures

1.1   The relationship between market share and return on investment   1
1.2   The floor-covering market   3
1.3   Segmentation archetypes in companies   12
1.4   The process of segmentation   18
1.5   Prioritising and selecting segments   19
2.1   A simple market map   29
2.2   Market map with contractor   30
2.3   Market map with business purchasing procedures   31
2.4   Market map with volumes and/or values on each route   32
2.5   Market map with influencers   34
2.6   Market map with different company/customer types, their volumes and/
       or values, number of each type and your market share   35
2.7   Leverage points on a market map for two junctions   42
3.1   Developing preliminary segments in the company car market   45
5.1   Who buys what, where, when and how cascade   68
5.2   A simplified 'who buys what' cascade for a manufacturer   72
6.1   Needs gap analysis in the 1960s car market   79
6.2   Needs gap analysis in the photocopier market   79
6.3   Extracts of a 'needs cascade' for the 'relief of pain and
       inflammation'   81
6.4   A perceptual map of the soap market   82
6.5   Perceptual map of the tabloid newspaper market   83
7.1   A micro-segment clustering report   97
9.1   The Boston matrix   104
9.2   The nine-box portfolio matrix   106
9.3   The four-box matrix   107
9.4   DPM for a portfolio of segments   107
9.5   Measuring segment attractiveness   109
9.6   Plotting segments on the portfolio matrix according to their
       attractiveness   115
9.7   Re-plotting segments on the portfolio matrix according to their
       attractiveness at the end of the planning period   116
10.1   Plotting a relative competitive score of 0.86   123
10.2   Plotting business positions on the portfolio matrix for each segment
       according to their relative competitive strength   123
10.3   The initial segment portfolio matrix   124
10.4   The DPM   125
11.1   Objectives and strategies in a corporate framework   132

11.2   The Ansoff matrix   131
11.3   Product life cycles within segments   135
11.4   Strategies suggested by portfolio matrix analysis   138
11.5   The importance of market share   141
11.6   Supply and demand curves   142
11.7   Cost versus differentiation matrix   143
11.8   The impact on unit costs of the learning curve   143
11.9   Cost/benefit matrix   145
11.10 Gap analysis   146
11.11 Technological and segment newness   148
11.12 Profit/division profit improvement option   149
12.1   The influence of size and diversity on the need for formalisation in marketing   160
13.1   Annual use of NPK fertilisers in the UK   187
13.2   Segments in the UK fertiliser market   192
13.3   ICIF's segment portfolio matrix   194
13.4   The sales organisation   197
13.5   Structure of the commercial organisation   198
13.6   The fertiliser product portfolio of ICIF   202
13.7   Relationship between plant utilisation and net margins   204

Please note:

1

Successful segmentation is the
product of a detailed understanding
of your market and will therefore
take time

2

Segmentation is appropriate for
those markets where it is essential
to combine individual customers/
consumers together into larger
buying 'units' to ensure your
marketing activity is both cost
effective and manageable

▌Foreword

One of the abiding principles of sound business practice is: 'Know your customer; know your market.'

The objective, of course, is to gain competitive advantage by building sustained customer loyalty, with products and services meeting, quite precisely, the demands of closely-defined markets.

As consumer markets have become more complex, so has this essentially basic process of market segmentation. It is the view of many that, in both the manufacturing and service sectors, the art of defining target markets rarely progresses beyond the assembly of somewhat dull demographics. The logical conclusion is that, if everybody is doing the same, differential advantage is difficult to attain.

Now, Professor Malcolm McDonald and Ian Dunbar have peeled away the layers of complexity and confusion to produce a step-by-step guide through the difficult terrain of market segmentation. The value of their book to business people everywhere is that it offers the kind of practical applications needed in today's intensely-competitive marketplace.

SIR COLIN MARSHALL
Chairman, British Airways, and President,
Chartered Institute of Marketing

January 1995

▌ Preface

This book is the result of a painstaking process of research into the difficulties that organisations experience in segmenting their markets.

We discovered that most of the academic work in this domain is prescriptive, with virtually no practical guidelines provided to enable managers to make sense of the confusing array of data and information available to them.

So we developed a process, which we tested on some of the best known companies in the world, amending the process until it was sufficiently robust for us to be able to share it with a wider audience.

The result is a piece of software called *The Market Segment Master*, and this book. Both are self-standing. If, however, readers feel that they would like the help of information technology in segmenting their markets, they can obtain details from Professor Malcolm McDonald, at the Cranfield University School of Management, Cranfield, Bedford, MK43 0AL, United Kingdom (fax +44 (0)1234 751806).

Returning to this book, we would like to stress that it is most definitely a practical book which, if used properly, will result in actionable market segments. To achieve this result will require time and resources. It is not a book just for reading. It is for reading and *doing*, and is best used by a team, rather than by an individual.

We both wish you happy and profitable segmentation!

Cranfield University School of Management
January 1995

MALCOLM MCDONALD
IAN DUNBAR

CHAPTER 1
Preparing for Segmentation

■ Summary

In this chapter, we discuss how to arrive at a definition of the *market* to be segmented and look at some examples of successful segmentation. The chapter also discusses a framework for looking at how companies currently define and segment their markets before moving on to a definition of segmentation, some views on who should be in the segmentation team, the rules and advantages of segmentation, and then giving a summary of the segmentation process contained in this book. Some useful definitions conclude the chapter.

■ Defining Markets

Market segmentation is easy to understand once an organisation has done it successfully! Examples such as BMW, Castrol GTX, Marks & Spencer and Mars are legendary in the history of marketing. *The problem is how to get there!*

Most business people already understand that there is a direct relationship between relatively high share of any market and high returns on investment, as shown in Figure 1.1.

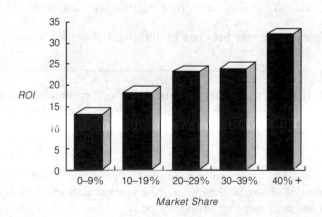

Figure 1.1 The relationship between market share and return on investment (ROI)

Source: PIMS database.

1

Clearly, however, since BMW are not in the same market as Ford, it is important to be most careful about how 'market' is defined. Correct 'market' definition is crucial for: measuring 'market' share and 'market' growth; the specification of target customers; re-confirmation of relevant competitors; and, most important of all, the formulation of marketing strategy, for it is this, above all else, that delivers differential advantage.

The general rule for 'market' definition is that it is the aggregation of all the products that appear to *satisfy the same need*. For example, we would regard the in-company caterer as only one option when it came to satisfying lunch-time hunger. This particular need could also be satisfied at external restaurants, public houses, fast food specialists and sandwich bars. The emphasis in the definition, therefore, is clearly on the word 'need'.

Aggregating currently available products/services is, however, simply an aid to arriving at the definition, as it is important we recognise that new products, yet to be developed, could better satisfy the users' need. For example, the button manufacturer which believed its 'market' was the 'button market' would have been very disappointed when zips and Velcro began to satisfy the need for fastenings! A needs-based definition for such a company would have enabled the management to recognise the fickleness of current products, and to accept that one of their principal tasks is to seek out better ways of satisfying their market's needs and to evolve their product offer accordingly. The founder of Revlon, Charles Revlon, is credited with one of the more famous needs-based definitions of a market. When he drew the distinction between products and needs for his company, he captured it by describing the factory as being the place where the company made chemicals, 'but in the store' he sold 'hope'.

In this book, we call 'market' definition market segmentation.

The following example may help you in defining the market your business is in:

Defining a market

A company manufacturing nylon carpet for the commercial sector wanted to check that it had a realistic definition of the 'market' it was in. The first step was to map out the total available market for all floor covering. This is summarised in Figure 1.2.

Clearly, it would be wrong to include the three types of floor covering used in the industrial sector in the company's market definition. The qualities required from such flooring cannot hope to be matched in a carpet made from any currently known type of fibre. Similarly, in both the commercial and domestic sectors, nylon carpet is not a competitor for the luxury end of the market. This luxury part of the market buys carpet made from natural fibres, particularly wool.

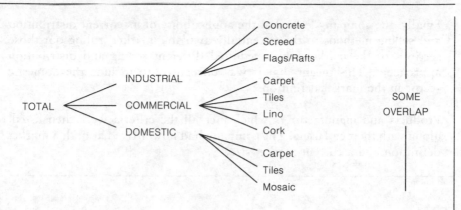

Figure 1.2   The floor-covering market

This leaves the non-luxury commercial and domestic sectors which, in total, represented the company's potential available market. It was potentially available because the company could, for example, produce nylon carpet for the domestic sector and extend its market this way. Similarly, the company could move into manufacturing nylon carpet tiles and extend its operation into this product for both the domestic and commercial sectors. There was also no reason why the company should not look at replacing lino, cork or mosaic flooring with nylon carpet.

Many of the opportunities in the potentially available market, however, represent possible strategies for the future. They would be considered during the marketing planning process when the future plans for the current business activity did not achieve the required financial targets. (See M. H. B. McDonald, *Marketing Plans – How to Prepare Them: How to Use Them*, 3rd edn (Oxford: Heinemann, 1995), Chapter 6, particularly 'Gap Analysis' and the 'Ansoff Matrix'.) The question now, therefore, is, what is the company's realistically available market?

To assist the company in this final stage of arriving at a market definition, the 'needs' being met by the current products, as highlighted by the current customers, were first listed. This revealed that the company's nylon carpet was bought because:

- It fell into a particular price range
- It was quiet underfoot
- It had a life expectancy of 15 years
- It was available in pleasant colours and textures
- The manufacturing plant was within a 60-mile radius

In addition to the obvious, this list removed lino, cork and mosaic from the company's available market.

Finally, the company looked at the applicability of its current distribution and selling methods to the potentially available market, ruling out those sections of the market which required different selling and distribution approaches. This meant that it was unrealistic to include the domestic sector in the market definition.

Products and manufacturers which met all the criteria were then listed, along with their end users. The company had now arrived at both a market definition and a current market size.

This example also illustrates the need to arrive at a meaningful balance between a broad market definition and a manageable market definition. Too narrow a definition has the pitfall of restricting the range of new opportunities segmentation could open up for your business. On the other hand, too broad a definition may overwhelm the segmentation exercise. For example, the television broadcasting companies are in the 'entertainment' market, which also consists of theatres, cinemas and theme parks, to name but a few. This is a fairly broad definition. It may, therefore, be more manageable for the television broadcasters, when looking at segmenting their market, to define their market as being the 'home entertainment' market. This could then be further refined into the pre-school, child, teenager, family, or adult home entertainment market. Similarly, companies supplying, for example, industrial lubricants may find segmentation more manageable if their market is defined in terms of the particular application of the product, such as heavy industrial use or precision engineering.

■ Segmentation Case Histories

This chapter continues with three case histories to illustrate how superior profitability results from successful market segmentation. The book itself goes on to take you through a logical process which will enable you to create differential advantage from market segmentation.

Case 1: A national off-licence chain

In the mid-1980s, a national off-licence chain, with retail units in major shopping centres and local shopping parades, was experiencing both a decline in customer numbers and a decline in average spend. The original formula for success of design, product range and merchandising, meticulously copied in each outlet, no longer appeared to be working.

The chain had become a classic example of a business comfortably positioned in the middle ground, attempting to be all things to all men, but managing to satisfy very few of them.

Rather than sit back in the belief that the business was just passing through a difficult patch, and what worked yesterday was bound to work again, the company embarked on a project designed to understand both their actual and potential customer base.

The first stage of this study turned to one of the more sophisticated geodemographic packages (CCN's MOSAIC) in order to understand the residential profiles of each shop's catchment area. Not unexpectedly, many geodemographic differences were found, and the business quickly accepted that it was unlikely the same retail formula would appeal to the different target markets found in them.

Rather than look at each shop separately, the catchment area profiles for each shop were subject to a clustering routine in order to place similar catchment areas together. This resulted in 21 different groupings, each of which were then profiled in terms of their potential to buy different off-licence products, using purchasing data from national surveys. (The company's own in-house retailing data would, of course, only reflect the purchasing pattern of their existing customers, or, at worst, only a proportion of their requirements if this was limited by the company's current product range.)

However, stocking the requisite range of products in their correct geographical location would not necessarily attract their respective target markets. The chain was already associated with one type of offer which, in addition to including a particular range of drinks, also included the basic design of the shops and overall merchandising.

The project, therefore, moved into a second stage, in which the market's attitudes and motivations to drinking were explored and relative values attached to the various dimensions uncovered. This was achieved through an independently commissioned piece of market research and resulted in the market being categorised into a number of psychographic groups. This included, amongst others, 'happy and impulsive' shoppers, 'anxious and muddled' shoppers, 'reluctant but organised' shoppers, and 'disorganised, extravagant' shoppers.

By ensuring this stage of the project linked the attitude and motivational findings to demographic data, the two stages could be brought together. This enabled the original 21 clusters to be reduced to five distinct segments, each of which required a different offer.

The company now had to decide between two strategies:

(a) to focus into one segment using one brand and re-locate its retail outlets accordingly through a closure and opening programme; or,

(b) to develop a manageable portfolio of retailing brands, leave the estate relatively intact, and re-brand, re-fit and re-stock as necessary.

They decided to pursue the second.

Realising that demographic profiles in geographic areas can change over time, and that customer needs and attitudes can also evolve, the company now monitors its market quite carefully and is quite prepared to modify its brand portfolio to suit changing circumstances. For the time being, however, the five retail brands of 'Bottoms Up', 'Wine Rack', 'Threshers Wine Shop', 'Drinks Store from Threshers' and 'Food and Drinks Store' sit comfortably within the five segments. They also sit comfortably together in the same shopping centre, enabling the group to meet effectively the different requirements of the segments found within that centre's catchment area.

Perhaps more importantly, this strategy sits comfortably alongside the financial targets for the business.

Source: J. Thornton, 'Market segmentation from Bottoms Up', *Research Plus – The magazine of the Market Research Society* (December 1993).

Case 2: Sodium tri-poly phosphate!

Sodium Tri-Poly Phosphate (STPP) was once a simple, unexciting, white chemical cleaning agent. Today, one of its uses is as the major ingredient of a sophisticated and profitable operation, appearing under many different brand names, all competing for a share of what has become a cleverly segmented market.

Ever wondered how the toothpaste marketers classify you in their segmentation of the market? Table 1.1, based on R. Haley's 'Benefit Segmentation: a decision-oriented research tool', *Journal of Marketing*, vol. 32 (July 1968), which presents the main segments, may assist you.

Table 1.1 Segments in the toothpaste market

	Worrier	Sociable	Sensory	Independent
Who buys				
Socio-economic	C1 C2	B C1 C2	C1 C2 D	A B
Demographics	Large families 25–40	Teens Young Smokers	Children	Males 35–50
Psy-chographics	conservative: hypochondriosis	high sociability: active	high self-involvement hedonists	high autonomy: value-oriented
What is bought				
% of total market	50%	30%	15%	5%
Product examples	Crest	McLeans Ultra Bright	Colgate (stripe)	Own label
Product physics	large canisters	large tubes	medium tubes	small tubes
Price paid	low	high	medium	low
Outlet	supermarket	supermarket	supermarket	independent
Purchase frequency	weekly	monthly	monthly	quarterly
Why				
Benefits sought	stop decay	attract attention	flavour	price
Potential for growth	nil	high	medium	nil

Case 3: Amber nectar

A privately owned brewery in the UK was enjoying exceptional profitability for its industrial sector. In terms of output, it was by no means the largest brewery in the UK, and in terms of geographic cover, it only operated within a particular metropolitan area.

At one of the regular meetings of the Board, it was agreed that the company had clearly developed a very successful range of beers and it was time to expand into new geographic areas.

The expansion programme met with aggressive opposition from other brewers, particularly the very large brewers. This came as no great surprise to the Board who, before setting on the expansion path, had built up a large 'war chest', largely made up of past profits, to finance the plan. The Board knew the competition would react in this way, because they were being challenged by a very successful range of beers, a 'success' that would ensure product trial, then customer loyalty, in the new areas.

As with all good marketing-focused companies, the progress of the marketing plan was regularly monitored against its target by a specially appointed Task Force headed by the Chief Executive. In addition, the Sales and Marketing Director, a key member of the Task Force, held regular meetings with his own key staff to ensure continuous evaluation of the sales and marketing strategies being followed.

The plan badly under-performed and was eventually abandoned.

In the post-mortem that followed, the brewery discovered why it had been so successful in the past, and why this success could not be extended to other areas of the UK. To its loyal customers, a key attraction of the beers manufactured by this brewery was the 'local' flavour. The 'market' for this company was the metropolitan area it already operated in, its competitors being other local brewers in the same area. Exporting this success was clearly, therefore, not going to work. Expansion could only be achieved by setting up new local breweries in other areas, or by acquiring already established local breweries.

Without this brewery realising it, the UK beer drinking market had already segmented itself. This brewer's segment was the 'Regional Chauvinist', and in the particular region where it operated, the company already had an overwhelming market share: hence its profitability.

With an earlier understanding of this segmentation structure, the company would have spent its war chest more effectively and achieved its growth objectives.

■ **Case History Conclusion**

These three case histories illustrate the importance of intelligent segmentation in guiding companies towards successful marketing strategies. However, it is easy to understand this success *after* the event, as occurred in one of the cases! The problem, for most of us, is how to arrive at a definition of 'market' (market segmentation) that will enable us to create differential advantage. That is the purpose of this book.

■ **Objective of this Book**

Market segmentation seems comparatively simple as a concept, yet it is a fact that, particularly in business-to-business marketing, as opposed to consumer goods marketing, companies still organise their marketing effort principally around the *products* they make, thereby missing many opportunities for creating competitive advantage. The reason is that segmentation is viewed as being extremely difficult to implement in practice, requiring, as it does, a *market-based* approach.

The problem with segmenting markets according only to the products offered, or the technology type, is that, in most markets, many *different* types of customers buy or use the same products. These different customer types, therefore, often get subsumed under one category. For example, if a mail company organises itself around express packages, or around mail sorting, it is unlikely that the company will ever get to understand fully the real and different needs of, say, universities, banks, advertising agencies, direct mail houses, manufacturing companies, retailers and so on.

However, before jumping to any early segmentation conclusions, reorganising your marketing effort along business classification lines is not necessarily the most creative segmentation structure for your market. The business classification approach could well be ignoring one or more of the following:

- Different divisions exist behind the business descriptor and these may have different applications for the product/service you supply. For example, does the Advertising and Promotions Department have the same requirements and specifications for mail services as the Sales Ledger Department?

- The requirements of, say, Advertising and Promotions Departments may well be the same regardless of business type.

- Even within a single division of a company, there may well be different applications for the product/service you supply which, in turn, may have different specifications attached to them. This could be associated with differences amongst their own customer base. For example, a decorating contractor buying gloss paint could vary its buying criteria according to:

- whether it is to be applied to the external or internal woodwork, to a public or private room; and/or,

- the different requirements expressed by their own customers.

- Segmentation along business classification lines assumes all the companies within the classification employ identical people with identical values. Businesses don't buy anything; it's their employees you have to sell to!

The objective of this book is to provide a logical process by which managers can explore whether there is any potential for new business opportunities as a result of re-examining the way in which they define their market segments. It then moves on to identifying the appropriate objectives and strategies for these segments and how segmentation fits into the marketing plan.

No computer program, let alone a book, however advanced, could ever cover all possible market segmentation outcomes. This particular book does not claim to provide the definitive answer to any organisation's segmentation problems. What it will do is to provide a logical process for you to follow. Above all else, however, it requires you to be creative and flexible in your thinking and asks you not to be hidebound by your current market segmentation definitions.

■ Definition of Market Segmentation

Not all customers have the same requirements and a marketing strategy which does not recognise this fact will result in a scatter-gun approach and dilute the marketing effort.

Market segmentation is the process of splitting customers into different groups, or segments, within which customers with similar characteristics have similar needs. By doing this, each one can be targeted and reached with a distinct marketing mix.

Segmentation is a creative and iterative process, the purpose of which is to satisfy customer needs more closely and, in so doing, create competitive advantage for the company. It is defined by the *customers'* needs, not the company's, and should be re-visited periodically.

The process of segmentation also helps identify new opportunities, for both products and markets.

Segmentation is the basic building block for effective marketing planning, and should reflect a market/customer-orientation rather than a product-orientation.

Most organisations will need to use more than one level of segmentation criteria to identify the customer types and to categorise their specific needs. Organisations are also likely to find that the process of segmentation needs to be carried out at more than one stage in the overall distribution chain, different stages having distinct customer types with their own specific needs.

Attractive market segments will be those that are growing and profitable, in which companies can effectively meet their customers' needs of today, or for which companies can develop their products/services to meet the needs of tomorrow.

Following the selection of market segments to be targeted, companies can then develop focused marketing strategies. This planned approach to meeting the needs of the customers helps companies to be proactive instead of reactive, enabling them to take advantage of market opportunities and gain competitive advantage.

It should be noted, however, that, whilst the segmentation process itself is externally focused in its consideration of the market 'out there', companies looking to 'meet their customer's needs effectively', should also consider how the company's own departments and staff relate to the chosen target segments. For example, when a customer from a particular segment contacts your company in the course of doing business with you, it could well negate the company's segmented approach in its external marketing activity if, in dealing with this customer's requirements, the applicable internal department subsumes the customer under one all-embracing procedure, and fails to match up to the external activity.

■ Segmentation Archetypes in Companies

The 'internal' and 'external' matching required for effective segmentation provides a convenient framework for looking at how companies currently define and segment their markets.

At one extreme is the company whose marketing activity is purely customer driven, but which takes no explicit account of the company's capabilities or structure. In such situations, the company will fail to deliver at the level of expectation engineered by their marketing department. At the other extreme is the company which bases segmentation on its own capabilities or structure, regardless of customer needs. With such an approach, the company may be unable to recognise changes in the market place, which, in turn, may undermine its entire marketing strategy.

These observations have been summarised in the form of a matrix by M. Jenkins and M. H. B. McDonald in their paper, 'Defining and Segmenting Markets: Archetypes and Research Agendas' (Cranfield University School of Management, 1994), as shown in Figure 1.3.

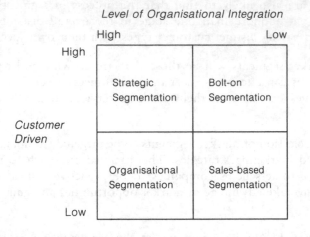

Figure 1.3   Segmentation archetypes in companies

■ Sales-Based Segmentation

This type of organisation would not recognise itself as having any form of market segmentation but, in terms of the fact that the organisation differentiates the way it deals with different customer groups, this is an implicit form of market segmentation.

The sales-based segmenter may have segments which are based on customer size (for example, national and local accounts) or particular territories. These are limited to the sales operation as opposed to providing a basis for the way in which the company interfaces with these customers as a whole. The segments are therefore determined by a historical structure of this particular function and are not reflected in the way the rest of the organisation sees the market place and the way in which strategies are developed.

Examples of this approach can be found in many of the world's airlines, who still look at their markets solely in terms of geographic territories.

■ Organisational Segmentation

Here, the organisational structure defines the segmentation approach. This may be through particular product divisions (for example, cars or trucks) or particular territory splits which are based around manufacturing capabilities. This form of segmentation underlies the organisational culture, with employees and structures being clearly differentiated by their allegiance to particular components of the organisation.

Effectively the marketing *effort* is segmented as these separate components of the organisation have their own marketing resources. Customers, however, may find themselves having to deal with separate parts of the organisation, each operating their own quite different marketing strategies. Divisionalisation based on product groups can be found, for example, in many chemical companies.

■ Bolt-On Segmentation

This archetype can often be found in companies which have recently 'discovered' marketing. The marketing activity is often quite sophisticated, with segments developed from both quantitative and qualitative data and often described in psychographic terms. The important aspect of this type of segmentation is that it exists exclusively within the marketing function. It is applied at an operational level for advertising campaigns and direct mail programmes. The segments are not, therefore, understood or applied in the many customer-facing activities of the business.

In this context, segmentation is a particular tool for applying marketing programmes. The segments developed are often task-specific and variable across differing projects and over time. As a consequence, this form of segmentation is unlikely to play a major role in product or market development at the strategic level.

Financial institutions in the UK have certainly demonstrated this characteristic. Many of them recruited external marketing professionals into their organisations when 'marketing' was seen as the activity to be pursuing at the time of liberalisation. Unfortunately, the customer-focused endeavours of the new marketing departments were all too often thwarted by the insistence of the banks that their branches didn't open their doors at times suited to the needs of their customers, or staff their branches during peak demand (because their staff needed to take lunch breaks as well).

■ Strategic Segmentation

In these companies, customer-driven segments permeate the entire organisation, both in its external marketing activity and in its internal structure. Resources are allocated on the basis of the segments, and strategies are based around these groupings.

Many multi-brand high street retailers operate their brands as different businesses, with not only distinct retail units but also with separate buying departments and administrative support. Such complete splits are not, however, essential for the successful delivery of strategic segmentation. For example, in-company training programmes are clearly distinguished from public programmes and extended courses at Cranfield University School of Management, but they are generally delivered and managed by the same teaching and administrative staff.

■ Segmentation Team

Before embarking on a segmentation project, a key question to answer concerns who should be involved in the segmentation team.

Whilst it is not unusual for short-term sales and profit pressures to prevent the allocation of time and resources to carry out market segmentation, it should be the primary responsibility of the general manager to ensure that it is done.

Ideally, a mixed team of representatives from the main functions of the company is required, because segmentation is central to corporate strategy and affects all areas of the business, and because each function has different contributions to make to the process. Within the team, a core group consisting of two to three individuals should be established. The function of this core group is to carry out all the detailed work required in the segmentation process, the core group reporting back to the full team for consultation, comment and guidance.

In some circumstances, there should also be an outsider, who knows nothing about the products and markets, to act as a facilitator for the process and to offer an objective and alternative viewpoint to the discussion. Team members from the functional disciplines should have had customer contact and have a good knowledge of the products, markets, customers and the company.

Sales and financial data and market research findings should also be accessible in order to provide extra information to help the decision making process.

Segmentation can be carried out at all levels of the organisation. Strategically, there needs to be a corporate segmentation which will fit within, or help companies develop, their mission statement. At lower levels within the organisation, there will be segmentation within the strategic business units (SBUs), and, finally, segmentation at a lower level, such as at customer group, product, or at geographic level. This book principally concerns segmentation at SBU and lower levels.

Segmentation is also a subject that should be periodically re-visited, as markets are dynamic, and changes in the macro-economy and the markets can alter the attractiveness of different market segments, especially in fast-changing markets. Also, there are benefits in being creative and innovative and developing new alternative approaches in order to gain competitive advantage.

As your selected team progresses through the process, you will need to answer the following questions:

- How should you segment the market?
- How detailed should your segmentation be?
- How do you define segments in the best possible way?
- Which segments are the most attractive?

■ Rules for Segmentation

The criteria used for segmentation must have the following characteristics:

(a) the ability to distinguish between segments, such that each segment has a unique set of common characteristics and can be served by an equally unique marketing strategy;

(b) each identified segment should have sufficient potential size to justify the time and effort involved in planning specifically for this business opportunity;

(c) each identified segment should be capable of being described or measured by a set of descriptors, such that the customers in that segment can be communicated with by means of a distinctive promotion, selling and advertising strategy;

(d) each identified segment should have relevance to its purchase situation (in other words it is a decision-making factor or affects the process of buying behaviour);

(e) Your company must be capable of making the necessary changes to its structure, information and decision-making systems so that they become focused on to the new segments.

■ The Advantages of Segmentation

These can be summarised as follows.

- Recognising customers' differences is the key to successful marketing, as it can lead to a closer matching of customers' needs with the company's products or services.

- Segmentation can lead to <u>niche marketing</u>, where appropriate, where the company can meet most or all of the needs of customers in that niche segment. This can result in segment dominance, something which is often not possible in the total market.

- Segmentation can lead to concentration of resources in markets where competitive advantage is greatest and returns are high.

- Segmentation can be used to gain competitive advantage by considering the market in different ways from your competitors.

- By means of segmentation, you can <u>market your company</u> as a <u>specialist</u> in your chosen market segments, with a better understanding of customers' needs, thus giving your products/services advantages over competitors' products.

The additional benefits of the approach to segmentation outlined in this book are:

- It checks your logic and your basic assumptions about your market.

- It helps with your team-building approach.

- It goes across vertical structures, often uncovering hitherto undiscovered customer needs.

■ The Segmentation Process

The first part of the process, which covers the essential steps you should follow to develop a segmented structure for your market, contains seven steps, and is applied to the *whole* market your business is operating in, not just to that bit of the market you are currently successful in. *It therefore looks at your competitor's products and/or services as well as your own.* A clear definition of your market is, therefore, essential. A guide for arriving at that definition was provided earlier in this chapter, namely, the aggregation of all the products that appear to *satisfy the same need*.

The first step, drawing a market map, requires you to present the market you are operating in as a diagram. It's rather like a flow chart along which your products flow to the final user and their cash flows back to you, the supplier. For many businesses, however, a flow chart simply tracking the physical delivery of their products/services is inadequate in covering the role played by 'influencers' on the purchase decision, and/or the purchase decision routines encountered by their business. The market map, in truth, is probably better described as an obstacle course.

Once the market map is complete, you are then required to determine at which stage(s) along the map segmentation should occur. The next three steps progressively enable you to look at any stage of this flow chart and to draw a two-dimensional picture illustrating who buys what, where, when and how.

Step 5 moves on from the mechanistic look at the market covered in the previous four steps to looking at the reasons why the various products are bought. These are then listed for each cell in the 'who buys what, where, when and how' cascade.

Step 6 then describes a technique of grouping these cells together in order to obtain the best fit. Options are also suggested in Step 6 which describe how you can group these cells in a number of alternative ways: by a selection of standard profiling descriptions, such as demographic, geographic and psychographic; attitudes; buying criteria; or any combination of these, in order to find if better 'fits' can be achieved.

The final step then subjects each 'cluster' to a segmentation test.

The process is primarily in a format designed to utilise information already held by your company. As you progress through the various steps, the process may, however, reveal information shortfalls which you will need to address. In many instances, the most appropriate method of addressing these shortfalls will be by commissioning market research. Guidelines on how to incorporate market research findings can be found in the text.

Diagrammatically, the first part of the process can be summarised as shown in Figure 1.4.

The second part of the process then looks at how to select those segments your business should be operating in and consists of a further five steps. These are summarised in Figure 1.5.

■ Useful Definitions

ACORN
: A Classification Of Residential Neighbourhoods (ACORN) according to a selection of factors such as home ownership, car ownership, health, employment, ethnicity and lifestyle to produce a picture of consumer status.

Benefit
: A perceived or stated relationship between a product feature and the need the feature is designed to satisfy. *See also* Differential advantage *and* Feature.

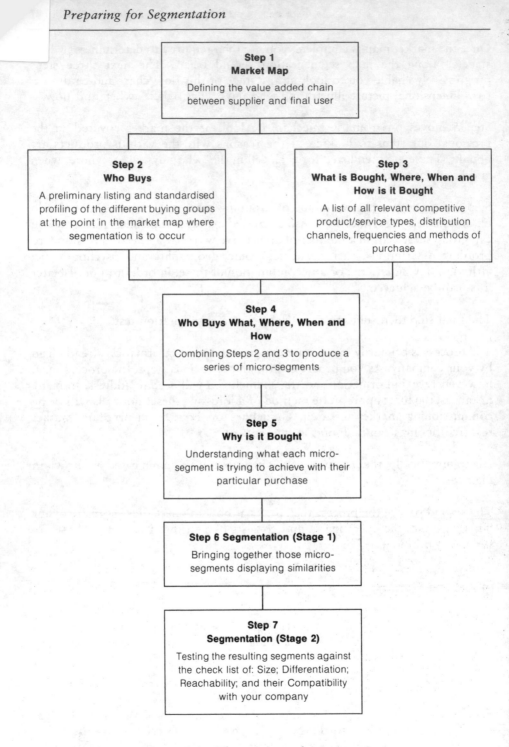

Step 1
Market Map

Defining the value added chain
between supplier and final user

Step 2
Who Buys

A preliminary listing and standardised
profiling of the different buying groups
at the point in the market map where
segmentation is to occur

Step 3
**What is Bought, Where, When and
How is it Bought**

A list of all relevant competitive
product/service types, distribution
channels, frequencies and methods of
purchase

Step 4
**Who Buys What, Where, When and
How**

Combining Steps 2 and 3 to produce a
series of micro-segments

Step 5
Why is it Bought

Understanding what each micro-
segment is trying to achieve with their
particular purchase

Step 6 Segmentation (Stage 1)

Bringing together those micro-
segments displaying similarities

Step 7
Segmentation (Stage 2)

Testing the resulting segments against
the check list of: Size; Differentiation;
Reachability; and their Compatibility
with your company

Figure 1.4 The process of segmentation

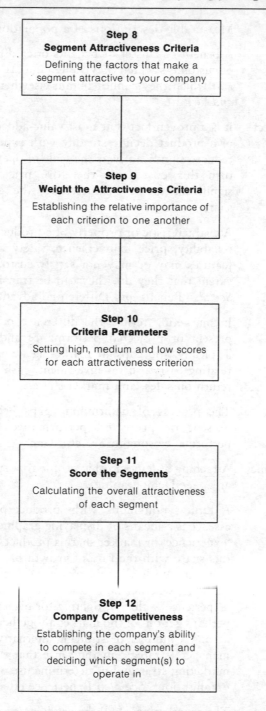

Figure 1.5   Prioritising and selecting segments

Demographics	Measurable descriptions of a population.
Differential advantage	A benefit or cluster of benefits offered to a sizeable group of customers which they value (and are willing to pay for) and which they cannot obtain elsewhere. *See also* Benefit *and* Feature.
Experience effect	It is a proven fact that most value-added cost components of a product decline steadily with experience and can be reduced significantly as the scale of operation increases. In turn this cost (and therefore price advantage) is a significant factor in increasing the company's market share.
Feature	A characteristic or property of a product or service such as reliability, price, convenience, safety and quality. These features may or may not satisfy customer needs. To the extent that they do, they can be translated into benefits. *See also* Benefit *and* Differential advantage.
Gap	In marketing terms, the difference between a product's present or projected performance and the level sought. Typically, the gaps in marketing management are those relating to return on investment, cash generation or use, return on sales, and market share.
Gap analysis	The process of determining gaps between a product's present or projected performance and the level of performance sought. *See also* Gap.
Geodemographics	Attaching a demographic profile to a specified geographic area. *See* Demographics.
Growth/share matrix	A term synonymous with 'product portfolio' which in essence is a means of displaying graphically the amount of 'experience' or market share a product has and comparing this share with the rate of growth of the relevant market segment. With the matrix, a manager can decide, for example, whether he or she should invest in getting more 'experience' – that is, fighting for bigger market share – or perhaps get out of the market altogether. These choices are among a number of strategic alternatives available to the manager (strategic in the sense that they not only affect marketing strategy but determine use of capital within the organisation). *See also* Experience effect.
Market	The aggregation of all the products/services that appear to satisfy the same need.

Marketing audit	A situational analysis of the company's current marketing capability. *See also* Situational analysis.
Marketing mix	The 'tools' or means available to an organisation to improve the match between benefits sought by customers and those offered by the organisation so as to obtain a differential advantage. Among these tools are product, price, promotion and distribution service. *See also* Differential advantage.
Marketing objectives	A statement of the targets or goals to be pursued and achieved within the period covered in the marketing plan. Depending on the scope and orientation of the plan – whether, for example, the plan is designed primarily to spell out short-term marketing intentions or to identify broad business directions and needs – the objectives stated may encompass such important measures of business performance as profit, growth and market share.
	Marketing objectives with respect to profit, market share, sales volume, market development or penetration and other broader considerations are sometimes referred to as 'primary' marketing objectives. More commonly, they are referred to as 'strategic' or 'business' objectives since they pertain to the operation of the business as a whole. In turn, objectives set for specific marketing sub-functions or activities are referred to as 'programme' objectives to distinguish them from the broader business or strategic objectives they are meant to serve.
Marketing plan	Contains a mission statement, SWOT (strengths, weaknesses, opportunities and threats) analysis, assumptions, marketing objectives, marketing strategies and programmes. Note that the objectives, strategies and policies are established for each level of the business.
Market segment	A group of actual or potential customers who can be expected to respond in approximately the same way to a given offer; a finer, more detailed, breakdown of a market.
Market segmentation	The process of splitting customers into different groups, or segments, within which customers with similar characteristics have similar needs. A critical aspect of marketing and one designed to convert product differences into a cost differential that can be maintained over the product's life cycle. *See also* Product life cycle.
Market share	The percentage of the market represented by a firm's sales in relation to total sales. Some marketing theorists argue

that the term is misleading since it suggests that the dimensions of the market are known and assumes that the size of the market is represented by the amount of goods sold in it. All that is known, these theorists point out, and correctly, is the volume sold; in actuality, the market may be considerably larger.

Mission The chief function of an institution or organisation. In essence it is a vision of what the company is or is striving to become. The basic issue is: 'What is our business and what should it be?' In marketing planning, the mission statement is the starting point in the planning process, since it sets the broad parameters within which marketing objectives are established, strategies developed, and programmes implemented. Some companies, usually those with several operating units or divisions, make a distinction between 'mission' and 'charter'. In these instances, the term 'mission' is used to denote the broader purpose of the organisation as reflected in corporate policies or assigned by the senior management of the company; the term 'charter', in comparison, is used to denote the purpose or reason for being of individual units with prime responsibility for a specific functional or product-marketing area.

Objective A statement or description of a desired future result that cannot be predicted in advance but which is believed, by those setting the objective, to be achievable through their efforts within a given time period; a quantitative target or goal to be achieved in the future through one's efforts, which can also be used to measure performance. To be of value, objectives should be specific in time and scope and attainable given the financial, technical and human resources available. According to this definition, general statements of hopes or desire are not true 'objectives'. *See also* Marketing objectives.

Planning The process of pre-determining a course or courses of action based on assumptions about future conditions or trends which can be imagined but not predicted with any certainty.

Positioning The process of selecting, delineating and matching the segment of the market with which a product will be most compatible.

Product

A term used in marketing to denote not only the product itself (its inherent properties and characteristics) but also service, availability, price, and other factors which may be as important in differentiating the product from those of competitors as the inherent characteristics of the product itself. *See also* Marketing mix.

Product life cycle

A term used in marketing to refer to the pattern of growth and decline in sales revenue of a product over time. This pattern is typically divided into stages: introduction, growth, maturity, saturation and decline. With time, competition among firms tends to reduce all products in the market to commodities – products which can only be marginally differentiated from each other – with the result that pioneering companies (those first to enter the market) face the choice of becoming limited volume, high-priced, high-cost speciality producers or high-volume, low-cost producers of standard products.

Product portfolio

A theory about the alternative uses of capital by business organisations formulated originally by Bruce Henderson of the Boston Consulting Group, a leading firm in the area of corporate strategy consulting. This theory or approach to marketing strategy formulation has gained wide acceptance among managers of diversified companies, who were first attracted by the intuitively appealing notion that long-run corporate performance is more than the sum of the contributions of individual profit centres or product strategies. Other factors which account for the theory's appeal are: (1) its usefulness in developing specific marketing strategies designed to achieve a balanced mix of products that will produce maximum return from scarce cash and managerial resources; and (2) the fact that the theory employs a simple matrix representation useful in portraying and communicating a product's position in the market place. *See also* Growth/share matrix.

Programme

A term used in marketing planning to denote the steps or tasks to be undertaken by marketing, field sales and other functions within an organisation to implement the chosen strategies and to accomplish the objectives set forth in the marketing plan. Typically, descriptions of programmes include a statement of objectives as well as a definition of the persons or units responsible and a schedule for completion of the steps or tasks for which the person or unit is responsible. *See also* Marketing objectives.

Psychographics	A consumer's inner feelings and pre-disposition to behave in certain ways.
Relative market share	A firm's share of the market relative to its largest competitor. *See also* Market share.
Resources	Broadly speaking, anyone or anything through which something is produced or accomplished; in marketing planning, a term used to denote the unique capabilities or skills that an organisation brings to a market or business problem or opportunity.
Situational analysis	The second step in the marketing planning process (the first being the definition of mission), which reviews the business environment at large (with particular attention to economic, market and competitive aspects) as well as the company's own internal operation. The purpose of the situational analysis is to identify marketing problems and opportunities, both those stemming from the organisation's internal strengths and limitations, and those external to the organisation and caused by changes in economic conditions and trends, competition, customer expectations, industry relations, government regulations and, increasingly, social perceptions and trends. The output of the full analysis is summarised in key-point form under the heading SWOT analysis; this summary then becomes part of the marketing plan. The outcome of the situational analysis includes a set of assumptions about future conditions as well as an estimate or forecast of potential market demand during the period covered by the marketing plan. Based on these estimates and assumptions marketing objectives are established, and strategies and a programme are formulated.
Socio-economic	A classification of individuals according to their level of income and occupation (or that of the head of household).

Part I

The Segmentation Process

CHAPTER 2

Market Mapping (Step 1)

Summary

This first step in developing a segmentation structure for your market consists of two parts. The first requires you to draw a market map for your business and the second determines at which stage(s) on this map you should be developing segments.

Constructing your Market Map

Draw a market map for the market in which your SBU operates that defines the value-added chain between supplier and final user. This should take into account the various buying mechanisms found in your market, including the part played by 'influencers'. (A definition of SBU follows.) Before you draw the map, however, it is suggested that you read the whole of this chapter.

This is a key step in the market segmentation process and you should spend as much time as necessary to complete the details.

It is not essential to draw the map starting from the supplier. In fact, it may even be easier to draw the map starting with the final user, back-tracking to the supplier. Do whatever you feel most comfortable doing.

An SBU:

(a) will have common customers and competitors for most of its products;

(b) is a competitor in an external market;

(c) is a discrete, separate and identifiable unit;

(d) will have a manager who has control over most of the areas critical to success.

In general, if an SBU's products or services go through the same channels to similar end users, one composite market map can be drawn. If, however, some products or services go through totally different channels and/or to totally different markets, there will be a need for more than one market map. For example, the domestic market may well be reached in an entirely different way from the business-to-business market.

Great care is needed in making the decision to exclude products or services from a market map. If in doubt, include them in your first pass.

A good point at which to start is to use your *current* SBU structure.

Such structures usually exist because the volume or value of business justifies such a specific focus. For example, in the case of a farming co-operative supplying seeds, fertilisers, crop protection, insurance and banking to farmers, it would be sensible to start, initially, by drawing a separate market map for each of these product groups, even though they all appear to go through similar channels to the same end users. In the organisation concerned, each one is treated as a separate SBU.

In other words, it is recommended that you start the mapping (and subsequent segmentation) process at the lowest level of disaggregation within the organisation's current structure.

Later on, it should be possible to use the same process for higher and higher levels of aggregation to check whether it may be possible to merge any of your current SBUs. Indeed, it may even be possible, eventually, to re-organise the whole company around 'new' groupings of either customers or products. This is covered at the end of Step 5 in Chapter 6.

The series of figures which follow progressively incorporate various points made in the text about market maps. Although the diagrams in these figures are a useful first stage in constructing market maps, it should be noted that, unless your business operates in a market with a very simple structure, this method of market mapping will only be an illustrative aid. For most businesses, you will find your market is too complex to be presented clearly in a diagram. The alternative is to construct your market map in a tabular format. This chapter contains guidelines designed to assist you in constructing your market map this way.

It is, therefore, recommended that you first read all of Step 1, using diagrams as a means of observing how the various steps in market mapping help develop a detailed picture of your market. You can then, if you wish, change to the tabular format and construct your market map this way. An example of a very basic market map is shown in Figure 2.1.

It is very important that your market map tracks your products/services, *along with those of your competitors*, all the way through to the final user, even though you may not actually sell to them direct.

In some markets, the direct customer/purchaser will not always be the final user. For example, a company (or household) may commission a third party contractor to carry out some redecoration, or an advertising agency to develop and conduct a promotional campaign, or a bank/accountant/financial adviser

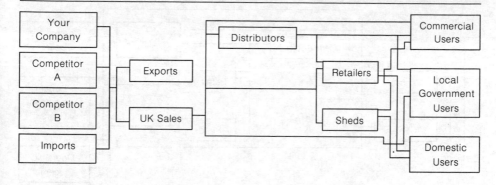

Figure 2.1 A simple market map

Note: This market map combines domestic and business-to-business end users. Some of the distribution channels are common to both of them.

to produce and implement a financial programme. For all of us, the doctor we visit when seeking treatment is, in many respects, a contractor when it comes to prescribing medicine. Although the contractor is strictly the direct buyer, he or she is not the final user. The distinction is important because, to win the commission, the contractor would have needed to understand the requirements of the customer and, in carrying out the commission, would have carried out those requirements on behalf of the customer. To miss out the final user from the market map would, therefore, have ignored an array of different needs which the supplier would need to be aware of (and have included in their product offer) if the supplier were to ensure that his or her company name appeared on the contractor's 'preferred supplier list'. The inclusion of a contractor on a market map is illustrated in Figure 2.2.

Ensuring your market map continues right the way through to the final user is also appropriate in those situations where final users have their products/ services purchased for them by their company's Purchasing Department. In such instances, the market map would track your products/services down the corridors of your business clients and continue beyond the Purchasing Department to the department(s) in which the final user(s) were found, each of which either utilised your product/service differently, or utilised it to achieve a different objective. Each of these final user departments would be listed separately on your market map. (Where a *single* final user department, or individual, puts your product/service to a number of different end-use applications, they should only appear on the market map once. Different end-use applications by single final users are captured in Step 3.)

Market research note: Ensure any market research project you commission uncovers and develops an understanding of different final user requirements.

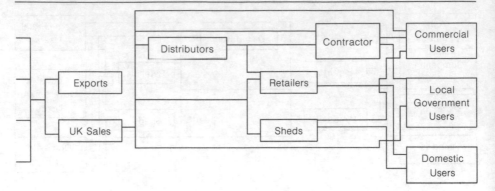

Figure 2.2   Market map with contractor

Note: In this particular market map the introduction of contractors has now reduced the similarity between the domestic and business-to-business end users quite notably. Sheds continue to be shared with a proportion of the commercial users, but this new contractor stage only operates in the business-to-business field.

Where appropriate, include in your market map the purchasing procedures, such as committees, authorisers, sealed bids and so on, encountered on the way, as shown in Figure 2.3.

The map in Figure 2.3 also illustrates a particular purchasing procedure which involves a Purchasing Committee and then the Financial Director. This has therefore been combined into one box.

For some businesses, it will also be important when drawing the market map to go beyond that stage in the value-added chain where their particular product becomes incorporated into another (and even becomes unrecognisable). For example, many chemical companies are switching to more environmentally friendly processes in the manufacturing of their products. However, few chemicals are seen in their raw state by their final user. As well as being good environmentalists, these companies need to be alert to the environmentally-aware consumers. These consumers are clearly a key target market for their products. It may, therefore, be in the interest of the chemical company to spend resources in this segment to ensure they buy products which incorporate the chemicals produced in an environmentally friendly way. One of the more recent, and apparently successful, examples of a company spending resources beyond the stage in their market map where their product becomes incorporated into another is Intel Corporation. Intel promote their microprocessors to the final user under the 'intel inside' logo.

If it is not obvious, mark on the market map the point at which your product becomes incorporated into another and begins to lose its own identity (an event which could, of course, occur in a single step).

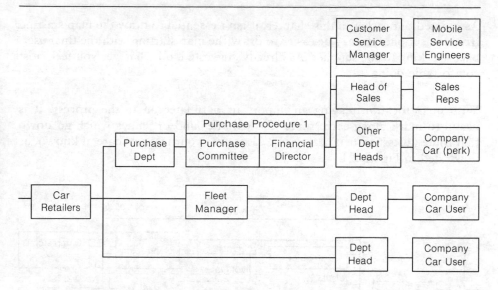

Figure 2.3 Market map with business purchasing procedures

Note: In this market map, the physical delivery of the product to the final user (car retailer to car user) is insufficient in representing the sales route and purchasing routines encountered. The market map also assumes that all the final users who appear beyond 'Purchase Procedure 1' are subject to the same purchasing routine. If this is not the case, ensure your market map reflects this. For example, all the departments in a company may use mail, but the advertising department may 'purchase' its mail through their direct mail agency and therefore bypass the normal purchase procedures.

As the figures have illustrated, most market maps will have at least two principal components:

- The channel (distribution channel)
- Consumers (purchasers/final users)

Be sure to draw a *total* market map rather than just the part you currently deal with. The purpose of this is to ensure that you understand your *market* dynamics properly. For example, beware of writing in only the word 'Distributor' if there are, in fact, different kinds of distributors that behave in different ways and that supply different customers. Similarly, avoid writing in only the word 'Buyer' if there are buyers who have different ranges of responsibilities (some may specify as well as buy) or who carry out their responsibilities in different ways. This is explained in more detail below under the heading, 'Market Leverage Points'.

As pointed out earlier in this chapter, it isn't essential to draw the map starting from the supplier. It may be easier to draw the map starting with the final user, back-tracking to the supplier. As already suggested, do whatever you feel most comfortable doing.

With quantification playing an important part later on in the process, it is useful to mark along each 'route' the volumes and/or values which go down that route (guesstimate if necessary). Also, note your market share, if known, as illustrated in Figure 2.4.

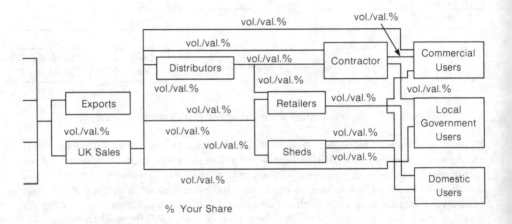

Figure 2.4   Market map with volumes and/or values on each route

Note: The market map could now be illustrating that the degree of commonality between the domestic and business-to-business end users based on volume and/or value is very small. In developing the market map further, It may now be preferable to treat them as different markets, each with their own market map. For the time being, however, we will continue to cover them with one map.

In implementing the directions which follow, you may find that you have to re-draw or amend your market map a number of times. All you are doing at this stage is creating a preliminary form of macro market segmentation. Later on, you will proceed to do more detailed segmentation.

Along the market map, ensure you include all the stages which play a part in the flow of products between suppliers and final users. These stages will, therefore, include points at which a transaction takes place and/or where influence/ advice/decisions occur (not necessarily a transaction) about which products to use.

For example, a co-operative may simply act as a buyer on behalf of its members (the members deciding on both the product type and specific manufacturer) and, once it has sourced the product, arrange for it to be distributed direct to its members. Alternatively, the members of a co-operative may decide on the generic product type they require, leaving the co-operative to decide on which specific manufacturer's product to buy, as well as arrange delivery either to a central depot or, again, direct to its members. Although, in the first instance, the role of the co-operative is quite passive and, in the second, quite active, the co-operative has played a part in the transaction and should therefore appear on the market map for both. Similarly, in both cases, the 'members' should appear on the market map.

Exactly the same situation can occur when, for example, accountants feature in financial transactions. In some transactions, accountants purchase or sell investments according to the instructions they receive from their client (the final user). In others, accountants may be authorised to make, and carry out, investment decisions on behalf of the client.

Another role for the accountant in the investment market could be purely that of an adviser contributing to the final decision, with the client carrying out the actual transaction. A more detailed look at the market in which the co-operative featured may have also revealed that the members referred to an outside consultant, such as an independent technical expert, for advice on which specific product to buy. In addition, for both the consumer and business markets, it is important you should not overlook in your market map the influence of specialist publications, or the influence of special reports in generalist publications (such as newspapers). Here, we are *not* referring to the power, or otherwise, of advertising. It is unusual for advertising to be deliberately sought out by the readers. We are referring more to the influence of well-researched articles on the buying behaviour of those final users who *deliberately* seek out such publications/articles as part of their buying process. For example, the range of '*Which?*' publications from the Consumers' Association (UK) can be a very powerful influence for some consumers on their choice of product, and even on their selection of investments. The important point here is that in all three instances, we are seeing an 'influencer' not directly featuring in any transaction. These influencers should also appear on the market map, as shown in Figure 2.5, just as if they were a transaction stage.

These transaction stages are referred to as '*junctions*', with each junction on a market map positioned hierarchically, according to how close it is to the final user. The last junction along the market map would, therefore, be the final user. The stages in the purchasing procedure found in business-to-business markets are regarded as a single junction (hence their enclosure in one box on the earlier example of a market map).

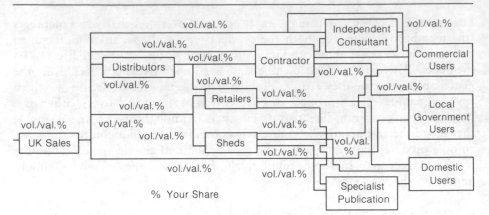

Figure 2.5   Market map with influencers

For most market maps, the decision on which junction a particular activity should be placed in will be very clear. However, there will be instances where the decision is not immediately apparent. Referring, again, to the co-operative example: a co-operative may simply replace a retail outlet or a wholesaler, in which case it could just as easily be placed in the same junction as the retailer or wholesaler, as appropriate. Alternatively, a co-operative may source its products from either a wholesaler, or direct from the manufacturer, in which case it is clearer to position the co-operative on the market map at a stage which is nearest to the final user. Following the same guidelines, the consultant would be placed in a junction one stage below the membership.

Note at each junction, if applicable, all the currently understood different types of companies/customers which occur there, along with the number (as suggested in Figure 2.6).

Allocate to these different company/customer types the volumes and/or values they deal with (again, guesstimate if necessary). Also, note your market share, if known.

The market mapping routine may already be challenging the traditional lists of company/customer types at the various junctions, around which you currently conduct your marketing effort. In such instances, replace what now appears to be the out-of-date list with the new list. The segmentation process you are now progressing through does, however, test the validity of your list during later steps.

What had started out as a fairly simple diagram has now become quite complex, even if the domestic and business-to-business markets are put on separate market maps. To continue using diagrams in this first pass, you may

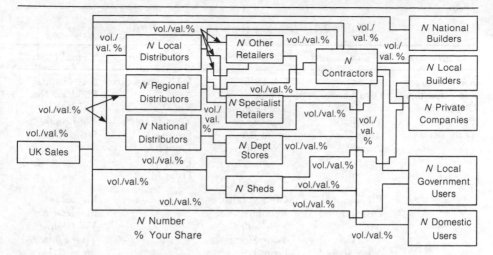

Figure 2.6 Market map with different company/customer types, their volumes and/or values, number of each type and your market share

Note: It is now clear that within the 'Commercial Users' group, only a proportion of local builders go to sheds for their supplies.

therefore need to sketch out the various junctions separately, and/or sketch out the various customers/consumers separately. It may also assist you if, in this first look at your market, you construct an outline (as opposed to a detailed) market map. The detail can be entered once you have determined at which junction(s) it is appropriate to develop a segmentation structure.

The alternative format for your market map is to construct it as a table, using letters to identify the flow of products.

The market map example in Figure 2.6, if constructed in the tabular format, would appear as in Table 2.1.

A simplified example of a completed market map in the tabular form appears in Table 2.2. For reasons of commercial confidentiality, the identity of the company and the specific market are not revealed.

To assist in developing your market map, apply letters to your diagram as illustrated in the tabular format example.

It should be emphasised that the market maps used to illustrate the text are relatively simplistic, especially for business-to-business markets, in both the identification of final user departments and in tracking through the various purchasing procedures that may be encountered (see earlier parts of Step 1).

Your market map should now be complete.

Table 2.1   Market map in tabular form

Suppliers	Distributors	Retailers	Contractors	Final Users
AA* Producers and Importers UK Sales: Vol./Val.: Your Share %:	BA Local Distributors: No. Vol./Val.: Your Share %: From AA	CA Other Retailers: No. Vol./Val.: Your Share %: From BA From BB	DA Contractors: No. Vol./Val.: Your Share %: From AA From BA From BB From BC	EA National Builders: No. Vol./Val.: Your Share %: From AA
	BB Regional Distributors: No. Vol./Val.: Your Share %: From AA	CB Specialist Retailers: No. Vol./Val.: Your Share %: From BA From BB		EB Local Builders: No. Vol./Val.: Your Share %: From CD From DA
	BC National Distributors: No. Vol./Val.: Your Share %: From AA	CC Department Stores: No. Vol./Val.: Your Share %: From AA From BC		EC Private Companies: No. Vol./Val.: Your Share %: From DA
		CD Sheds: No. Vol./Val.: Your Share %: From AA		ED Local Government: No. Vol./Val.: Your Share %: From AA From DA
				EE Domestic Users: No. Vol/ Val: Your Share %: From CA From CB From CC From CD
Total: Vol./Val.	Total: Vol./Val.	Total: Vol./Val.	Total: Vol./Val.	Total: Vol./Val.

* If you prefer, you can, of course, allocate separate codes to each producer and each source of import (AA, AB, AC and so on), and then illustrate where each distributor obtains their supplies.

Note: Any or all of the non-domestic final-users could be extended beyond one type if it was known that more than one purchase procedure existed in any of them. For example, if there were two different purchasing procedures known to exist with national builders, there would be two sets of national builders. Companies could additionally be extended further along the map if there were different departments using the product/service you supply.

Table 2.2 A completed market map for a UK manufacturing company (the units are in thousands)

Manufacturer and Brand	Distributor	Fitter	Consultants	Final Users
AA The Company – brand X 1365 units	**BA** National Distributors *No.* 16 1560 units *Co. share:* X – 70.2% Y – 21.2% From AA: 1095 From AB: 330 From AC: 75 From AD: 55 From AE: 5	**CA** National Fitters *No.* 3 280 units *Co. share:* X – 50.4% Y – 18.1% From BA: 175 From BB: 105	**DA** Consultants *No.* 2000 330 units *Co. share:* X – 44.2% Y – 16.3% From CA: 17 From CB: 100 From CC: 183 From CE: 30	**EA** Residential – type A *No.* 600 000 per annum 1535 units *Co. share:* X – 38.2% Y – 15.1% From CA: 220 From CB: 1205 From CC: 65 From CD: 45
AB The Company – brand Y 515 units	**BB** Large Independents *No.* 275 1315 units *Co. share:* X – 17.5% Y – 12.9% From AA: 230 From AB: 170 From AC: 270 From AD: 160 From AE: 150 From: AF 335	**CB** Local Independents *No.* 17 500 1655 units *Co. share:* X – 36.9% Y – 15.0% From BA: 635 From BB: 810 From BC: 210		**EB** Residential – type B *No.* 53 000 per annum 480 units *Co. share:* X – 47.3% Y – 16.7% From CB: 30 From CC: 450
AC Competitor 1 – brand R 365 units	**BC** Small Independents *No.* 5500 355 units *Co. share:* X – 11.3% Y – 4.2% From AA: 40 From AB: 15 From AC: 20 From AD: 75 From AE: 25 From AF: 180	**CC** Contractors *No.* 3500 1145 units *Co. share:* X – 48.0% Y – 16.8% From BA: 680 From BB: 325 From BC:140		**EC** Public – type A *No.* 1800 660 units *Co. share:* X – 43.3% Y – 16.2% From CA: 30 From CB: 235 From CC: 300 From CE: 95
AD Competitor 1 – brand 5 290 units	**BD** Superstores *No.* 9 45 units *Co. share:* nil From AF: 45	**CD** Domestic do-it-yourself *No.* 16 000 (per annum) 45 units *Co. share:* nil From BD: 45		**ED** Public – type B *No.* 1800 60 units *Co. share:* X – 42.1% Y – 16.8% From CE: 60 With 50% via DA

Table continued overleaf

Table 2.2 *continued*

Manufacturer and Brand	Distributor	Fitter	Consultants	Final Users
AE		CE		EE Commerical
Competitor 2		Organisation's		No. 45 000
– single brand		own dept.		540 units
180 units		No. 1200		Co. *share:*
		150 units		X – 44.4%
		Co. *share:*		Y – 16.3%
		X – 42.1%		From CA: 30
		Y – 16.8%		From CB: 180
		From BA: 70		From CC: 330
		From BB: 80		With 55% via DA
AF (Imports)				
560 units				
Total: 3275	**Total: 3275**	**Total: 3275**	**Total: 330**	**Total: 3275**

Note: The market information accessible to this company was limited. The above table was produced by using well-informed guesstimates, linked into data that was available. As in many companies, the nearer they came to the final users, the less they actually knew.

■ Identifying the Junction(s) where Segmentation should Occur (Market Leverage Points)

First, note those junctions where decisions are made about which of the competing products/services should be purchased. It is not necessary for *all* the various buying types (companies/customers) listed at each junction to make this decision.

The segmentation process does not concern itself with the actual decision to satisfy a particular need, only with the decision about which particular product/service to purchase in order to satisfy that need (see 'market' definition in Chapter 1).

Although the segmentation process detailed in Steps 2 to 7 should, ideally, occur at each junction along the market map where decisions are made (as long as the volume/value or number of customers/consumers at that junction justifies it: for example, if there are 5 or more), it is recommended that you first segment the junction *furthest* away from the supplier (manufacturer) *where decisions are made*. Once the segmentation process has been completed for this particular junction, the process can then be repeated for each successive junction where decisions are made, progressively back-tracking along the market map away from the final user towards you, the supplier. This will be particularly important for those businesses where the sales force is required to deal with buyers who act on behalf of final users.

It is possible to start this stage of the segmentation process at junctions other than the one furthest away from the supplier (manufacturer), though it is suggested that starting at the furthest junction will help in segmenting the junctions closer to the supplier.

For businesses where their particular product/service becomes incorporated into another and is both unrecognisable and has little or no influence on decisions at the final user junction, a consensus will need to be arrived at to determine where along the market map the segmentation process outlined in this book should occur.

At the junction selected on the market map where you are proceeding with the segmentation process, mark in *bold* the company/customer types which make decisions about which product to have. These are known as *Market Leverage Points*. If, at this stage of the process, the selected junction is seen as consisting of only one type of company/customer, mark the whole junction in bold if it is where decisions are made about which products to have. Note at each junction the number of customers/consumers that exist there, if known.

If the selection of which product to have at any junction is influenced by decisions at other junctions further along the map towards the final users, the earlier junction does *not* contain any leverage points. To explain this, let us return to the case of the co-operative once more and use this as an example: When the co-operative just buys what it is instructed to buy by its members, the members represent the leverage point. The leverage point, however, reverts to the co-operative in those instances where the co-operative decides which manufacturer's product to buy. On some occasions, especially in business-to-business marketing, this distinction is not always so clear cut. For example, the purchasing procedure for any department (final user) wishing to acquire any 'substantial' items may require the department to obtain three quotes and submit these to a 'purchasing committee' for a final decision. The principle leverage point clearly lies with the department selecting the three alternative suppliers, because if your company's product is not included at this stage there is no possibility of progressing any further. However, because the department wishing to make the purchase has its freedom of action constrained by a company policy, the leverage point is 'shared' with this policy. The requirements of both have to be taken into account.

When discussing whether a particular company/customer type (or a junction as a whole) is a leverage point or not, if it appears that in some instances it is and in some instances it isn't, this could be indicating one of two things:

(a)   that beyond this leverage point and further along the map, the market must split in two (or more). For example: Consumer Group 1 will buy any brand of toothpaste stocked by their preferred retailer, because they trust the retailer to supply good quality products. If this retailer drops a particular brand, it makes no difference to these particular consumers. Here, the retailer is a leverage point. At the same time, however, Consumer Group 2 visit the same retailer as Group 1, but will only buy a particular brand of toothpaste. If the retailer doesn't stock it, then Group 2 will find an alternative retailer that does. Here, the *consumer* is a leverage point. Consumer Groups 1 and 2 are clearly different, and the retailer is a leverage point for one but not for both groups. (Also see the 'Note' at the end.)

A typical instance where this can be seen in a business-to-business stage of a product's flow from manufacturer to final user is when a junction appears on the market map for 'contractors'. Contractors normally do business with a variety of customers, and it is unlikely these customers will demonstrate the same approach to buying the services of a contractor. Take a building contractor as an example. Customers of the building contractor will include local authorities, health authorities, private hospital groups, private house builders, commercial property builders, new developments, renovations, industrial concerns and central government. Some of these customers will specify which products the contractor should use (making the 'customer' the leverage point), whilst others will leave product specification to the contractor (making the 'contractor' the leverage point). It may help you in your discussions about contractors to review the specifications they issue for different types of jobs. Contractors will reflect the different requirements of those customers with whom the leverage point lies in the specifications issued to their suppliers. This may well, of course, have been picked up while constructing the market map. It also illustrates the importance of carrying out the first segmentation pass at the junction of the final user.

To cover these situations, write the name of that particular company/customer type or junction twice. Add a number to the letter code, for example, CB1, CB2, to identify separately the name written in bold from the name written normally. Using the same letter code indicates that it is physically a single company/customer type or junction, but one that performs two roles. Do not be put off by the fact that it is, for example, the same distributor or customer type. This merely indicates that a *single* operating policy to that distributor or customer is unlikely to be effective.

Note: In the example above, which refers to Consumer Groups 1 and 2 buying toothpaste through retailers, it is possible that, although Group 2 have a brand preference, if it is out of stock at their preferred retailer they will opt for one of the alternative brands in stock. This does not mean that, in constructing the market map, the leverage point lies with the retailer for both consumer groups. The leverage point for Group 2 still rests with them, but it is a very weak one. This situation will be covered in Step 5, which allocates values to the reasons for purchase.

(b)   there are different types of consumers/business units at this leverage point. For example: In constructing the market map for hi-fi products, a particular junction may have been labelled 'retailers', but this could well be too broad a description and should be split between, say, specialist retailers and department stores. If this is the case, separate letter codes should be applied to the different types: for example, CB and CC.

Taking the toothpaste example above, if, in constructing the market map, a discussion about leverage points had not occurred at the retailer junction (and therefore hadn't identified Consumer Groups 1 and 2 at this stage), a discussion could occur at the consumer junction and identify the two consumer groups at this later stage. If this is the case, and because we are dealing with two distinct physical entities, each performing a single role, the map should now show the two consumer types identified by separate letter codes, as opposed to the addition of a number to the same letter code, together with the associated volumes/values. (In addition, to assist with segmentation of the retailer junction at a later stage, the map should now be amended to show the retailer twice, once as a leverage point, with a number added to the letter code of the retailer to distinguish the different roles (as above), together with the associated volumes/values).

Don't forget to mark those which warrant it in *bold*. Attach to each type the approximate number of business units/individual purchasers found in it. Clearly, in those instances where one type has been split into two in order to distinguish between a leverage point and a non-leverage point – for example, CB1 and CB2 – only a total number for the CB type as a whole can be entered.

The inclusion of leverage points is illustrated in Figure 2.7.

Returning to the market map presented in the tabular form earlier in this chapter in Table 2.2, the number and proportion of units bought by final users selecting their own brand in this market is summarised in Table 2.3.

At this stage of the process, you may find that your discussions have revealed some differences between the products included in one of your SBUs. Later stages of the process separate out the specific products and enable you to note the reasons why each one is bought. A re-grouping procedure then takes place based on similarities. This should be sufficient to overcome any problems observed at this stage. (In extreme cases, where progressing to the next stage of the process is held up because of these differences, it is, of course, possible to split the products between different market maps.)

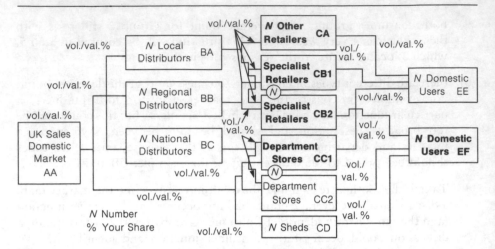

Figure 2.7   Leverage points on a market map for two junctions (also illustrating the use of letter codes)

Note: The market map has now been split between the domestic and business-to-business end users.

Table 2.3   Brand specification by final users from the market map for a UK manufacturing company (thousands of units)*

Final Users	Number of units with brand specified	Proportion of total units bought
Residential – type A	1235	80.5%
Domestic – type B	nil	–
Public – type A	630	95.5%
Public – type B	30	50.0%
Commercial	150	27.8%
Total	**2045**	**62.4%**

* See Table 2.2.

Market research note: The market map provides important guidelines for any market research project commissioned to improve your understanding of the market your business is in. It identifies the different target groups to be included in the sample frame.

So far, we have mapped out the different transactions that take place in your market all the way through to the final user, and seen how the transactions relate to each other. By quantifying these various 'routes' and determining your company's share along them, we have identified the most important routes and seen your company's position along each of them.

By then looking at where decisions are made between the products/services of competing suppliers, we have identified a number of stages (junctions) where segmentation could occur. For most companies, it is recommended that segmentation should first take place at the junction *furthest* away from the supplier/manufacturer, *where decisions are made*.

We are now going to proceed to draw up a preliminary segmentation structure for the selected junction. This preliminary structure could well benefit from taking into account the existence of leverage and non-leverage customer groups, assuming both exist at the selected junction. You may also wish to take into account the different purchasing 'routes' highlighted for this junction on the market map, although there is an opportunity to cover this in Steps 3 and 4.

CHAPTER 3

Who Buys (Step 2)

■ Summary

The second step consists of two parts. The first requires you to draw up a preliminary list of 'who buys' using demographic, geographic or psychographic descriptions. The second contains an optional routine which enables you to attach additional demographic, geographic and psychographic descriptors to each 'who', if there are any. This profiling data will be used later in the process.

■ The Preliminary List of Who Buys

At the junction on the market map selected for this pass of the segmentation process, which, in the first instance, should be the junction *furthest* away from the supplier (manufacturer), *where leverage points occur*, draw a *preliminary* segmentation structure as long as you answer '*No*' to the following question:

Are *all* the consumers/business units the same?

A 'Yes' answer should be seriously challenged.

Now draw up a draft list of 'who buys', using demographic, geographic or psychographic descriptions for this preliminary segmentation. Avoid using descriptions at this stage which represent 'what' is bought, 'where' it is bought, 'when', 'how' or 'why' it is bought, as these are addressed in subsequent steps.

The descriptions allocated to each 'who' can consist of a single characteristic or a combination, whichever is appropriate to the market being looked at. The descriptions could be built up by cascading through the characteristics you believe, at this stage, to be determinants of different buying behaviour (or wish to test as determinants of different buying behaviour), as illustrated in Figure 3.1.

A list of possible descriptions is given later in this chapter.

Although the title of this chapter is 'Who Buys', it is important to note that in many situations, those *who buy* are not necessarily those *who specify*, and the junction being looked at may consist of both buyers and specifiers. For example, the employees entitled to a company car would not necessarily carry

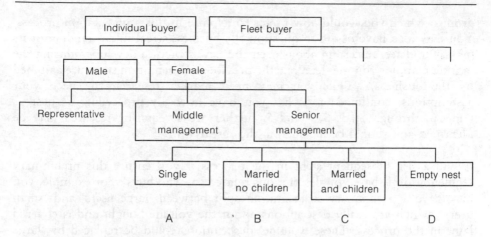

Note: The letters are used to identify the preliminary segments.

Figure 3.1 Developing preliminary segments in the company car market

out the buying transaction, though they could specify the car model they wished to have bought on their behalf. The term 'who buys' should therefore be seen as including specifiers in such circumstances.

Market research note: In any market research carried out as a requirement for segmentation, questions should be included which collect standard descriptive segmentation information about each respondent. This will be used later in the segmentation process.

This preliminary list of 'who buys' could be just a simple division between leverage and non-leverage groups. It is, however, unlikely that all the members in either one of these groups have homogenous requirements. This could, of course, have already been established by your business, with sub-groups and their different 'requirement packages' already identified. (A detailed look at the reasons why your customers buy takes place in Step 5, which can be found in Chapter 6.) If this is the case, the preliminary 'who buys' segmentation can be the one currently in use by the business, for example, location (rural/built-up), Standard Industrial Classification (SIC) or your own business classification (doctors in private GP practice/group practice/partnership or in nationalised hospital/private hospital; professional/manufacturer; arable farm/grassland farm); size of business (big/small); age; lifestyle; family cycle and so on.

Alternatively, it could well be that, in constructing the market map, you have already developed the basis of a new segmentation structure at the junction being looked at (beyond a simple division between leverage and non-leverage groups) which you would now prefer to explore in this segmentation process. You may also have begun to question the business's real understanding of its market and feel uncertain about even the new structure developed during the market mapping routine (let alone the previous segmentation structure assumed by the business). While you may need market research to check your assumptions, continue with what you have now. By proceeding as best as you can through Steps 3, 4 and 5, further areas requiring research may be identified and should be included in the research brief.

It will assist subsequent steps in the process if you ensure this preliminary segmentation is based on descriptions related to 'who buys'. For example, you may have a preliminary segmentation split between 'large users' and 'small users', which are really descriptions about the volume bought and is covered later in the process. These 'volume' descriptions could be replaced by 'large companies' and 'small companies' (or 'large families' and 'small families'), or even combined under a common SIC code (or common stage in the Family Life Cycle), assuming any of these were the case, with the split into different usage levels carried out during Step 3.

This list of preliminary segments simply forms a base from which to work as the segmentation process contained in this book takes the segmentation team from the *preliminary* guess to a thought-through conclusion.

If, at this stage, you know (or suspect) there are lapsed users who have completely opted out of the market (those who no longer buy your products/ services or any of those on offer from the competition) and/or non-user prospects who, on the face of it, appear to have the 'need' being looked at, open up preliminary segments for each of them as appropriate. Although 'unmet requirements' are looked at in more detail during Chapter 6 (where these two preliminary segments re-enter the process), capturing the fact at this stage will assist you later on.

To further help you develop a preliminary list of 'Who Buys', it may be useful to review some of the standard methods of demographic, geographic and psychographic segmentation in use today. These can be found at the end of this chapter. A detailed breakdown of both the UK's and USA's SIC and the full list of the UK's 120 postcode areas appears in Appendices 2 and 3.

At junctions where you have already distinguished between groups who are leverage points and those who are not, you should just focus the segmentation process on to the group(s) which have been identified as being leverage points. However, you may be in a situation where your knowledge about this junction is, in truth, inadequate. In such circumstances, this preliminary segmentation should cover *all* the businesses/individuals who make up the market at this particular junction. It therefore includes those who are and those who are not leverage points. We suggest you continue down this track, because you may uncover opportunities existing for the non-leverage groups, if only the right offer were put together.

For example, consumers who depend on their retailer for the selection of which brand to buy should still be grouped as a segment; or even segments – there could be different reasons for this dependence, resulting in different 'requirement packages' to be met by the retailer, and there could be varying degrees of dependence, any of which could be a reflection of shortfalls in the products on offer. By addressing these shortfalls, the leverage point may well be moved away from the retailer to the consumer. Such a move may be very important to the business strategically and affect the distribution of power in its market place. This was certainly the case for a manufacturing company whose products were installed in domestic, industrial and commercial premises by trade professionals. An analysis of the total UK market for their product line illustrated that around half the total volume went to final purchasers who, they believed, were not leverage points. Key in this group were the domestic users who were heavily dependent on a very diverse group of installers who, in turn, were heavily dependent on the purchasing policies of powerful distributors. In looking for opportunities to develop 'pull through' for their product, this company researched both the non-leveraging domestic and non-leveraging installer groups. The findings of the research had important strategic implications, and to have ignored these two non-leverage groups in developing their segmentation structure, would have been clearly very short-sighted.

For another manufacturing company, a market research project commissioned to assist them in their market segmentation process identified that 11 per cent of the total market went to final users, who simply bought whatever their local distributor stocked. This same research exercise, however, also identified that if a manufacturer were to put together a product range specifically targeted at this group (a group previously ignored by all the manufacturers) a pull-through effect would be generated, thereby shifting the leverage point away from powerful buyers.

As a guide to the number of preliminary segments to be used here, the following questions may help:

> For up to how many is it commercially sensible to offer tailored products and/or services?

Alternatively,

> At what number would we need to start grouping individual customers/ consumers together in order to manage our offer to them in a viable way?

However, whatever number you arrive at in answer to these questions, it would be quite safe to double it at this early stage of the process. It is too early to be unnecessarily restrictive. This is better suited for the procedures in Step 6 of the process.

At the other extreme, you may well be in a business which only deals with, say, 12 purchasers at a particular junction, all of whom are leverage points. In such circumstances, a segmentation process along the lines being described here is unlikely to be required, as a one-to-one bespoke service would be offered anyway.

It is worth noting here that when large numbers of purchasers are involved and impersonal contact, such as advertising, is likely to be the method of communication in the promotional plan, the resulting segments could end up being quite loosely defined. However, large numbers of purchasers still warrant a sophisticated approach to segmentation. Valuable niche opportunities could be uncovered.

You should now finalise your list of 'who buys' and attach to each of them a distinct 'label' such as 'A', 'B', 'C' and so on, as appeared in Figure 3.1.

■ Adding Further Profile Information to the List of Who Buys

The second part of 'who buys' is purely optional and enables you to build up the standard segmentation profiles of each preliminary segment by attaching to them any further descriptions you are aware of. This profiling data will be used later in the process and it is *not* restricted to those characteristics you believe to be (at this stage) determinants of different buying behaviour. They may be useful at a later stage for identifying the concluding target segments when deciding whether they are reachable or not. For example, you may have used 'large companies', 'medium companies' and 'small companies' as descriptions for three of your preliminary segments in Part 1 of this Step. All the large companies and small companies may also be car manufacturers, so this additional (SIC) information should be attached to their profiles. This will enable you to check later on in the process whether car manufacturers have, in fact, common needs, and whether the size of company is, in fact, irrelevant. Before attaching additional demographic, geographic or psychographic information you need to be able to answer '*Yes*' to the following question:

Is this additional description applicable to *all* the buying units to be found in that particular preliminary segment?

You will also need to take into account your answer to the following question:

Can this description be found in *any*, though not necessarily all, of the buying units found in any of the remaining preliminary segments?

If your answer to the second question is 'No', nothing further needs to be done. If, however, your answer is 'Yes', it is essential you attach this description to the appropriate buying units. An opportunity for doing this occurs in Chapter 5 (Step 4). Please, therefore, note this requirement on a separate piece of paper.

In the next chapter, we will move to the next stage of the segmentation process.

The following list of standard segmentation descriptions may be useful in completing the stage outlined in this chapter.

■ Standard Approaches to Business Market Segmentation

■ Demographic Characteristics

• SIC: The latest details are available from the appropriate statistical office. A summary appears below and a detailed listing appears in Appendix 2.

United Kingdom

Agriculture, Forestry and Fishing (0)
Agriculture and Horticulture (01)
Forestry (02)
Fishing (03)

Energy and Water Supply Industries (1)
Coal extraction and manufacture of solid fuels (11)
Coke ovens (12)
Extraction of mineral oil and natural gas (13)
Mineral oil processing (14)
Nuclear fuel production (15)
Production and distribution of electricity, gas, and other forms of energy (16)
Water supply industry (17)

Extraction of Minerals and Ores Other Than Fuels; Manufacture of Metals, Mineral Products and Chemicals (2)
Extraction and preparation of metalliferous ores (21)
Metal manufacturing (22)
Extraction of minerals not elsewhere specified (23)
Manufacture of non-metallic mineral products (24)
Chemical industry (25)
Production of man-made fibres (26)

Metal Goods, Engineering and Vehicle Industries (3)
Manufacture of metal goods not elsewhere specified (31)
Mechanical engineering (32)
Manufacture of office machinery and data processing equipment (33)
Electrical and electronic engineering (34)
Manufacture of motor vehicles and parts thereof (35)
Manufacture of other transport equipment (36)
Instrument engineering (37)

Other Manufacturing Industries (4)
Food manufacturing industries (41)
Sugar, confectionery, animal feeds, drink and tobacco manufacturing
    industries (42)
Textile industry (43)
Manufacture of leather and leather goods (44)
Footwear and clothing industries (45)
Timber and wooden furniture industries (46)
Manufacture of paper and paper products; printing and publishing (47)
Processing of rubber and plastics (48)
Other manufacturing industries (49)

Construction (5)
Construction (50)

Distribution, Hotels and Catering; Repairs (6)
Wholesale distribution, except dealing in scrap and waste materials (61)
Dealing in scrap and waste materials (62)
Commission agents and commodity brokers (63)
Retailing: food, CTN, off-licences, chemists, leather, clothing, footwear,
    home furnishings and household goods (64)
Other retailing: cars, fuel, books, mixed retailers and so on (65)
Hotels and catering (66)
Repairs of consumer goods and vehicles (67)

Transport and Communications (7)
Railways (71)
Other inland transport (72)
Sea transport (74)
Air transport (75)
Supporting services to transport (76)
Miscellaneous transport services and storage not elsewhere specified (77)
Postal and telecom services (79)

Banking, Finance, Insurance, Business Services, Leasing (8)
Banking and finance (81)
Insurance, except for compulsory social security (82)

Business services (83)
Renting of movables (84)
Owning and dealing in real estate (85)

Other Services (9)
Public administration, national defence and compulsory social security (91)
Sanitary services (92)
Education (93)
Research and development (94)
Medical and other health services; veterinary services (95)
Other services provided to the general public (96)
Recreational services and other cultural services (97)
Personal services (98)
Domestic services (99)
Diplomatic representation, international organisations and allied armed
    forces (00)

United States of America

Agriculture, Forestry and Fishing (0)
Agricultural production – crops (01)
Agricultural production – livestock (02)
Agricultural services (07)
Forestry (08)
Fishing, hunting and trapping (09)

Mining and Construction (1)
Metal mining (10)
Anthracite mining (11)
Bituminous coal and lignite mining (12)
Oil and gas extraction (13)
Mining, quarrying non-metallic materials, excluding fuels (14)
Building construction – general contractors (15)
Construction, excluding buildings, general contractors (16)
Construction – special trade contractors (17)

Manufacturing (2)
Food and kindred products (20)
Tobacco products (21)
Textile mill products (22)
Apparel and other finished fabric product manufacturers (23)
Timber and wood products, excluding furniture (24)
Furniture and fixtures (25)
Paper and allied products (26)
Printing, publishing and allied industries (27)
Chemical and allied products (28)
Petroleum refining and related industries (29)

Manufacturing continued (3)
Rubber and miscellaneous plastics products (30)
Leather and leather product manufacturers (31)
Stone, clay, glass and concrete products (32)
Primary metal industries (33)
Fabricated metal products, excluding machinery and transportation
    equipment (34)
Machinery manufacture, excluding electrical machinery (35)
Electrical, electronic machinery, equipment and supplies (36)
Transportation equipment manufacture (37)
Measuring, photographic, medical instruments, watches and clocks (38)
Miscellaneous manufacturing industries (39)

Transportation and Communications (4)
Railway transportation (40)
Local public transport and intercity buses (41)
Road freight transportation and warehousing (42)
Postal services (43)
Transportation by water (44)
Air transport (45)
Pipe lines, excluding natural gas (46)
Transportation services (47)
Communication (48)
Electric, gas and sanitary services (49)

Wholesale and Retail (5)
Wholesale trade – durable goods (50)
Wholesale trade – non-durable goods (51)
Building materials, garden supply, mobile home dealers (52)
General merchandise retailers (53)
Food retailers (54)
Motor vehicle dealers and petrol stations (55)
Clothing and accessory retailers (56)
Furniture, home furnishings and equipment retailers (57)
Eating and drinking places (58)
Miscellaneous retail trade (59)

Finance, Insurance and Real Estate (6)
Banking (60)
Credit agencies other than banks (61)
Security, commodity brokers, dealers, exchanges and allied services (62)
Insurance (63)
Insurance agents, brokers and service (64)
Real estate (65)
Combination of real estate, insurance, loans, law offices (66)
Holding and other investment offices (67)

Services (7)
Hotels, guest houses, camps and other lodgings (70)
Personal services (72)
Business Services (73)
Automotive repair, services and garages (75)
Miscellaneous repair services (76)
Motion pictures (78)
Amusement and recreation services, excludig cinemas (79)

Services continued (8)
Health services (80)
Legal services (81)
Educational services (82)
Social services (83)
Museums, art galleries, botanical and zoological gardens (84)
Membership organisations (86)
Private households (88)
Miscellaneous services (89)

Public administration (9)
Executive, legisaltive, general government, excluding finance (91)
Justice, public order and safety (92)
Public finance, taxation and monetary policy (93)
Administration of environmental quality and housing programmes (95)
National security and international affairs (97)
Unclassified establishments (99)

- Size of company

Very small	Small	Small–Med.	Medium
Med.–Large	Large	Very Large	Very Large +

- Department/section

Manufacturing	Distribution	Customer Service
Sales	Marketing	Commercial
Financial	Bought Ledger	Sales Ledger
Personnel	Estates	Office Services
Planning	Contracts/Purchasing	Information Technology (IT)

Where appropriate, use more specific descriptions, such as specialist purchasing units, general purchasing units.

■ Geographic

- Postcode (the 120 postcode areas of the UK are listed in Appendix 3)
- City, town, village, rural
- County
- Region: frequently defined in the UK by television region (see Standard Approaches to Consumer Market Segmentation)
- Country
- Economic/political union or association (for example, ASEAN)
- Continent

■ Psychographics (Buyer Characteristics)

- Personality: stage in its business life cycle (start-up, growth, maturity, decline, turn-round); style/age of staff (formal, authoritarian, bureaucratic, disorganised, positive, indifferent, negative, cautious, conservative, old fashioned, youthful)
- Attitude: risk takers or risk avoiders; innovative or cautious, and bear in mind that many of the adjectives used to describe different types of personality can also express a company's attitude towards your product line (as opposed to their distinctive personal character)
- Lifestyle: environmentally concerned; involved with the community; sponsor of sports/arts

■ **Standard Approaches to Consumer Market Segmentation**

■ **Demographic Characteristics**

- Age

< 3	3 – 5	6 – 11	12 – 19
20 – 34	35 – 49	50 – 64	65 +

- Sex: male, female
- Family life cycle: Bachelor (young, single), split into dependants (living at home or full time student) and those with their own household; Newly married (no kids); Full nest (graded according to the number and age of kids); Single parent; Empty nesters (children left home or a childless couple); Elderly single.

- Family size

  1-2   3-4   5 +

- Type of residence: flat/house; terraced/semi-detached/detached; private/ rented/council; number of rooms/bedrooms.

- Income (£k)

  < 10   10-15   16-20   21-30   31-50   > 50

- Occupation: operatives; craftsmen, foremen; managers, officials, proprietors; professional, technical; clerical, sales; farmers; retired; students; housewives; unemployed; white-collar (professional, managerial, supervisory, clerical); blue-collar (manual).

- Education (highest level): secondary, no qualifications; GCSE; graduate; postgraduate.

- Religion: Christian; Jewish; Muslim; Buddhist; Other.

- Ethnic origin: African; Asian; Caribbean; UK, Irish; Other European.

- Nationality

- Socio-economic (a guide on social grading appears in Appendix 1). The following definitions are those agreed between Research Services Ltd, and National Readership Survey (NRS Ltd).

  A   Upper middle class (higher managerial, administrative, professional)
  B   Middle class (middle managerial, administrative, professional)
  C1   Lower middle class (supervisory, clerical, junior management, administrative, professional)
  C2   Skilled working class (skilled manual workers)
  D   Working class (semi and unskilled manual workers)
  E   Subsistence level (state pensioners, widows with no other earner, casual or lowest-grade workers)

- Multi-demographic: combining a selection of demographic criteria. For example, Research Services Ltd have combined each of four life cycle stages (Dependent, Pre-family, Family and Late) with the two occupation groupings of White-collar (A, B, C1) and Blue-collar (C2, D, E), producing eight segments. They have then further split out 'Family' and 'Late' into 'Better Off' and 'Worse Off', producing a total of twelve segments in their 'Sagacity' model. The basic thesis of the model is that people have different aspirations and behaviour patterns as they go through their life cycle. Their definition of these life cycle stages is as follows:

Dependent	Mainly under 24s, living at home or full-time student.
Pre-family	Under 35s, who have established their own household but have no children.
Family	Housewives and heads of household, under 65, with one or more children in the household.
Late	Includes all adults whose children have left home or who are over 35 and childless.

■ Geographic

- Postcode (the 120 postcode areas of the UK are listed in Appendix 3)
- City, town, village, rural
- Coastal, inland
- County
- Region (frequently defined in the UK by the 15 ITV regions: Carlton, Meridian, Central Television, HTV Wales, Anglia, Scottish Television, Grampian Television, Granada Television, Yorkshire, Tyne Tees, Westcountry, LWT, Border Television, Ulster Television, and Group in the Channel Islands)
- Country
- Economic/political union or association (for example, NAFTA)
- Continent
- Population density
- Climate

■ Geodemographics

- ACORN produced by CACI Information Services Ltd is one of the longer established geodemographic classifications, updated in 1993 using the 1991 Census data. It consists of 54 types summarised into 17 basic groups, which in turn are condensed into six broad categories. These six broad categories act as a simplified reference to the overall household classification structure. The categories are:

| *Category 'A'* *'Thriving'* | Accounts for 19.8% of all households in the UK |
| *Category 'B'* *'Expanding'* | Accounts for 11.6% |

Category 'C'   7.5%
'Rising'

Category 'D'   24.1%
'Settling'

Category 'E'   13.7%
'Aspiring'

Category 'F'   22.8%
'Striving'

(Unclassified   0.5%)

- PIN from Pinpoint, which combines geodemographics and financial data.

Other, more recent, classifications have been developed by some of the larger database companies which, as well as linking residential areas with selected demographics, also add psychographic factors (see 'Multi-dimensional' on p. 59).

■ Psychographic Characteristics

- Personality: compulsive, extrovert, gregarious, adventurous, formal, authoritarian, ambitious, enthusiastic, positive, indifferent, negative, hostile. Specific ones by sex have also been developed, such as Wells' eight male psychographic segments:

Quiet Family Man	Self-sufficient, shy, loner; lives for his family; practical shopper; low education, low income.
Traditionalist	Conventional, secure; has self-esteem; concerned for others; conservative shopper, likes well-known brands and manufacturers; low education, low/middle income.
Discontented	Nearly everything (job, money, life) could be better; distrustful, socially aloof, price conscious; lowest educational and socio-economic group.
Ethical Highbrow	Content with life and work; sensitive to others; concerned, cultured, religious; social reformer; driven by quality; well educated; middle/upper socio-economic group.
Pleasure Oriented	Macho, self-centred; views himself as a leader; dislikes his work; impulsive buyer; low education and socio-economic group.

Achiever	Status conscious; seeks success (power, money and socially); adventurous in leisure time pursuits; stylish (good food, music, clothes); discriminating buyer; good education; high socio-economic group.
He-Man	Action, excitement, drama; views himself as capable and dominant; well educated; middle socio-economic group.
Sophisticated	Attracted to intellectual and artistic achievements; broad interests; cosmopolitan, socially concerned; wants to be dominant and a leader; attracted to the unique and fashionable; best educated; higher socio-economic groups.

Source: W. D. Wells, *Lifestyle and Psychographics* (American Marketing Association, 1978).

- Attitude: degree of loyalty (none, total, moderate), risk takers or risk avoiders, likelihood of purchasing a new product (innovator, early adopter, early majority, late majority, laggard), and many of the adjectives used to describe different types of personality can also express an individual's attitude towards your product line (as opposed to their distinctive personal character). Some companies have also developed specific behavioural groups, such as 'Monitor' from Taylor Nelson Ltd which has seven social value groups, each with a distinct pattern of behaviour.

- Customer status: purchase stage (aware, interested, desirous, ready for sale), user classification (non-user, lapsed user, first time, potential).

- Lifestyle: consists of three main dimensions –

Activities	Work, hobbies, social events, vacation, entertainment, club membership, community, shopping, sports.
Interests	Family, home, job, community, recreation, fashion, food, media, achievements.
Opinions	Selves, social issues, politics, business, economics, education, products, future, culture.

In the UK, the three main providers of Lifestyle data are NDL (National Demographics and Lifestyles), CMT (Computerised Marketing Technologies) and ICD (International Communications and Data). Each obtains its information from consumer questionnaires. NDL's 'questionnaires' are product registration guarantee forms containing questions on household demographics, income and leisure interests, and distributed with durable goods such as electrical equipment. This has enabled NDL to collect over 10 million deduplicated 'questionnaires' which can be matched up to census data in order to produce accurate (for the census data) geographic profiles.

- Multi-dimensional: combining psychographic profiles with selected demographic data and identifying geographic areas where the resulting segments are to be found. For example, CCN Marketing have developed 20 Persona behavioural types using CMT's National Shoppers Survey database. These types range from so-called 'Bon Viveurs' to 'New Teachers' and 'Craftsmen and Homemakers'. CCN's MOSAIC system now also extends into certain mainland European markets, classifying neighbourhoods into ten lifestyle types:

Elite Suburbs	Well-established suburban neighbourhoods in large and medium-sized cities, consisting of residential properties in large grounds. Wealthy but living in restrained luxury.
Average Areas	Average in age, income and family composition. Usually found in small market towns and local centres. Low poverty level.
Luxury Flats	Found in the centre of large conurbations, whose occupants set the country's fashion style and cultural agenda. Stylish accommodation for the political, artistic and media elite.
Low Income Inner City	Poor quality older housing, mixed with bars, cinemas, take-aways and football clubs, in the industrial and commercial inner city areas of large towns and cities.
High Rise Social Housing	Many social problems with a reliance on welfare caused by unemployment, divorce and illness.
Industrial Communities	Older terrace housing occupied by blue-collar workers in the traditional heavy industries.
Dynamic Families	Higher income families living in modern, privately-owned housing. Materialistic and up-to-date with the latest gadgets.
Lower Income Families	Living in both private and social housing in regional centres and average-sized towns. A good market for strongly branded packaged goods.
Rural/Agricultural Areas	Occupied by older, conservative, traditional people, not commuters, very dependent on agriculture, keen supporters of the independent retailer.
Vacation/ Retirement	Mix of tourists, second homers and the retired. Both seasonal and week day changes in population.

CHAPTER 4

What, Where, When and How (Step 3)

■ Summary

This chapter is Step 3 in the process of developing a segmentation structure for your market. It breaks down the current activity in the market under four headings: what is bought; where it is bought; when it is bought; and how it is bought. For some markets, these lists could be quite extensive, so the chapter contains guidelines on how to restrict these lists without losing their contribution to the segmentation process. Breaking down the market's activity this way enables you to identify all the different purchasing combinations that take place within it, each of which could be reflecting different needs.

■ What is Bought

As a separate step, list *all* relevant competitive products/services purchased, whether or not you manufacture/supply all of them. Ensure you 'unbundle' all the components of a purchase so that you arrive at a comprehensive breakdown of 'what is bought'.

Avoid covering a number of different product/services with what is really a description of either the advantage or the benefit being provided. For example, 'next day delivery' is a description of what is obtained by buying first class postage or certain types of courier service. The list should therefore contain 'first class post' and 'next day courier service'. It may, however, assist you in drawing up the list of competitor's and your own products/services if they are categorised by the advantage or benefit being provided.

To assist in the distinction between a 'feature', 'advantage' and 'benefit' the following summary may help you:

- Feature: what it is, or is made from

- Advantage: what it does

- Benefit: what the customer gets that they need (or want)

A more detailed discussion of features, advantages and benefits occurs at the end of Chapter 6.

The role of 'influencers', as defined in Step 1 (Chapter 2), along with technical advisers and consultants, should be included in the lists of 'what is bought' (as opposed to appearing in the list of 'who buys') when they are used by the junction being segmented (and are therefore located at junctions closer to your company on the market map). Influencers/advisers/consultants and so on should be separated out, where applicable, between those purposely brought into the buying process (independents), and those included in ('bundled' together with) the purchase by the supplier (manufacturer), regardless of whether the buyer wants them or not.

Ensure the level of detail used to describe the products/services equates to the level of aggregation being looked at in the market map. A finely defined market would have the individual products listed, while a more generally defined market would have broader product/service groups listed, possibly using generic descriptions. For example, if looking at family cars, it is essential to list the different types and makes of car available. However, if looking at the passenger transport market between major cities, types and makes of cars being used would be unnecessary as this level of detail would complicate the process (particularly in the next Step). A list of alternative modes of transport would be more appropriate for this level of aggregation.

Features to take into account when drawing up your list include:

- Type of product: cleaners, galvanisers, installed, flat pack, made up, resident engineers, on-call engineers, bundled with a service package, and so on.

- Specification: 100% purity, 98% purity, tolerance levels, percentage failure rate, and so on.

- Colour: red, white, blue, pastel, garish and so on.

- Size of package: single, multiple, family pack, 5 litre, 10 litre, 20 kgs, bulk and so on.

- Volume used: small, medium, large, very large and so on.

- Level/intensity of use: high, medium, low and so on.

- Type of service: testing service, technical advice (which is sometimes, unintentionally, provided by the sales force), evaluation, analysis.

- End-use application: where a single final user department or individual utilises your product/service for a number of different end-use applications, these should be listed here. For example, the office services department may require cleaning services, but the cleaning requirements of the public areas, general office areas and the manufacturing plant (particularly if the manufacturing process involves precision instruments) could all be different. Another example has been identified in the domestic paint market, where the selection process for paint differs according to the type of room it is being bought for (the buying criteria for gloss in the lounge being different from the buying criteria for gloss in the bedroom).

- Brand: manufacturer's, own label, single brand only, any major brand, only local brands, high profile brand.
- Country of origin: UK, German, French, EC, Scandinavian, Western European, Eastern European, Japanese and so on.
- Independent influencers, advisers, consultants (complementing or competing with the technical/advisory services provided by the manufacturers/suppliers): specialist publications, consumer publications, accountants, financial advisers, consultants and so on, if they appear at junctions used by buyers at the junction being segmented.
- Type of delivery: next day (or a listing of the competing products which provide this, for example, courier, first class), within four hours, collected, automatically triggered via links with inventory control systems, and so on.
- Volume of purchase: large, medium, small (or by a more precise breakdown if appropriate).
- Value of purchase: high, medium, low (or by a more precise breakdown if appropriate).
- Range of products: all, single, across the range, those at the top/middle/bottom of the range, and so on.

The resulting list could be as follows:

Lawnmowers	Hover, cylinder, rotary, petrol driven, manual, electrically driven, 12″ cut, 16″ cut, any mower with a branded engine, extended warranty, with after sales service, and so on.
Paints	Emulsion, gloss, non-drip, one coat, 5 litre cans, 2 litre cans, environmentally friendly, bulk and so on.
Petrol Stations	Self-service, forecourt service, with loyalty programme, and so on.

■ Where it is Bought

As a further separate step, and without attempting at this stage to link this step with the earlier step, list all the channels (if appropriate) where the listed range of products/services are bought. Please note that this only refers to the products/services supplied/manufactured by you and your competitors. It therefore excludes the sourcing details for independent influencers, advisers, consultants and so on.

The channels list could include:

> Direct/mail order, distributor, department store, national chain, regional chain, local independent retailer, tied retailer, supermarket, wholesalers, shed, specialist supplier, street stall, through a buying group, through a buying club, door-to-door, local/high street/out-of-town shop and so on

■ When it is Bought

Draw up a list which covers the different frequencies of purchase experienced for your own, and your competitors' products/services.

The purchase frequency list could include:

> Daily, weekly, monthly, seasonally, every two years, at 50 000 miles, occasionally, as needs, only in emergencies, degrees of urgency, infrequently, rarely, special events, only during sales, at the bottom of the market, and so on

■ How it is Bought

Finally, draw up a further separate list covering the different methods of purchase and, if applicable, the different purchasing organisations and procedures observed in your market.

Examples which may help in drawing up your list include:

- Methods of purchase: credit card, charge card, cash, direct debit, standing order, credit terms, Switch, outright purchase, lease-hire, lease-purchase, negotiated price, sealed bid and so on.

- Purchasing organisation: centralised or decentralised; structure and distribution of power in the decision-making unit (DMU), which could be equally applicable in a household as in a business (for example, decision to purchase made at one level, with the choice of suitable suppliers able to meet the specification/price and so on made at a technical level, negotiation of price left to the purchasing department and the final decision left to senior management).

■ Reducing the Complexity of the 'What', 'Where', 'When' and 'How' Lists

At this stage, it is usually advisable to restrict the contents of each list to a more manageable number of variants through any of the following:

- If there is data to hand, based on market research conducted amongst a statistically sound number of customers at the junction being looked at, which has identified the influential components of 'What', 'Where', 'When' and 'How' – in other words those included in the buying criteria (for example, packaging, size) – and/or influence the attitude of buyers (for example, brand, technical advisers), all the other items in the various lists can be dropped.

- Statistically sound research information may go further and enable you even to restrict the list appearing in one of the categories of buying criteria. For example, one product could have eight different pack sizes and four different pack types. Research may show that only two are relevant in demonstrating differences between segments.

- Further research data may be to hand which enables you to merge different items within any one list together. For example, you may have data which enables you group a number of similar products together because the product type has no relevance to market segmentation (for example, lemonade and orangeade could be grouped together as 'pop' because, listed separately, they indicate nothing more about possible segmentation splits). On the other hand, attitudes towards mixers, such as tonic water, are different from attitudes towards pop (as mixers are added to expensive spirits) and so would be listed under 'what' separately in a drinks market. Likewise, the breakdown of retail outlets into specialist stores, department stores and so on may be irrelevant to the buying process when listed separately because 'local store' is the pertinent description. It may also be possible to combine products into different groupings such as 'full range', 'premium services', 'blends', for example, as long as these combinations reflect buying patterns in the market place. Combinations may also be possible for your list of different purchasing organisations.

It may also be possible to use your judgement to restrict the list to a manageable number, but take care to ensure that the rationale behind any restriction is *market based*.

At this stage, neither attempt to list 'what is bought' nor 'where, when or how it is bought' according to who might/might not buy, and do not attempt to list the real needs being met by the product. For example, some customers may be buying quality/reliability, which they obtain by buying well-known brands, or by buying goods produced in a particular country (for example, Japan): this will be covered in Step 5. Just list product types, channels used, purchase frequencies and buying methods *as they are nothing more than comprehensive lists*.

When you have completed the 'what', 'where', 'when' and 'how' for those customers who are leverage points at the junction in the market map being looked at, you can now do the same exercise for non-leverage points. This needs to be done unless the reader is absolutely certain that it is pointless (in other words, that there is nothing to learn about these customers and nothing will change their buying habits).

■ A Brief Comment about Price

It is *not* appropriate at this stage in the process to include price in the list of 'what is bought', even though a number of your customers may simply buy the cheapest. Price is better covered in Step 5, 'why is it bought', when it can be allocated an importance rating, relative to the product/service being bought.

CHAPTER 5

Who Buys What, Where, When and How (Step 4)

■ Summary

Here, we are presenting a comprehensive picture of the market as it is today by identifying, for each currently active 'who', all the unique combinations of 'whats', 'wheres', 'whens' and 'hows' observed in their particular buying activity. The resulting cascade arrived at in this fourth step produces a large number of micro-segments, often too many to handle manually. These can be reduced by re-arranging the layers of the cascade into a descending order of importance and determining a cut-off point to separate the important from the less important. Further screening may be possible by removing items seen to appear across all the preliminary segments (the 'whos'), by removing superfluous items and/or removing micro-segments known to be unattractive to your company (segment attractiveness is looked at in Chapter 9).

Once complete, the concluding micro-segments should have a volume or value figure attached to *each* of them. In addition, if you have 'removed' any micro-segments from the process because they are unattractive to your company, a volume or value figure should be attached to this group of micro-segments as a whole. You may have to re-visit this 'rejected' group later in the process if you need to look for additional sources of revenue.

From this point, whenever you see 'what' followed by an asterisk ('what*'), please assume that it also includes 'where', 'when' and 'how'.

■ Developing Micro-segments in your Market

For each 'who' (preliminary segment) you concluded with in Chapter 3, Step 2, first list on a separate piece of paper all the applicable 'whats*' identified in Step 3 under their appropriate heading. For those 'whos' relying on what is available, or what is in stock at their suppliers, exclude those product elements which are irrelevant (for example, brand). If, however, *within* a particular preliminary segment it is known that some individuals/groups regard a particular item or heading (for example, 'what' – brand) as irrelevant, but

others believe it is relevant, capture that situation in
including 'irrelevant' as one of the options. Ensure that
are listed. Attach one selected unit of measurement (fo
value; guesstimate where necessary).

A possible list may look like the one in Table 5.1.

Table 5.1 A 'what, where, when and how' list for a prelimi⸺ ⸺..t
(Who – Large families)

Applicable categories	Appropriate variants
'What' product type	DIY kits, made up
'What' colour	Teak, mahogany, pine, for painting
'What' brand	High profile, own label
'What' country of origin	Scandinavia, Germany, UK
'What' type of delivery	Collected, delivered
'Where'	Department stores, direct mail, sheds
'When'	As needs
'How'	Credit terms, outright purchase

Compile similar lists for each of the other 'whos'.

Review each list appearing for each 'who' and combine the variables which are
highly correlated by removing those which are unnecessary. For example, in the
list just compiled in this chapter, it may well be that *only* goods sourced by
direct mail are delivered. Either 'direct mail' or 'delivered' should therefore be
removed. Similar combinations can be carried out if, for example, it was only
very rarely that any of the other retail outlets delivered, as this would mean
'direct mail' and 'delivered' were highly correlated.

If every possible permutation of each entry opposite 'what', 'where', 'when' and
'how' takes place in the market for this particular 'who' (and you have no
evidence to support the alternative hypothesis), you can now construct your
'who buys what*' cascade. For the example appearing in Table 5.1, this would
produce 576 different combinations, each of which could be regarded as a
'micro-segment'. Pictorially, this would look as shown in Figure 5.1.

On the other hand, you may know, for example, that large families only ever
buy UK products when they want to paint something themselves. This reduces
the number of combinations to 480. You may also know that when a customer
buys an own label brand, they always assume it is made in the UK, as all the
distribution sources are UK companies. This further reduces the combinations

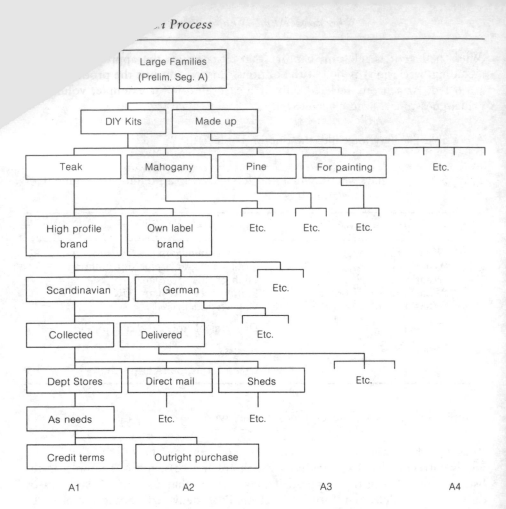

Figure 5.1 Who buys what, where, when and how cascade

Note: A1, A2, A3 and so on are the micro-segment labels, the prefix indicating the preliminary segment they originated from. This labelling serves as a useful check later in the process, because it indicates the source of all the micro-segments which have come together to form each of the final segments.

to 312. In addition, it may also be the case that the Scandinavian and German products are regarded as being the same thing (because they are perceived as offering the same level of quality, and it is in order to obtain this particular benefit that large families buy this product line from these two countries). This allows you to combine these two countries and list them as Scandinavian/ German. The combinations are now reduced to 156.

Do not substitute at this stage any of the 'what*' entries by the benefit they deliver. This is better tackled in the next step, Step 5.

Whilst working through this particular Step, you may be able to enhance the demographic, geographic and/or psychographic profile attached to each preliminary segment. It is possible that the various constituents of 'what', 'where', 'when' and 'how', or any of their combinations, could be associated with particular profile descriptions. For example, mahogany furniture could be associated with the 'A', 'B' and 'C1' socio-economic groups. If any such opportunities occur, note them on a separate piece of paper so that they can be used later in the process. These are in addition to those already noted at the end of Chapter 3, 'who buys'.

In most markets, the cascade you are required to draw in this step will produce a large number of micro-segments, almost certainly too many in number to satisfy segmentation criteria. Step 6 in the process provides the mechanism for reducing the number of micro-segments, with Step 7 providing the test for satisfying segmentation criteria. However, some initial screening may be possible at this point before proceeding further.

Market research note: In any research project commissioned to assist the segmentation process, 'what', 'where', 'when' and 'how' data should be collected for each completed interview.

■ Screening within a Preliminary Segment through Prioritising

Using either market research data or reasoned judgement, preferably the former, you may be able to re-arrange for each 'who' their 'what*' lists into a descending order of importance. It may then be possible to decide a cut-off point which separates out those purchase categories which play an important part in the buying process from those which, to all intents and purposes, play only a secondary part. In this book we refer to those items which play an important part in the buying process as *Critical Purchase Influences* (CPIs). They play a particularly significant role in Step 5.

To help determine the cut-off point, once you have re-arranged the purchase categories into a descending order of importance, allocate 100 points between them in a way which represents their relative importance to each other *from the market's perspective*. It's as if the preliminary segment put a value on the product/service of £100 and was then asked to indicate its preference between the purchase categories by indicating how it would allocate this total sum. Draw a cut-off point at, say, where the score comes to 80. An example appears in Table 5.2.

Table 5.2   Scoring the purchase categories (Who – Large families)

Purchase categories	Individual score	Cumulative score
'What' colour – Teak, Mahogany, Pine, For painting	35	35
'What' country of origin – Scandinavian/German, UK	25	60
'What' product type – DIY kits, Made up	15	75
'Where' – Department stores, Direct mail, Sheds	10	85
'What' brand – High profile, Own label	5	90
'What' type of delivery – Collected, delivered	4	94
'How' – Credit terms, outright purchase	3	97
'When' – As needs	3	100

In this particular example, the cut-off point could be after 'What product type' or after 'Where'. Either way, the number of combinations now entering into Step 5 has been quite substantially reduced.

If in carrying out this prioritising routine you do not believe all the individual customers in this preliminary segment would produce the list in the same order (which will certainly be the case if you have included 'irrelevant' in one of the headings), split the preliminary segment up into the appropriate number of different groups. Produce a priority table for each of them and now regard them as distinct preliminary segments with their own identification prefix. This will also require you to re-allocate the volume/value figure attached to the original preliminary segment between the two (or more) resulting preliminary segments.

■ Screening across the Preliminary Segments by Eliminating Repeated Items

Screening may be appropriate if, at this stage, you begin to notice that certain items (purchase 'variants' in Table 5.1) appear under several of the preliminary segments, making it necessary to ask whether these particular 'whats*' are really segmentation determinants. Before arriving at any conclusions on this, it is essential that you are able to answer 'No' to *all* the following questions:

● Is the product/service applied in the same way?

   Although 'end-use application' was addressed earlier in the process, it is appropriate to re-visit it here. An example given concerned the domestic paint market, where it has been determined that the selection process for paint differs according to the type of room it is being bought for (the buying criteria for gloss in the lounge being different from the buying criteria for gloss in the bedrooms).

- Is its importance rating and relative value the same in each preliminary segment (as well as the same in each micro-segment)?

  For example, some individuals will only ever buy goods from a well known manufacturer, even if it means going without. This would become apparent during the CPI routine earlier in this Step.

- Is the product/service used to achieve the same end result, the same benefit? (Although this third question was also addressed earlier in the process it, too, is appropriately re-visited here.)

  For example, some people may buy first class postage (the product feature) to secure next day delivery (the advantage) and therefore prompt receipt by the addressee (the benefit). Others may buy it for reasons of personal status or to imply importance (alternative benefits).

You may well find that you are able to answer 'No' to all three and therefore remove the repeated items from the cascade, thereby reducing the number of micro-segments. For example, each preliminary segment may buy 5 litre and 25 litre containers. This could be indicating one of two things:

(a) that customers are demonstrating nothing of significance in selecting one size or the other, and the two sizes can be deleted from the 'who buys what*' cascade; or,

(b) the two sizes are a significant segmentation factor and will play a major part in re-defining the market structure.

■ Further Screening by Removing Superfluous Items

Additional screening may be possible by challenging some of the splits built into the cascade once more, even though they survived the scrutiny test suggested at the end of Step 3 in Chapter 4. In the example appearing in Figure 5.2, it may well be that the split between 'general distributor' and 'specialist supplier' is superfluous in determining segments. Instead, 'local proximity' could be the criteria determining which retail outlet is used, and it is this which should appear in the cascade. 'General distributor' and 'specialist supplier' would therefore be combined and re labelled 'local proximity'. This would reduce the number of micro-segments by one third. Figure 5.2 also identifies a group who regard 'brand' as irrelevant.

Particularly useful in determining which items should appear in the cascade is market research data. The findings of past research projects may indicate which 'whats*' are considered in the buying process by each of the preliminary segments. Without such data, great caution should be exercised when considering how to reduce the number of micro-segments. Be particularly alert to items being removed because *you* would prefer them not to be important!

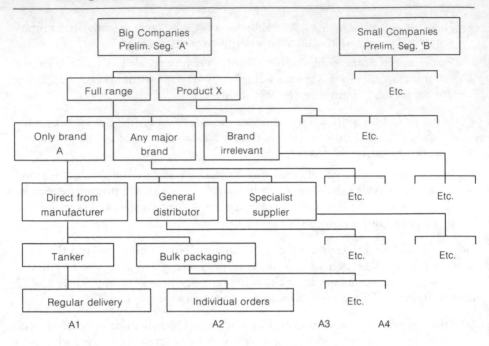

Figure 5.2   A simplified 'who buys what*' cascade for a manufacturer

■ Removing 'Unattractive' Micro-Segments

If, despite the screening routines, the number of micro-segments remaining are still too many to handle, those which are known to be unattractive to your company may be removed from the detailed analysis which follows this Step by combining them into one group. It is important they are not removed from the process completely because to do so would distort the picture of the market being looked at.

Great care should be taken when removing micro-segments from the detailed analysis this way. Micro-segments may be unattractive today, but could well be the attractive segments of tomorrow:

(a)   some micro-segments may be currently unattractive because no supplier has put the right offer together to stimulate demand from this particular group and/or obtain the required margins from it;

(b)   some micro-segments may be unattractive today because they only account for a small volume/value of business, but this may be because they are at an early stage of their development.

Individually, micro-segments may represent only a small volume/value, but their *needs* may be the same as those of micro-segments found in other preliminary segments. Later stages of the process would see these micro-segments combined and, as a group, they may then represent a significant volume/value. To remove them from the detailed analysis appearing in later stages of this process would lead to this possibility being overlooked, especially as these 'similar' micro-segments would probably be combined in a group which also contained 'dissimilar' micro-segments.

Only combine micro-segments this way if you feel satisfied with the selection criteria you propose to use and/or you simply have to rationalise the number of micro-segments like this in order to progress with the next steps. The resulting group of micro-segments can always be re-visited later, which is an option you may need to consider when looking for opportunities to achieve the company's revenue targets.

As you will need to attach a volume/value figure to this group, leave this method of reducing the number of micro-segments until after the next section. (Segment attractiveness criteria for your company is looked at in Chapter 9.)

■ Attaching Volumes or Values to each Micro-Segment

For each preliminary segment, you are now required to allocate the volume and/or value attributed to each preliminary segment between the items listed for all the applicable categories of 'what*'. Therefore, if your volume total for a particular preliminary segment is 2000, and you have listed three different items for 'What product' in this preliminary segment, you will need to split the 2000 between these three entries. *Don't forget to take account of any particular relationships between the 'what', 'where', 'when' and 'how' entries,* just as there were in the example seen earlier in this Step. For instance, while looking at 'large families' it was revealed that they only ever bought UK products when they wanted to paint something themselves. They also mentioned that if it was an 'own label' brand, it was made in the UK. If you have no information to assist you in how to split your volume/value between the entries, assume an even split and attach the appropriate figures. An example appears in Table 5.3. In this particular example, the most appropriate figures to deal with were 'volume' figures.

The example in Table 5.3 has assumed the full permutation for the 'large family' preliminary segment. The purchase categories could, of course, be limited to those you have identified as being CPIs.

Table 5.3   Allocating volume (or value) in the 'who buys what*' cascade

Market: XYZ
Preliminary Segment: A   Large Families
Volume: 2000   Value:

'What' variants*			*Volume*	*Value*
'What' product type	DIY		500	
	Made up		1 500	
	Kit			
		Total	**2 000**	
'What' colour	Teak		750	
	Mahogany		200	
	Pine		500	
	For painting		550	
	Formica			
	White			
		Total	**2 000**	
'What' brand	High profile		1 550	
	Own label		450	
		Total	**2 000**	
'What' country of origin	Scandinavian/German		1 450	
	UK		550	
	Far East			
		Total	**2 000**	
'What' type of delivery	Collected		1 600	
	Delivered		400	
		Total	**2 000**	
'Where'	Department stores		1 100	
	Direct mail		200	
	Sheds		700	
	Warehouses			
	Specialists			
		Total	**2 000**	
'When'	As needs		2 000	
	Sales periods			
	Planned replacement			
		Total	**2 000**	
'How'	Credit terms		300	
	Outright purchase		1 700	
		Total	**2 000**	

Note: The list includes all the 'what*' variants for this market, and therefore contains some which are not appropriate for the 'large family' preliminary segment.

On completing all the entries for each preliminary segment, you will now be able to calculate how many micro-segments have been created. Attach a unique alpha-numeric label to each micro-segment by adding a number to the unique alpha label already allocated to each preliminary segment (as illustrated earlier). Also ensure each micro-segment has a volume or value figure.

■ Completing the Profile for Each Micro-Segment

If you have any additional demographic, geographic and/or psychographic profile descriptions you now wish to include, either from Chapter 3 or from earlier in this chapter, ensure they are now linked up to their respective micro-segment(s). For example, it may be the case that large families who buy mahogany are to be found in the 'A', 'B' and 'C1' socio-economic groups, if so, all the micro-segments generated from this combination should have this further profiling information attached to them.

If this further profiling information is a new category of description in addition to those used in the initial profiling of preliminary segments in this market (as opposed to refining a category initially applied), it is also helpful if the other micro-segments have their profiles enhanced by attaching to them their applicable description from this same category. Using the example given in the previous paragraph, this would mean attaching to the other micro-segments their applicable socio-economic groups (C2, D and/or E). This particular piece of information may be useful in identifying the concluding segments for marketing purposes.

CHAPTER 6

Why is it Bought (Step 5)

▪ Summary

Step 5 consists of four parts: the first is designed to ensure the real needs in your market are fully understood and, in doing so, uncover any unmet needs. Part two then looks at the different attributes your market may attach to individual 'whats', 'wheres', 'whens' and 'hows' (in addition to any used to reduce the number of micro-segments in Step 4, such as combining different retail outlets into 'local stores' because proximity was the determining criteria). The third part then identifies the key CPIs *across all* the preliminary segments in your market, with the final part requiring you to attach relative values to these CPIs for each micro-segment. Part four also sees 'price' introduced into the process and requires a relative value to be attached to it whilst attaching values to each micro-segment's CPIs.

▪ Understanding the Real Needs, the Real Benefits

The primary purpose of this first stage is to develop the attributes list required later in this step and to uncover any unmet needs in your market. This will help in correctly capturing the importance of 'price' in the buying process.

First, draw up, separately, a complete 'benefits' list which covers all the reasons the market has given for buying, including the reasons given by those who depend on another junction in the market map to select the products they eventually purchase. This benefits list should cover both tangible and intangible benefits.

To ensure the distinction between 'feature', 'advantage' and benefit' is clear, a section on features, advantages and benefits is included at the end of this chapter.

If you created preliminary segments for lapsed buyers and/or prospects in Chapter 3, an understanding of their unmet needs should be developed in this step using the procedures suggested.

The question, 'Why is it bought?', really only provides answers to the status quo. To help uncover the real needs, we must also be able to answer the question, 'What are they trying to achieve?' For example, in the agricultural market for a particular product line, the focus of some farmers was to buy products which produced lush, green grass for their livestock to graze on. For another group of farmers, their concern was how well their livestock looked (the appearance of the grass being a minor concern). In the arable sector, one group of farmers concentrated solely on producing crops which met the needs of the market they were selling into, again regardless of how the crop looked whilst in the field. This particular group also demonstrated another important point when looking at the reasons 'why' particular products are bought.

This point concerns the 'market oriented' arable farmers, who bought a great deal of this product in its constituent parts, rather than already mixed (which was how the majority of it was sold in various standard combinations), and they always looked for the cheapest buys. The initial conclusion was that this group bought on price, a conclusion which, it was later discovered, combined them with another group of farmers who *were* driven by price. However, on probing what they were really trying to achieve, it became apparent that they were combining the constituent parts in a variety of ways to make up a number of different mixes. This was being done because the standard, off-the-shelf combinations produced by the manufacturers were not sophisticated enough for the needs of this particular group of farmers. These bespoke combinations improved their farm's output and had nothing to do with price. In addition, a further driving force for this group of farmers was innovation, and their own bespoke mixing operation was also seen to be innovative.

In yet another market, one segment was found to consist of unenthusiastic buyers who stated they were not really interested in the product class and only made purchases in this product class for the functional needs it satisfied. For example, they bought cars simply to travel between 'A' and 'B'. However, a research project discovered that this segment did have aspirations, in addition to the functional requirements, which could be met by the product if only it was designed and specifically targeted at this distinct group (which, usefully, had a distinct demographic profile). An example of this would be a car specifically designed to meet the requirements of businesswomen and specifically positioned to appeal to this segment. A motor manufacturer who has pursued a strategy similar to this is Jaguar (Ford): in the USA they positioned the XJS model as one targeted at (wealthy) women.

Thus, it is crucial at this stage to be alert to any possible unsatisfied needs manifesting themselves in the guise of something else, rather than accepting the status quo. For example, 'price' may be given as the sole or major criteria for choice, but it *could* be hiding the fact that customers/consumers are dissatisfied with the currently available offers, as their real needs are not being met. What they are having to buy in order to meet a functional need is, therefore, second rate, for which they certainly would not pay a premium. For example, there is a functional need of (most) garden owners to mow the grass. To meet this need, there were once only cylinder mowers available. Despite a close cut, a collecting box and roller providing an attractive finish, the cylinder mower was regarded as cumbersome by some gardeners and, because of this, they would buy cheap versions. Then came the hover mower, which was light and quick, thus enabling a substantial amount of the time previously allocated to a chore to be better spent. This group, therefore, has a need for a fast method of keeping their grass in check. In contrast, the group choosing to use a cylinder mower has a need, in many instances, to present the lawn as a 'show piece'.

To assist in identifying whether there are any unsatisfied needs in a market, two techniques are available, 'needs gap analysis' and 'perceptual mapping'.

■ Needs Gap Analysis

This concept is best described using examples.

Needs Gap Analysis in Motor Car Manufacturing

A simple example of needs gap analysis occurred in the 1960s when Bayerische Motoren Werke, a motor company struggling to survive, desperately set out to uncover whether there were any unmet market opportunities in an already seemingly saturated market.

After undertaking extensive market research to uncover both the needs of car buyers and how well the models available at that time met these needs, it became apparent that buyers of motor cars in the 1960s made their choice of model based mainly on two criteria, speed and price. The company then sat down and plotted out on a simple, two-dimensional, matrix a 'picture' of the total car market as it was then, as shown in Figure 6.1.

The resulting picture revealed that there was a gap in the market, a gap with sufficient sales potential to justify the required capital investment, so the company set about building cars for it.

Today, this motor company has only a small share of the total motor car market, but has a large share of the particular segment its namesake brand has become associated with. Only once has the brand stepped outside its specialist segment, but it quickly withdrew the specific model in question. Today, the major car manufacturers have fluctuating financial results, but BMW, as it is better known, continues to be a profitable, niche car brand.

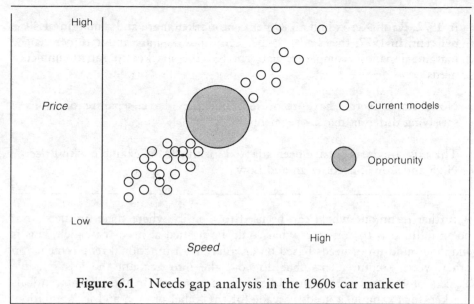

Figure 6.1 Needs gap analysis in the 1960s car market

Needs Gap Analysis in the Photocopier Market

Another example of needs gap analysis can be seen in Figure 6.2.

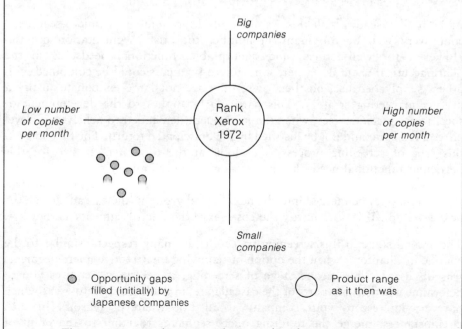

Figure 6.2 Needs gap analysis in the photocopier market

In 1972, Rank Xerox had an 80 per cent market share and a margin of 40 per cent. In 1977, they had a 10 per cent market share and a 10 per cent margin. Japanese companies had entered the market to satisfy unmet needs.

Now, Rank Xerox have recovered, but they have separate divisions satisfying different market segments.

The axis could easily have been adapted for the BMW example with Price: High and Low; Speed: High and Low.

A further technique which can be used to identify where there are needs not being fulfilled is to construct what could be termed a 'needs cascade'. This is simply a build-up of needs based on an analysis of functional requirements: in other words, requirements that do not take into account the less tangible aspects of buying such as attitudes and perceptions. In the pharmaceuticals market, for example, a needs cascade for the 'relief of pain and inflammation' could be constructed as illustrated in Figure 6.3.

The precise structure of this cascade could differ, of course, by sex, and further differ by age. Separate cascades would therefore need to be constructed for each of these different user groups, who could well have entered the segmentation process earlier as preliminary segments.

As with all cascades built this way, the resulting number of 'micro-segments' could very well be too many in number to satisfy segmentation criteria. However, for well-defined, and quantifiable, functional needs, as in the pharmaceutical example earlier, some micro-segments could be combined with others simply because, on their own, they are not large enough to justify a distinct marketing strategy. This particularly applies to the development of specific products/services, when the investment demanded to achieve this level of requirement could not be justified by the anticipated return. The first stage in this type of screening process is to look at the total market size for this particular functional need (that is, across all the preliminary segments). If that still does not justify product development costs, then these particular micro-segments should be merged into the next logical group in the cascade (often the next level up). If it does justify the cost, leave the micro-segments as they are.

The second stage in this screening process is, in many respects, similar to the routine in Chapter 5 when the option of removing unattractive micro-segments was discussed. This second stage of screening, if necessary, requires you to determine whether any parts of the cascade are, in truth, going into areas which have no interest to your company at all (for whatever reason). In such circumstances, merge the resulting micro-segments together to the point of aggregation where your lack of interest starts. Do not, however, remove them

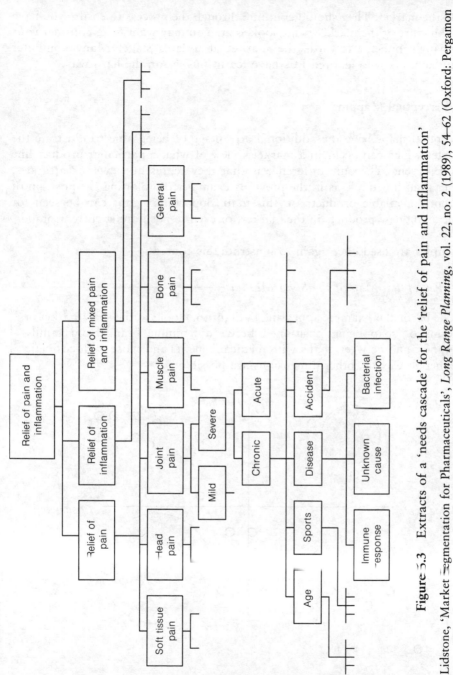

Figure 5.3 Extracts of a 'needs cascade' for the 'relief of pain and inflammation'

Source: J. Lidstone, 'Market Segmentation for Pharmaceuticals', *Long Range Planning*, vol. 22, no. 2 (1989), 54–62 (Oxford: Pergamon Press).

from the market. They should continue through the process to ensure you have a full picture of the market being looked at. You may want to re-consider your company's policies towards the market at a later stage! Many computer manufacturers who ignored PCs have learnt this lesson the hard way.

■ Perceptual Mapping

Perceptual maps have the additional advantage of being able to illustrate the changes which can occur in a market's view of what a particular product line can represent. The only difference is that they represent views, or attitudes, rather than functions, as in the previous examples. By plotting the position of currently available products on this map, opportunity gaps can be seen for positioning new products in the market, or even re-positioning current brands.

Examples are used once again to illustrate this concept.

A Perceptual Map of the Soap Market

The particular example appearing in Figure 6.4 looks at the soap market in terms of soap being positioned between feminine brands and family brands, and between soaps with medical benefits and those with cosmetic benefits. Clearly, other dimensions are possible.

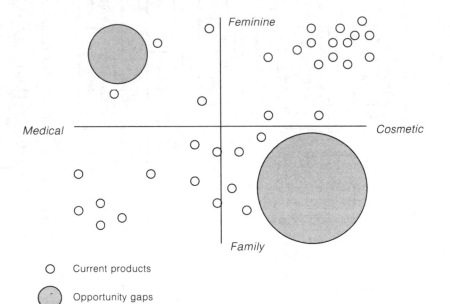

Figure 6.4   A perceptual map of the soap market

There appear to be two areas of opportunity in the soap market as represented above. These new opportunities would clearly have to be evaluated before resources were committed to developing and launching suitable products (in case they were actually representing areas where little or no demand existed). It is interesting to note that in the male toiletries market, there is an increasing flow of new products positioned as having a cosmetic value. There has clearly been a major shift in this market which has opened up the 'cosmetic' area of the male's perceptual map.

Tabloid Newspapers in the UK as a Perceptual Map

The dimensions used for the map in Figure 6.5 show the extremes of 'up-market' and 'down-market' (which can, in some cases, be associated with socio-economic group) and 'serious' or 'entertaining', the latter often being associated with 'exclusive' reports highlighting the activities of individuals which the individuals concerned would often prefer not to have highlighted!

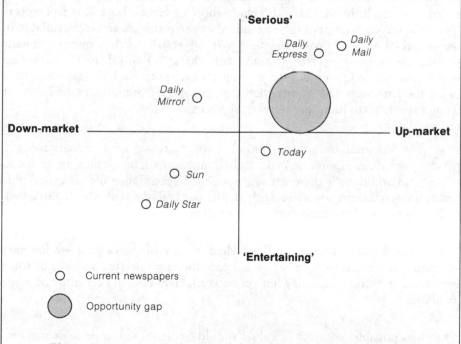

Figure 6.5   Perceptual map of the tabloid newspaper market

Source: Partially developed from the *National Readership Survey* of April–September 1993.

The tabloid newspaper market is a good example of a market in which brands (titles) have been steered towards new positions. For example, the *Daily Mail* has gradually been steered towards its current 'up-market' position. The *Today* newspaper has also changed position and become more 'serious'. It is important, however, that we don't confuse deliberate re-positioning with drifting. The danger of drifting is that it can often take a product into the weak, middle ground.

Market research note: If, at this stage, you now consider your company's understanding of its market is inadequate, there is clearly a need to fill the information gaps by commissioning some independent market research. It is, however, recommended that you finish reading through Step 5 before finalising your research brief, as there may well be other areas you would want to include in that brief.

To cover the existence of unmet needs, such as those uncovered by market research – which, in turn, could include those of lapsed buyers and prospects (potential buyers who appear to be suited to the products/services available in the market but who aren't buying anything yet) – further micro-segments should be opened up to account for these potential new marketing opportunities. Each should have a unique alpha-numeric label attached to it (with the letter selected from either the appropriate preliminary segment, or from a newly introduced preliminary segment).

It is now essential to attach to each new micro-segment the appropriate psychographic descriptions in order to help uncover what it is they are trying to achieve. In addition, if there are any specific demographic and/or geographic descriptions you can associate with them, particularly with the 'unattached' micro-segments, these should also be attached.

For each new micro-segment not 'attached' to any of the original preliminary segments, you are now required to allocate the appropriate 'whats*'. In some instances, of course, these may not yet be available, but could certainly be made available.

As best as possible, volumes or values should be attributed to these new micro-segments made up, if appropriate, of volumes/values from other micro-segments, or preliminary segments, along with any potential extra volume/value which could be generated by meeting these currently untapped needs.

■ Attributes

Just as there may be different needs being met by the same product, there could well be different attributes attached to some of the individual features appearing in your 'what', 'where', 'when' and 'how' lists. For example, 'brand' could mean quality, and/or reliability, and/or good service, dependable R&D, good sales representatives, good complaint handling, and so on. A similar list could be drawn up for 'country of origin'. Unless *all* your micro-segments attach the same attributes to each feature listed in Step 3, you can now move to Part 3 of this Step.

Market research note: At this stage you may, once again, believe there is a need to commission some independent market research. Further requirements may still be identified whilst reading through the whole of Step 5. Completing the research brief should therefore be delayed until then.

For each appropriate feature appearing in Step 3, draw up on a separate piece of paper the list of attributes your market attaches to them. If there is any uncertainty in drawing up this list, simply note the information shortfalls. The opportunity to compile a full research brief appears shortly.

It could be the case that within an individual micro-segment, one or more of the features may have different attributes attached to them. To accommodate this, further new micro-segments should be opened up and the volume/value re-distributed between them.

■ The Key CPIs

Part 3 consists of two stages: the first re-arranges the 'what', 'where', 'when' and 'how' categories selected for each preliminary segment into an order of importance and then highlights those which play a significant role in the buying process across the market. The buying criteria now seen as being 'significant' can then be extended, where appropriate, by attaching the different attributes associated with them. The optional second stage allows you to allocate the final list of purchase requirements into either 'buying criteria' or 'attitude' groups.

■ Ranking the 'What', 'Where', 'When' and 'How' Items

For each preliminary segment, including any new ones created earlier in this step, re-arrange their 'what', 'where', 'when' and 'how' categories into a descending order of importance. Use market research data or reasoned judgement to do this.

If you carried out this procedure in Step 4 for *all* your preliminary segments, 'Screening within a preliminary segment through prioritising', and you have not created any new preliminary segments, you can move to the next part of this step, 'Creating market CPIs'.

It may now be possible to decide a cut-off point which separates out those items which play an important part in the buying process from those which, to all intents and purposes, play only a secondary part. In this segmentation process, as already mentioned, we refer to those items which play an important part in the buying process as CPIs.

Here is a quick refresher on how to determine the cut-off point which divides the significant items from the insignificant: once you have re-arranged the items into a descending order of importance, allocate 100 points between them in a way which represents their relative importance to each other *from the market's perspective*, as illustrated in Table 6.1. Draw the cut-off point at, say, where the score comes to 80.

Table 6.1   Determining the CPIs ('Who' – high technology companies)

Purchase categories	Individual score	Cumulative score
'What' product type – Complete unit, Main part only	35	35
'What' service level – 4 hours, 24 hours	30	65
'What' country of origin – UK, mainland Europe, ROW*	20	85
'What' brand – Specialist, General technology company	5	90
'How' – Lease-purchase/hire, Outright purchase	4	94
'What' type of delivery – Collected, delivered	3	97
'When' – As needs, 3 years, 5 years	3	100

*ROW = Rest of the world.

In this particular example, the cut-off point would be after 'What country of origin'. All the items up to the cut-off point would now be regarded as CPIs.

If, in carrying out this prioritising routine, you do not believe all the micro-segments within a particular preliminary segment would produce the same order, note the different orders that occur in separate tables and determine the cut-off point for each of them.

You now have a series of CPI lists, one (or more) for each preliminary segment.

■ **Creating Market CPIs**

First, for those features now appearing as CPIs *and* for which you have developed different attributes in the second part of this step, ensure the appropriate attribute is attached to that particular feature in each applicable preliminary segment. For example, 'brand' may be listed as a CPI and you have developed two attributes for brand: 'quality' and 'R&D'. For each preliminary segment which lists 'brand' as a CPI, extend the feature by adding 'quality' or 'R&D' as appropriate.

Whenever a feature is extended in this way, this also extends the total number of CPIs. In the example, therefore, 'Brand – quality' and 'Brand – R&D' are now separate CPIs.

Now compile one CPI list for the whole market by bringing each separate list together. *These are now your market CPIs.*

■ **Optional: Allocating the Market CPIs into 'Buying Criteria' or 'Attitude' Lists**

This optional process allows you to test segmentation results obtainable from the data by separately grouping your micro-segments by buying criteria and by attitude.

Re-arrange your market CPIs into two groups. The first group, 'buying criteria', should be made up of the physical components of the purchase such as size, packaging, shed and so on. The second group, 'attitude', should be made up of the intangible components of the purchase, such as brand.

■ **Price**

Clearly, 'price' has an important part to play in the buying activity of segments and is obviously a component of 'buying criteria'. Everything has its price!

However, 'price', as a distinct topic, has been deliberately kept out of the process up until now because it can too easily be used as a 'catch all' or 'get out' in answer to some of the more difficult questions posed by this segmentation process. All too often, 'price' is given as the reason for particular buying activity. Not everyone buys the cheapest, and for those that do, it could be because there is nothing available in the market that really meets their requirements, as was pointed out earlier in this chapter. Produce the product/ service they are looking for, and price becomes less of an issue.

'Price' is simply a measure of value placed by the buyer on both the tangible and intangible components of a purchase. A simple example should suffice to illustrate this point: a company launched a new pure juice product on the market after tests had indicated an overwhelming acceptance by the target group. When sales fell far short of expectations, research indicated that the target group simply did not believe that the claims on the can about the product could be true at such a low price. So the company doubled the price and re-launched it, and the product was a resounding success.

For the purposes of segmentation, we are concerned with the relative importance of price to the other components of the purchase: in other words, to what extent will the purchaser let their requirements be bought out by lower prices? Alternatively, when will they start trading in their requirements in order to keep the price at an acceptable level? The ability of one supplier to supply the market at lower prices than everyone else is not the issue we are addressing here, or need to address, when segmenting markets.

To conclude these comments on price, it is worth noting that, in some instances, the role played by price can be distorted (as in the case, for example, of company car purchases by individuals). This will certainly be true when none of the options available are really what the employee wants, yet they 'have' to spend their allowance! Ideally, however, this would have been picked up earlier in this chapter.

■ Attaching the CPIs and their Values to the Micro-segments

This is achieved by apportioning between all the market CPIs for every micro-segment a total of 100 to attach to the CPIs a relative value relationship. Wherever a particular market CPI is irrelevant, attach a zero score. *Do not forget to include a relative score for price.*

Market research note: At this point, you may have identified another area of weakness in your market research data. It is now timely to complete your research brief and commission some independent market research. Information gaps identified earlier in the process should also be included in this research project. In addition, and assuming it has not been already identified as an information gap in the process so far, it will help Step 7 if the research gathers demographic, geographic and psychographic profile data from the companies/individuals interviewed.

As the market research project progresses, the implications of any new findings should be incorporated into the segmentation steps taken so far and the necessary amendments made. The 'attitudes' and 'needs' data can then be fed directly into the process so that the clustering routine detailed in Step 6 can take place. Alternatively, it may be possible to include in the specification for the research project this clustering procedure, with the resulting segments tested against the checklist appearing in Step 7.

This stage may be helped by identifying for each micro-segment the top 3–5 market CPIs – in other words, the 3–5 most important – and list them in rank order, including price, with the most important first. (Three to five is a guideline figure. It could be more, or it could be less: what you are focusing on at this stage are the CPIs which account for around 80 per cent of the decision. Only on very rare occasions is the number likely to be above this.) Then apportion between each micro-segment's CPIs a total of 100 in order to remove the linear relationship implied by the rank order (and unlikely to be the case) and attach a relative value relationship *from the micro-segment's perspective*.

For example, the three most important CPIs could be:

1. Brand – quality.
2. Three-litre size.
3. Recyclable container.

The relative values of these three CPIs to each other, along with price, may have been found to be:

1.	Brand – quality:	40
2.	Recyclable container:	35
3.	Three litre size:	15
4.	Price.	10
	Total	100

If market research data is available, particularly if it has used the technique of requesting respondents to allocate between their buying criteria a pre-specified sum, such as 100, attach the values obtained through this exercise to the CPIs.

At this stage, you may discover that the CPIs and their values for your products are almost identical. If this is the case, segmentation by product bought is irrelevant and you should reduce the number of product types at this micro level.

If you are in a business with a number of SBUs, and have, so far, been looking at only one of them, although the intention is to take all the SBUs through the process, this point can be a useful stage in the process to take stock and tackle the remaining SBUs, bringing them through Steps 1 to 5. This is because Step 6 is where the process seeks to group common micro-segments. If all your SBUs are, therefore, included in Step 6, it will enable you to see whether your current SBU structure is the most appropriate for the market, or whether a re-organisation of your business is required. You may, of course, prefer to take the first SBU through the whole process in order to become familiar with it, after which the remaining SBUs are taken through Steps 1 to 5, with the first SBU taken through Step 6 again, once the remaining SBUs are ready.

A key question to re-address at this point is: are you absolutely sure that the reasons listed are not hiding any underlying needs which are not being met? If your answer is 'No', it is recommended that you, or a professional market research interviewer, conduct face-to-face interviews with a small sample (five or six) of those customers you are still unsure about. This should be sufficient to indicate whether or not there are any unmet needs yet to be discovered. If necessary, this check should then move on to a larger scale project in order to quantify the extent and value of these unmet needs.

■ **Features, Advantages and Benefits**

Customers buy products and services because they seek to acquire a range of benefits that go with them. For example, the motivation behind employing a surveyor when contemplating moving into a new house is not to preserve the sub-species *homo sapiens surveyorcus*; analgesics are not bought to keep the pharmaceutical manufacturers in business; and the do-it-yourselfers do not buy drill bits out of an interest in preserving the precision engineering industry of the Lower Don Valley! Purchasers are rarely motivated in the first instance by the technical features or attributes of a service or product, but rather by the benefits those features or attributes bring with them. Therefore, the surveyor is employed because the buyer wants to be assured the proposed new property is structurally sound; analgesics are bought to relieve pain; and, as a drill manufacturer is quoted as saying, 'Last year we sold one million quarter-inch drills, not because people wanted quarter-inch drills, but because they wanted quarter-inch holes' (although this could be seen as a blinkered understanding of the need, which is basically to attach two items together and could therefore be achieved by using an appropriate glue!). Understanding benefits is therefore as important as knowing about the products or services themselves. It is equally important to realise that different customers may attach different values to these benefits.

■ **Standard Benefits**

These are the basic benefits that arise from the features of the product, but are not in any way unique to any particular manufacturer/supplier: for example, 'the aerosol propellant is one that does not damage the ozone layer'. Even if all aerosols contained such propellants, it is still worth noting as it could be an important consideration in the purchasing decision for your market. Its importance may also differ between segments.

■ **Company Benefits**

Whenever a purchase is made, the transaction links the customer to the company supplying the item. Links will be forged between the two at many levels. For example, in business-to-business transactions their accounts departments will be in contact to deal with payment or financial matters; people on installation work or after-sales servicing will interact with the personnel at the buyer's company; delivery men with storemen; designers with technicians, and so on. When a buyer selects one of a number of competing suppliers, there ought to be some benefits to that buyer for making that choice.

Customers will prefer to deal with companies that, for example, provide better customer service, inspire confidence, have a reputation for fair trading policies, are known to be flexible, or even have a particular image associated with them. Company benefits are a means of differentiating your products/services from competing ones if, to all intents and purposes, they are similar. Take UK banks, for example: some are trying to establish specific identities for the benefits they supply. Hence there is the 'action bank', the 'bank that likes to say yes' and the 'listening bank'. There are now even banks which are 'open when their customers want them to be'!

■ **Differential Benefits**

In a competitive market place, most suppliers vying for the available customers will not be able to claim that their standard, or company, benefits are, in truth regarded as being very different from those of the competition. The benefits that only your products or services provide, which are also benefits in the eyes of the customer, give your company its competitive advantage and are known as 'differential benefits'. To understand your market dynamics fully, however, particularly in the context of developing a segmentation structure for it, you not only need to be able to list your own company's differential benefits, you also need to list those differential benefits of your competitors which attract some of the market to them, as opposed to you. Differential benefits could include, for example:

(a)   the only breakdown service genuinely open 24 hours a day and therefore available at any time to get the customer back on the move;

(b)   the only product with self-cleaning heads, so once installed there are no maintenance worries.

It is important to note, however, that a particular feature may have more than one benefit, and the most appropriate benefit(s) to highlight could well differ by segment. For example, an airline's non-stop service between two cities could mean:

(a)   a better use of time because less of it is spent at 35 000 feet;

(b)   less opportunity to go missing at transit airports and get left behind (an important concern for expatriates sending their children back home for the school term);

(c)   a better chance of arriving on time (a transit stop is an opportunity for delaying incidents to occur).

■ Distinguishing between Features, Advantages and Benefits

To get from a feature to an advantage, and then to a benefit, the phrase 'which means that' can be helpful. For example, 'This product is coated in new formula paint (*feature*) which means that the colour will never fade (*advantage*)'. If you *know* this is what the customer *needs*, then you have also arrived at a *benefit*.

Sometimes the expression 'which means that' can sound rather clumsy. When this happens, an alternative linking word is 'because': for example, 'You can be sure of personal attention from us because we are a small family business.'

To check if you have arrived at a benefit and not just an advantage, apply the 'so what?' test. Ask this question after the benefit. If the 'so what?' prompts you to go further, it is likely you have not yet reached the real benefit: for example, 'The products are hand-made (*feature*), which means they are better quality than machine-made ones (*benefit?*) – 'so what?' – which means they last longer (*the real benefit*).

■ Developing the Benefits List for your Market

In arriving at the pertinent list of benefits for the whole market you will initially need to concern yourself with 'customer appeal'. The first step in arriving at the final benefits list is, therefore, to determine what issues are of particular concern to the customer. This can then be developed into a list of the feature(s) that enable the product/service to appeal to the customer, then the advantage(s) they provide and, finally, the benefits. Table 6.2 contains a structure for a benefits analysis sheet which will assist this process, and three examples.

Table 6.2 Benefit analysis sheet

Customer appeal	Features	Advantages	Benefits
What issues are of particular concern for this customer? For example, reliability, availability, safety, simplicity, fashionable, leading edge and so on.	What features of the product/service best illustrate these issues? What are they? How do they work?	What advantages do these features provide? In other words, what do they do for the customer?	How can tangible benefits be expressed to give maximum customer appeal? In other words, what does the customer get *that he/she needs*?
Credit cards Ease of use. Safer than carrying money. Less bulky than cash or cheque book. Speedy transaction. Provide credit. International.	Access credit card.	Enables purchases to be made world-wide.	Eliminates the need to carry large amounts of cash. Eases cash flow problems and so on.
Saucepans Ease of use. Ease of washing up. Attractive end product.	Teflon coated.	Non-stick.	Trouble-free cooking. Quicker washing up. Better presentation of food and so on.
Office Service Bureaux Accuracy. Speedy turnround of work.	Latest software. Very skilled staff.	Extremely versatile.	Minimum of errors. Cost saving on overheads.

■ **Summary**

- Feature – what it is, or is made from

- Advantage – what it does

- Benefit – what the customer gets that they need (or want)

CHAPTER 7

Segmentation: Stage 1 (Step 6)

■ Summary

This step discusses the routine required for building the micro-segments back up into market segments. With a manageable number of micro-segments it is possible to carry this out manually. However, in many instances the assistance of a computer, suitably programmed, may be required. A program for this already exists. It is called *The Market Segment Master*. For further details, contact Professor Malcolm McDonald at Cranfield University School of Management, Cranfield, Bedford, MK43 0AL, United Kingdom (fax +44 (0)1234 751806).

■ Size and Number of Market Segments

Before proceeding to combine similar micro-segments, two important decisions need to be made:

- What is the economical minimum number of customers/consumers needed for each segment, or what is the economical value or volume of sales needed for each segment?

  'Value' could, of course, be represented by volume multiplied by margin. Ensure whatever 'measurement' you use corresponds to that used so far in the process, particularly in measuring the micro-segments.

- What is the manageable number of segments the business can handle?

  Whatever the number you arrive at, increase it by, say, one-third. It is unlikely you will be able to operate in all the resulting segments successfully and so you will need to select the most promising segments for your business. Chapters 9 and 10 contain routines which enable you to select the most appropriate segments.

The importance in Step 5 of creating micro-segments for those customers in the market with unmet needs, along with a forecast of their additional sales volume/value, should now be apparent. Step 6 could see them being absorbed into macro-segments unnecessarily, purely to meet the criteria listed above. Equally, you should at this point be alert to micro-segments which presently only have a small volume/value, but which are seen as offering growth potential for the future and therefore are of great strategic importance. To protect these micro-segments from being absorbed unnecessarily, attach to them a projected volume/value rating to reflect their potential. Note the alpha-numeric reference of all the micro-segments which have their size increased this way.

The future size of segments is a topic covered in Chapter 9.

■ Clustering Micro-Segments into Market Segments

The micro-segments should now be subject to the first clustering routine (the mechanics of a clustering routine are discussed later in this chapter).

Routine 1   This routine produces an overall 'best fit' report showing the degrees of similarity in each resulting segment of the demographic, geographic and psychographic descriptions, in addition to the market CPIs (including 'price'). You will have to do this manually if you do not have the computer program.

Depending on how satisfied you are with the degree of 'fit' obtained in this first clustering routine, you may wish to explore alternative clustering routines to see whether or not this 'fit' can be improved upon. Up to four further clustering routines can be available if you followed the process in its entirety (up to two if you did not opt to divide the CPIs between 'buying criteria' and 'attitudes'). The four clustering routines are as shown below.

Routine 2   A demographic, geographic and psychographic 'best fit' report which shows how good a 'demographic, geographic and psychographic fit' was achieved, as well as showing the degree of similarity between the CPIs in each resulting segment.

Routine 3   A CPI 'best fit' report which shows how good a 'CPI fit' was achieved, as well as showing the degree of similarity between the demographic, geographic and psychographic descriptions in each resulting segment.

Routine 4   A buying criteria CPI 'best fit' report which shows how good a 'buying criteria CPI fit' was achieved, as well as showing the degree of similarity between the attitude CPIs and demographic, geographic and psychographic descriptions in each resulting segment.

Routine 5   An attitude CPI 'best fit' report which shows how good an 'attitude CPI fit' was achieved, as well as showing the degree of similarity between the buying criteria CPIs and demographic, geographic and psychographic descriptions in each resulting segment.

Two options can be looked at when running these clustering routines with the aid of a computer:

- Option 'A': taking the clustering routine through its various stages, step by step.

- Option 'B': leaving a computerised clustering routine to proceed straight to the final reports. This would produce 1–5 reports (depending on whether you have opted to divide the CPIs between buying criteria and attitudes).

Option 'A' is the only routine available if you are carrying out this step manually, using the guidelines contained in this chapter.

■ Progressively Building your Market Segments (Option A)

The clustering reports you wish to produce can be progressively built using this option.

The example which follows relates to Routine 3 and suggests one approach which could be adopted for manual clustering. You may, however, prefer to adopt a slightly different approach, but one which follows the same principle of gradually merging the micro-segments together. The other reports would be built in a similar way.

First, cluster together all the micro-segments which have the same CPIs and CPI values. On completing this first pass, determine the size of each cluster based on a count of the customers/consumers or value/volume of the micro-segments which have been clustered together. To assist the next stage, the clusters should appear in groups, the group being determined by the highest-valued CPI. All those micro-segments which have, for example, 'available at my local retailer' as the highest-valued CPI will now appear together, broken down into their unique second and third CPI combinations, as illustrated in Figure 7.1.

Each cluster should list the micro-segments which have gone into making up that cluster, using the unique label attached to each of them in Step 4 as the identifier. It is useful if the labels are arranged in alpha-numeric order.

Cluster Group A: Highest-ranked CPI, 'Available at my local retailer':

Cluster 1

Local availability:	40
Colour required:	35
Well-known brand:	25
Total value:	£1.250m

Micro-segments included from Step 4: A1 A2 A7 B4 C1 C3

Cluster 2

Local availability:	55
Colour required:	35
Delivery:	10
Total value:	£0.950m

Micro-segments included from Step 4: B1 C2 C7 C8 D1 E3

Cluster 3

Local availability:	35
Colour required:	33
On demand:	32
Total value:	£0.650m

Micro-segments included from Step 4: B2 B3 D2 D3 E9

Cluster Group B: Highest-ranked CPI, 'Colour required':

Cluster 1

Colour required:	75
Well-known brand:	25
Total value:	£1.200m

Micro-segments included from Step 4: A3 A4 B5 C5 E4 E10

Cluster 2

Colour required:	70
Local availability:	25
Well-known brand:	5
Total value:	£1.100m

Micro-segments included from Step 4: A6 B9 D5 E5 E6

Figure 7.1 A micro-segment clustering report

A summary of this first pass should be made, such as:

Total number of concluding segments: 86 (76 above specification, if ten was decided as being the maximum)

Number of concluding segments matching the minimum value specification (for example, £1.25 million):   1 (with 85 below specification)

After reviewing the results of the first cluster pass, any resulting segments which meet the value specification should be put to one side and omitted from the next pass. They will, however, be reviewed at the close of the subsequent passes.

For the second and subsequent clustering passes through the micro-segments, the values attributed to each benefit in each segment should be progressively expanded. For example, the next pass may have the following specification:

> *Expand the value attributed to all third ranked CPIs by one point either side, leaving the values attributed to the first and second benefits as they are.*

The results of this pass would then be listed as detailed above. Wherever expanding the values produces clusters which now match segments put aside in previous passes, they will need to be highlighted and a decision is required on whether to merge them or keep them separate.

Another possibility is that for some clusters, expanding the value of the third ranked benefit could make it match or even exceed the value attributed to the second ranked benefit. Although this does not change the order of benefits, a further report is useful here which is generated by a further clustering routine. This extra routine would need to run through the micro-segments and, where necessary, expand the value of the second ranked benefit by the amount required to match the higher value which the expansion has given to the third benefit. For example, take Group A, Cluster 3 (A3) as listed earlier. When the clustering routine has expanded the values attributed to 'on demand' by two on either side, this produces the range 30–4. In A3, however, the second ranked benefit is 'colour required' and has a value of 33. The extra routine should run through the micro-segments and produce a clustering report which gave a value range of 32–4 to 'colour required' in A3. A decision would then be required on whether to accept or reject the clustering produced by this further routine.

This iterative process should continue until all the micro-segments are swept up, inevitably with ever-weakening specifications.

Profiles of each concluding market segment would now be built up by listing the demographic, geographic and/or psychographic descriptions associated with each micro-segment it now contained. In order to determine how representative each of these descriptions were for their market segment, they should be 'weighted' by adding up the size of each micro-segment now accommodated in the market segment carrying that description. For example, age profiles may have been allocated to each micro-segment, as in Table 7.1, thus enabling an age profile to be drawn up for each concluding segment.

Table 7.1   Age profiles of segments in a market

Segment 1 (vol./val. 2050)			Segment 2 (vol./val. 3050)		
Micro-segment	Age		Micro-segment	Age	
	30–40	40–50		30–40	40–50
A2	300		A1	500	
B3		1 000	A4	300	
D2	250		D5		250
D3		500	E1	2 000	
Total	550	1 500	Total	2 800	250
	26.8%	73.2%		91.8%	8.2%

From Table 7.1 you could state that, 'Segment 1 was predominantly in the age group 40–50', and that 'Segment 2 was predominantly in the age group 30–40'. If, however, the concluding segments had a less focused age structure, you would then conclude that 'age' was not a discriminator between segments in the market being looked at.

A summary of demographic profiles for the concluding segments in a study of the USA's historical romance novel market appear in Table 7.2.

Table 7.2   Segment demographics of the historical romance novel market (USA)

	Segment 1 (Movers and shakers)	Segment 2 (Isolated readers)	Segment 3 (Young swingers)	Segment 4 (Laggards)
Age	Average age: 30–40	Average age: 40–50	Average age: under 30 years	Average age: over 50 years
Children	One or no children	At least one child	Most have no children	Most have grown children
Education	High school education	High school education	One-third have college degree	Least education
Employment and income	Most employed; family income of $20 000	Half are employed; family income of $20 000	Most employed; income less than $20 000	More unemployed; lowest income

Source: S.P. Schnaars and L.G. Schiffman, 'An application of segmentation design based on a hybrid of canonical correlation and simple cross tabulation', Journal of the Academy of Marketing Science, 12 (Autumn 1984).

CHAPTER 8

Segmentation: Stage 2 (Step 7)

■ Summary

To conclude this stage of the segmentation process, each market segment is checked against size, differentiation, reachability and company compatibility.

■ The Segmentation Checklist

For the concluding segments in Step 6, apply the segmentation checklist as follows:

- Volume/Value The 'size' test for each segment should already have been cleared in Step 6. Segments have to be measurable.

- Differentiated Is the offer required by each segment sufficiently different from that required by the other segments? This is where the marketing strategies appropriate for one segment are checked to ensure they are distinguishable from the marketing strategies developed for the other segments.

- Reachable This is where the different marketing strategies are checked to ensure that they can be directed towards their applicable segments. Each segment must therefore have a distinctive profile, for example:

  - distinct television viewing, radio listening, newspaper or magazine reading profiles; and/or
  - distinct characteristics which can classify them by a geographic area, such as post codes; and/or
  - distinct purchasing patterns; and/or
  - distinct distribution channels; and/or
  - distinct benefits they are looking for; and/or
  - distinct responses to prices.

If it is not clear whether your segments meet this requirement, first check you have explored all the possible distribution and communication alternatives available. Once this is complete, it may be necessary to review the profiles of each micro-segment appearing in the final clusters. You then need to use your judgement to decide whether the cluster is reachable.

Before rejecting any cluster that is not sufficiently homogeneous in terms of their descriptions, ensure that there are not some different descriptions that you have overlooked that would enable them to be reached cost effectively by your marketing effort, such as:

– demographic characteristics;
– geographic characteristics;
– psychographic characteristics.

The lists appearing in the segmentation summaries in Chapter 3 (Step 2), supplemented by the Appendices, could be of use here.

● Compatibility   This is where you rigorously check your own company's ability to focus on the new segments by structuring itself around them organisationally, culturally, in its management information systems and in its decision-making processes. Such changes may not be possible immediately, therefore the organisation's ability to evolve to the required structure should be tested.

To help you through this checklist, the following procedure may be of use. For *every* segment generated, carry out the following (of the five questions, questions 2, 4 and 6 are the most important; it is therefore *essential* they each can be answered by a 'Yes'):

1. Can this segment be measured by a set of measurable parameters? (For example, volume, value, number of customers.)

Yes [ ]   No [ ]

2. Has the segment achieved sufficient size to make it worth being considered a significant business opportunity? (This should have been covered in Step 6, which will also have ensured you have not excluded those segments with strategic potential, either because of unmet needs or because they are at an early stage of their growth curve.)

Yes [ ]   No [ ]

3. Can this segment be served by a common sales and distribution channel? Please note, If there is any reason why you do not want a 'No' answer to reject this segment (for example, customers with similar requirements may use different distribution channels), mark the answer 'Yes'.

Yes [ ]   No [ ]

4. Can you identify and reach customers in this segment by means of a distinctive and cost effective communications strategy (for example, promotion, selling, advertising)?

Yes [ ]   No [ ]

5. Can this segment be clearly identified by a set of common characteristics, and can you describe it?

Yes [ ]   No [ ]

6. Can your company adopt a structure and information system which will enable you to serve this segment effectively?

Yes [ ]   No [ ]

Developing the segments for the market in which your business operates is now complete. You can now move on to Chapters 9 and 10 which enable you to prioritise and select the segments in which your business should focus its resources.

CHAPTER 9

Segment Attractiveness (Steps 8–11)

■ Summary

Now the segments in your market have been defined, it is essential that you determine how attractive each segment is to your company. This, along with an analysis of your competitiveness in each segment (Chapter 10), will help you decide how best to distribute your financial and managerial resources between them.

In this chapter we start by suggesting some attractiveness factors you may wish to consider and then move on to attach weightings to your selected factors in order to gauge their relative importance to each other. 'High', 'medium' and 'low' parameters are then defined for each attractiveness factor, with each segment finally scored against the selected factors. The chapter starts, however, with a summary of portfolio analysis, followed by a brief discussion about the planning period over which you should be assessing the segments.

■ Portfolio Analysis

Portfolio analysis, for the purposes of this book, is simply a means of assessing a number of different segments, first of all according to the potential of each in terms of achieving an organisation's objectives, and second according to the organisation's ability to take advantage of the identified opportunities.

The idea of a portfolio is for a company to meet its objectives by balancing sales growth, cash flow and risk. As individual segments grow or shrink, then the overall nature of the company's portfolio will change. It is therefore essential that the whole portfolio is reviewed regularly and that an active policy towards the move into new segments and the exiting of old segments is pursued.

Widely referred to as the *Directional Policy Matrix* (DPM), portfolio analysis offers a detailed framework which can be used to classify possible competitive environments and their strategy requirements. It uses several indicators to measure the dimensions of 'segment attractiveness' on the one hand, and 'company competitiveness' on the other. These indicators can be altered by management to suit the operating conditions of particular markets.

The purpose of the matrix is to diagnose an organisation's strategy options in relation to the two composite dimensions outlined above.

Portfolio analysis initially came out of the work of the Boston Consulting Group, begun in the 1960s, and it has had a profound effect on the way management think about their market and their activity within it.

There are basically two parts to the thinking behind the work of the Boston Consulting Group. One is concerned with *market share* and the other with *market growth*, which we would translate into *segment share* and *segment growth*. These are brought together into a single matrix (the Boston matrix), which has important implications for the firm, especially in respect of *cash flow*. Cash is a key determinant of a company's ability to develop its segment portfolio.

For the purposes of this book, the Boston matrix can be used to classify a firm's position in each segment found in the market according to their cash usage and their cash generation along the two dimensions described above, namely relative segment share and rate of segment growth. This is summarised in Figure 9.1.

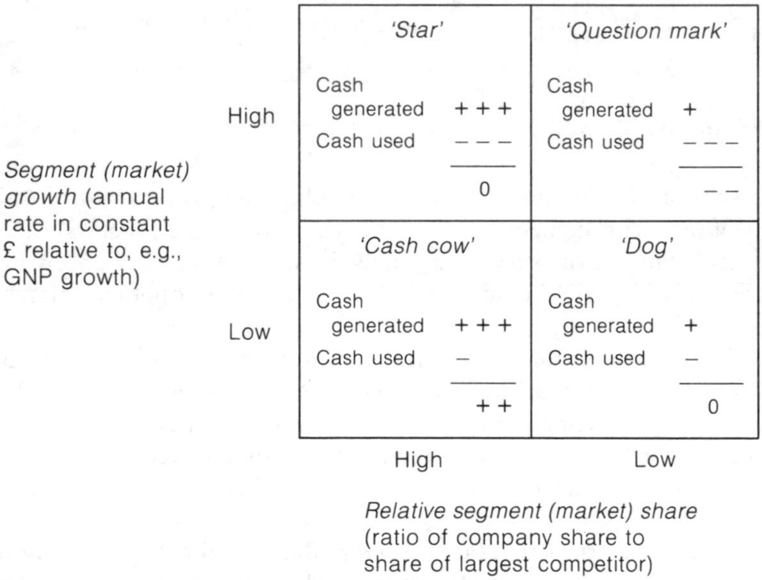

	'Star'	'Question mark'
High	Cash generated + + + Cash used − − − ————— 0	Cash generated + Cash used − − − ————— − −
Low	'Cash cow' Cash generated + + + Cash used − ————— + +	'Dog' Cash generated + Cash used − ————— 0

Segment (market) growth (annual rate in constant £ relative to, e.g., GNP growth)

High   Low

Relative segment (market) share (ratio of company share to share of largest competitor)

Figure 9.1   The Boston matrix

The somewhat picturesque labels attached to each of the four categories give some indication of the prospects for the *company* in each quadrant. Thus, the 'question mark' is a segment in which the company has not yet achieved a dominant position and, therefore, a high cash flow, or perhaps it once had such a position but has slipped back. It will be a high user of cash because it is a growth segment. This is also sometimes referred to as a 'wildcat'.

The 'star' is probably a newish segment in which the company has achieved a high share and which is probably more or less self-financing in cash terms.

The 'cash cows' are leaders in segments where there is little additional growth, but a lot of stability. These are excellent generators of cash and tend to use little because of the state of the segment.

'Dogs' often have little future and can be a cash drain on the company. They are probably segments the company should exit, although it is often very difficult to leave 'old friends'.

The art of managing segments as a portfolio now becomes a lot clearer. What we should be seeking to do is to use the surplus cash generated by the 'cash cows' to invest in our 'stars' and also to invest in a selected number of 'question marks'.

The approach of the Boston Consulting Group is, however, fairly criticised because of its dependence on two single factors: relative segment share and segment growth. To overcome this difficulty, and to provide a more flexible approach, General Electric (GE) and McKinsey jointly developed a multi-factor approach using the same fundamental ideas as the Boston Consulting Group.

The GE/McKinsey approach uses *industry attractiveness* and *business strengths* as the two main axes, and builds up these dimensions from a number of variables. When applying this to segments, the first (vertical) axis is re-labelled *segment attractiveness*. We have also re-labelled the horizontal axis *company competitiveness*. Using these variables, and some scheme for weighting them according to their importance, segments are classified into one of nine cells in a 3 × 3 matrix. Thus, the same purpose is served as in the Boston matrix (namely, comparing investment opportunities among segments) but with the difference that multiple criteria are used. These criteria vary according to circumstances, but generally include those shown in Figure 9.2.

It is not necessary, however, to use a nine-box matrix, and many managers prefer to use a four-box matrix similar to the Boston box, while using the GE/McKinsey definitions for the axes. This is the preferred methodology of the authors as it seems to be more easily understood by, and useful to, practising managers.

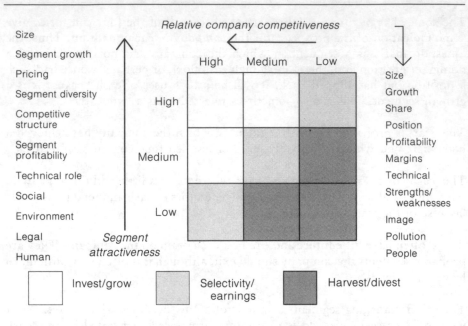

Figure 9.2   The nine-box portfolio matrix

The four-box matrix is shown in Figure 9.3. Here, the circles represent sales into a segment, with each circle being proportional to that segment's contribution to turnover. The position of each segment on the matrix is determined by its attractiveness and the company's competitive position within it.

The difference in this case is that, rather than using only two variables, the criteria which are used for each axis are totally relevant and specific to each company using the matrix. It shows:

- Segments categorised on a scale of attractiveness to the company
- The company's relative strengths in each of these segments
- The relative importance of each segment to the company

An example of an actual segment portfolio directional policy matrix is presented in Figure 9.4. The procedures contained in this chapter and Chapter 10 will equip you to produce your own DPM.

Portfolio analysis is discussed in more detail in Chapter 5 of *Marketing Plans – How to Prepare Them: How to Use Them*, M. H. B. McDonald, 3rd edn (Oxford: Heinemann, 1995).

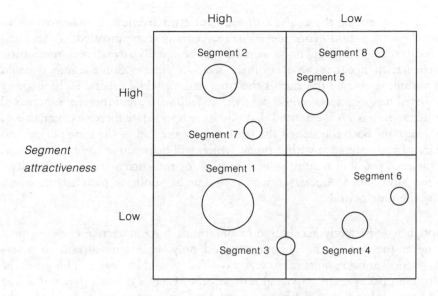

Figure 9.3 The four-box matrix

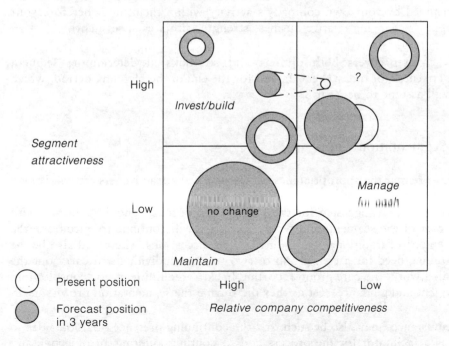

Figure 9.4 DPM for a portfolio of segments

■ Time Horizon

Prior to commencing the analysis of segment attractiveness, it is important to define the time period being scored (three years is recommended). A segment that is attractive today will not automatically be equally attractive in the future. A particular change that can occur is the size of segments. Some segments could have shrunk in size by the end of the time period, while others, including any anticipated new segments, could have increased in size, and therefore increased their attractiveness. It is essential that you have up-to-date forecasts available to help determine both the size of the segments by the end of the time period and the size of your presence within them, which will help you in the next chapter. To this end, you will require sales forecasts for the current products/services, and for any new products/services your current policies plan to introduce during the time period.

Although it is perfectly acceptable to determine how attractive each segment will be at the *end* of the planning period only, it is quite useful to assess attractiveness at two points in time: today (Year 0) and in Year 3. This gives the resulting portfolio matrix a visual indication of each segment's dynamics. The DPM presented in Figure 9.4 has segment attractiveness calculated only for the final year. In such circumstances, segments can only move horizontally – that is, along the same level of attractiveness – with their direction of movement determined by your own company's activity within them (and therefore your company's changing relative business strength within each segment).

This chapter covers both options and so looks at determining segment attractiveness for today (Year 0), and for the end of the planning period, which we will assume to be Year 3.

■ Segmentation Team

To ensure that the appropriateness of the selected attractiveness criteria is high and that the scoring is realistic, it is recommended that the same cross-functional team suggested for the segmentation process should continue with this part of the segmentation work. This mix will continue to encourage the challenging of traditional views during their discussions. There will also be the continuing need for a core group of two to three individuals to carry out the detailed work, the core group reporting back to the full team for consultation, comment and guidance, just as they did during the segmentation process itself.

Circumstances may also be such that the continuing presence of an outsider to act as a facilitator for the process and to continue offering an objective and alternative viewpoint to the discussion could still be warranted.

■ Definition

Segment attractiveness in Year 3 is a measure of the potential of a segment to yield growth in sales and profits during the next three years (that is $t0$ to $t+3$, where t represents time), with Year 0 representing the current attractiveness of a segment based on the past three years (that is $t-3$ to $t0$). It is important to stress that this should be an objective assessment of segment attractiveness using data *external* to the organisation. The criteria themselves will, of course, be determined by the organisation carrying out the exercise and will be relevant to the objectives the organisation is trying to achieve, but the criteria should be *independent* of the organisation's position in its segments.

Put another way: imagine you have a measuring instrument, something like a thermometer, which measures not temperature but segment attractiveness. The higher the reading, the more attractive the segment. The instrument is shown in Figure 9.5. Estimate the position on the scale *each* of your segments would record (should such an instrument exist) and make a note of it.

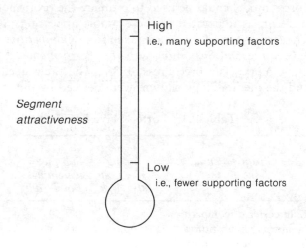

Figure 9.5   Measuring segment attractiveness

■ Segment Attractiveness Factors (Step 8)

Here, you should list the factors you wish to consider in comparing the attractiveness of your segments. This will be a combination of a number of factors, though they can usually be summarised under three headings.

Growth rate	Average annual growth rate of revenue spent by that segment (percentage growth of 1995 over 1994, *plus* percentage growth of 1996 over 1995, *plus* percentage growth of 1997 over 1996, with the total divided by three: in other words, the number of years being looked at). If preferred, compound average growth rate could be used. Clearly, in determining segment growth rates, you will need to take into account the supportiveness (or otherwise) of the overall business environment.
Accessible segment size	An attractive segment is not only large, it also has to be accessed. One way of calculating this is to estimate the total revenue of the segment during the selected time span, *less* revenue impossible to access, *regardless of investment made*. Alternatively, total segment size can be used, which is the most frequent method, as it does not involve any managerial judgement to be made that could distort the true picture. This latter method is the method advised here.
Profit potential	This is much more difficult to deal with and will vary considerably, according to segment. For example, Porter's Five Forces model could be used to estimate the profit potential of a segment, as illustrated in the example appearing in Table 9.1. The factors for this table are taken from *Competitive Advantage – Creating and Sustaining Superior Performance*, M. E. Porter (New York: The Free Press, 1985). The table itself, however, and the methodology shown, were devised by the authors.

Table 9.1   Porter's Five Forces model

Profit potential sub-factors	*Segment rating* $10=Low$ $0=High$	*Sub-factor weightings (Total−100)*	*Weighted factor scores (rating × weight)*
1. Intensity of competition		50	
2. Threat of substitutes		5	
3. Threat of new entrants		5	
4. Power of suppliers		10	
5. Power of customers		30	
		Profit potential factor score	

Alternatively, a combination of these and segment specific factors could be used. In the case of the pharmaceutical market, for example, the sub-factors could be those appearing in Table 9.2.

Table 9.2 Profit potential sub-factors in the pharmaceutical market

Sub-factors	High	Med.	Low	× Weight	Weighted sub-factor score
Unmet medical needs (efficacy)				30	
Unmet medical needs (safety)				25	
Unmet medical needs (convenience)				15	
Price potential				10	
Competitive intensity				10	
Cost of segment entry				10	
				Profit potential factor score	

These are clearly a proxy for profit potential. Each is weighted according to its importance. The weights add up to 100 in order to give a *profit potential factor score*, as in the Porter's Five Forces example (Table 9.1).

Naturally, growth, size and profit will not encapsulate the requirements of all organisations. For example, in the case of an orchestra, artistic satisfaction may be an important consideration. In another case, social considerations could be important. In yet another, cyclicality may be crucial.

It is possible, then, to add another heading, such as 'risk' or 'other' to the three headings listed earlier.

A generalised list of possible attractiveness factors is shown below. It is advisable to use no more than an overall total of five or six factors between your selected headings, otherwise the exercise becomes too complex and loses its focus.

Market factors
Size (money, units or both)
Growth rate per year
Sensitivity to price, service features and external factors
Cyclicality
Seasonality
Bargaining power of upstream suppliers
Bargaining power of downstream suppliers

Competition
Types of competitors
Degree of concentration
Changes in type and mix
Entries and exits
Changes in share
Substitution by new technology
Degrees and types of integration

Financial and economic factors
Contribution margins
Leveraging factors, such as economies of scale and experience
Barriers to entry or exit (financial and non-financial)
Capacity utilisation

Technological factors
Maturity and volatility
Complexity
Differentiation
Patents and copyrights
Manufacturing process technology required

Socio-political factors
Social attitudes and trends
Laws and government agency regulations
Influence with pressure groups and government representatives
Human factors, such as unionisation and community acceptance

Source: M. H. B. McDonald, *Marketing Plans – How to Prepare Them: How to Use Them,* 3rd edn (Oxford: Heinemann, 1995).

■ Weighting the Factors (Step 9)

For each of the factors for segment attractiveness, weight their relative importance to each other according to your own particular requirements.

Given that the overall aim of a company is usually represented in a profit figure, and that profit is a function of:

Segment Volume × Margin × Growth

it would be reasonable to expect a weighting against each of the attractiveness factor headings listed earlier in this chapter to be along the lines shown opposite:

Growth Rate	40
Accessible Segment Size	20
Profit Potential	40
Total	100

An even higher weighting for growth could be understandable in some circumstances (in which case, the corresponding weightings for the others should be reduced). These factors could then be combined with market-specific factors, resulting in a table along the lines shown in Table 9.3.

Table 9.3   Weighting segment attractiveness factors

Market: XYZ	
Segment Attractiveness Factors	*Weight*
1. Volume growth potential	25
2. Profit potential	25
3. Potential segment size (£m)	15
4. Vulnerability	15
5. Competitive intensity	10
6. Cyclicality	10
Total	100

It is important to note that the segment attractiveness factors and their weightings for the market being evaluated cannot change whilst constructing the DPM. Once agreed, under no circumstances should they be changed, otherwise the attractiveness of your segments is not being evaluated against common criteria and the matrix will become meaningless.

■ Defining the Parameters for each Attractiveness Factor (Step 10)

You now need to select high, medium and low parameters for each of the factors selected, where very high scores 10 and very low scores zero. An example is given in Table 9.4.

■ Scoring Segments (Step 11)

For each of the concluding segments arrived at in Steps 1 to 7, you can now establish how attractive each is to your business by using the attractiveness factors and their weightings relative to each other, scoring the segments individually against each factor, multiplying the percentage weighting by the score, and adding the resulting figures together in order to arrive at a total. A worked example of this quantitative approach to evaluation is given in Table 9.5.

Table 9.4   Parameters and their scores for the segment attractiveness factors

Market: XYZ

Segment Attractiveness Factors	Parameters		
	High (10–7)	*Medium (6–4)*	*Low (3–0)*
Growth	GNP* + 5%	GNP	GNP −5%
Profitability	> 15%	10–15%	< 10%
Size	> £5m	£1m–£5m	< £1.0m
Vulnerability	Low	Medium	High
Competitiveness	Low	Medium	High
Cyclicality	Low	Medium	High

* GNP = Gross National Product.

Table 9.5   Segment attractiveness evaluation (for Year 0)

Market: XYZ

Attractiveness	Weight	Segment 1		Segment 2		Segment 3	
		Score	*Total*	*Score*	*Total*	*Score*	*Total*
Growth	25	10	2.5	7	1.75	8	2.0
Profitability	25	8	2.0	8	2.0	6	1.5
Size	15	5	0.75	7	1.05	6	0.9
Vulnerability	15	6	0.9	4	0.6	7	1.05
Competition	10	6	0.6	7	0.7	5	0.5
Cyclicality	10	2.5	0.25	3	0.3	2.5	0.25
Total	100		7.0		6.4		6.2

In this example, an overall score of 7 out of 10 places Segment 1 in the highly attractive category for Year 0.

It should be noted that if in carrying out Steps 1 to 7 you concluded your market had less than five segments, there is little point in using the DPM.

■ Plotting the Position of Segments on the Portfolio Matrix

Transpose the results of your segment attractiveness evaluation on to the matrix, writing the segments on the left of the matrix. Still using the matrix, draw a dotted line horizontally across from each segment, as shown in Figure 9.6.

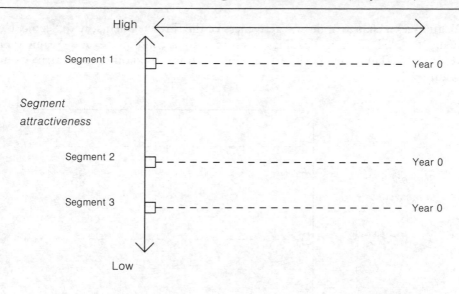

Figure 9.6 Plotting segments on the portfolio matrix according to their attractiveness

In considering the position of each segment on the 'attractiveness' axis at some time in the future, it is important to remember that they can only move vertically *if* the matrix also shows their current level of attractiveness. This implies carrying out one set of calculations for the present time using the agreed segment attractiveness factors, in order to locate segments on the vertical axis for Year 0, then carrying out another set of calculations for a future period (say, in three years' time) based on your forecasts using the same segment attractiveness factors. A re-worked Table 9.5, illustrating the position of each segment in Year 3, appears in Table 9.6.

Table 9.6 Segment attractiveness evaluation (for Year 3)

		Market: XYZ					
		Segment 1		Segment 2		Segment 3	
Attractiveness	*Weight*	*Score*	*Total*	*Score*	*Total*	*Score*	*Total*
Growth	25	6	1.5	5	1.25	10	2.5
Profitability	25	9	2.25	8	2.0	7	1.75
Size	15	6	0.9	5	0.75	8	1.2
Vulnerability	15	5	0.75	6	0.9	6	0.9
Competition	10	8	0.8	8	0.8	4	0.4
Cyclicality	10	2.5	0.25	3	0.3	2.5	0.25
Total	100		6.45		6.0		7.0

Year 3 sees a change in the attractiveness of the three segments, with Segment 1 being toppled from its leading position into second place and Segment 3 replacing it. These new positions can now be transposed on to the matrix, as in Figure 9.7.

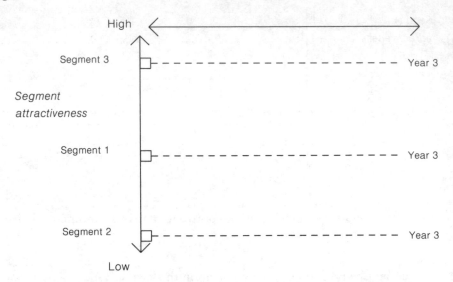

Figure 9.7   Re-plotting segments on the portfolio matrix according to their attractiveness at the end of the planning period

It has to be said that, in practice, it is quicker and easier to carry out only the calculations for the final year of the planning period, in which case the circles can only move horizontally with changes to your company's relative strength in each segment.

It is worth repeating that, once agreed, under no circumstances should segment attractiveness factors be changed, otherwise the attractiveness of your segments is not being evaluated against common criteria and the matrix becomes meaningless. Scores, however, are specific to each segment.

It is also worth stressing that segments positioned in the lower half of the matrix should *not* be treated as unattractive. All this means is that they are relatively less attractive than segments positioned in the top half of the matrix. In addition, it should not be forgotten that the cash generated from those segments in the lower half of the matrix (particularly the lower left quadrant) will be an important contribution to the investment required in those segments appearing in the top half of the matrix.

In the examples shown in Tables 9.5 and 9.6, it can be seen that the weighted scores for all three segments is above 5.0. If the vertical axis was scaled from 0 to 10, this would put all three segments in the 'highly attractive' quadrant. Should you have only three segments, which is unlikely, this would obviously be a nonsense. To overcome this problem in cases such as this, where all weighted scores are above 5.0, it is suggested that the scale on the vertical axis be amended so that 4.0 becomes the point of origin and, in the example given, 8.0 becomes the highest point. This will always ensure a spread, which is, of course, the whole point of using the device in the first place. Table 9.7 shows a more likely spread of weighted attractiveness scores.

Table 9.7 The range of weighted attractiveness scores in a market with nine segments

Market: ABC

Attractiveness	Weight	Segment 1 Score	Total	Segment 2 Score	Total	Segment 3 Score	Total
Profitability	35	8	2.8	9	3.15	6	2.1
Growth	30	3	0.9	4	1.2	4	1.2
Size	15	9	1.35	5	0.75	7	1.05
Competition	20	3	0.6	5	1.0	5	1.0
Total	100		5.65		6.1		5.35

Attractiveness	Weight	Segment 4 Score	Total	Segment 5 Score	Total	Segment 6 Score	Total
Profitability	35	7	2.45	7	2.45	5	1.75
Growth	30	7	2.1	8	2.4	2	0.6
Size	15	8	1.2	7	1.05	5	0.75
Competition	20	4	0.8	6	1.2	2	0.4
Total	100		6.55		7.1		3.5

Attractiveness	Weight	Segment 7 Score	Total	Segment 8 Score	Total	Segment 9 Score	Total
Profitability	35	5	1.75	2	0.7	3	1.05
Growth	30	3	0.9	1	0.3	5	1.5
Size	15	2	0.3	2	0.3	8	1.2
Competition	20	9	1.8	2	0.4	2	0.4
Total	100		4.75		1.7		4.15

■ When the Final Result is not what you Expected

The first time managers try using the DPM, they frequently find that the points of intersection from the two axes for their individual segments do not come out where expected. One possible reason for this is a misunderstanding concerning the use of market attractiveness factors. Please remember, you will be most concerned about the *potential* for *growth in volume, growth in profit*, and so on for your company in each of your 'segments'. For example, even if a 'segment' is mature (or even in decline), if the *potential* is there for your company to grow in this mature segment, then it would obviously be more attractive than one in which there was little or no potential for you to grow. (As would be the case, for example, if you already had a high share in a segment.) Likewise, even if a 'segment' is currently very profitable for your company, if there were little or no *potential* for profit growth, this segment might be considered less attractive than one which was currently not so profitable to your company, but which offered good *potential* for profit growth.

CHAPTER 10

Company Competitiveness and the Portfolio Matrix (Step 12)

▮ Summary

It can now be very tempting to simply focus on those segments obtaining the highest attractiveness ratings (despite the cautionary comments at the end of Chapter 9), which could also be the chosen strategy of your competitors. This, however, fails to acknowledge that your company's ability to be successful in each segment will differ according to how strong you are in it *relative to the competition*. This chapter therefore presents a format for you to follow which can be used to determine where your relative strengths lie.

Your company's ability to deliver the CPIs for each segment needs to be weighed up against your competitors' ability to deliver these very same CPIs. The results can then be plotted on the portfolio matrix to determine the point of intersection with the attractiveness weightings.

To complete the matrix, a circle is drawn at the point of intersection, the size of which represents either the volume/value of that segment or your company's volume/value within it.

▮ Definition

Company competitiveness is a measure of an organisation's actual strengths in each segment (in other words, the degree to which it can take advantage of an opportunity). Thus, it is an objective assessment of an organisation's ability to satisfy the needs of each segment, relative to competitors.

▮ Competitiveness Factors

These factors will principally be a combination of an organisation's relative strengths versus competitors in connection with customer-facing needs in each segment, namely those that are required by the customer. These were identified in Chapter 6 as CPIs, with each concluding segment having its own rank order and relative value of the market CPIs. To win the business in any particular segment, therefore, the company has to be relatively more *successful* than its competitors in matching up to the segment's CPIs. In constructing a portfolio matrix, the CPIs are therefore often referred to as *Critical Success Factors* (CSFs); this is the term most often found in marketing text books and papers when describing this technique.

The CSFs can often be summarised under the following headings:

- Product/service requirements
- Price requirements
- Promotion requirements
- Place (distribution and service) requirements

In your review of how well your company can meet the requirements of each segment, you may well need to consider questions such as:

- Are we big enough?
- Can we grow?
- How large is our market share?
- Do we have the right products?
- How well are we known in this market?
- What image do we have?
- Do we have the right technical skills?
- Can we adapt to changes?
- Do we have enough capacity?
- How close are we to this market?

It should be stressed, however, that the answers to these questions should not be confused with customer-facing CSFs. They will only tell you in what ways you have to change to satisfy your customer's needs.

It will be clear that a company's relative strengths in meeting customer-facing needs will be a function of its capabilities in connection with the CSFs relative to the capabilities of the best competitor. For example, if a depot is necessary in each major town/city for any organisation to succeed in any segment, and the company carrying out the analysis doesn't have this, yet the competition does, then it is likely that this will account for its poor performance under 'customer service'. Likewise, if a major component of 'price' is the cost of feedstock, and it is necessary in some segments to have low prices in order to succeed, any company carrying out the analysis which doesn't have low feedstock costs, while competitors do, will find that it is this which accounts for its poor performance under 'price'.

Clearly, this type of assessment of a company's capabilities in respect of CSFs could be made in order to understand what needs to be done in the organisation in order to satisfy customer needs better. This assessment, however, is quite separate from the quantification of the business strengths/position axis, and its purpose is to translate the analysis into actionable propositions for other functions within the organisation, such as purchasing, production, distribution and so on.

It is worth emphasising that for the purposes of the portfolio matrix, it is usually only necessary to work with the top 3–5 CSFs (CPIs) in your analysis of company competitiveness.

■ Weighting the Factors

The weightings allocated to the factors appearing under the heading 'critical success factors' will, of course, be specific to each segment and will reflect their relative values to each other as observed in Chapter 6. An example is shown in Table 10.1.

Table 10.1 Weighting CSFs

Market: XYZ *Segment:* A	
Critical Success Factors	*Weight*
1. Price	50
2. Product technical performance	25
3. Service (delivery reliability)	15
4. Image (leading edge/forefront)	10
Total	100

■ Scoring your Company and your Competitors

The parameters for each CSF are very straightforward, as they are common to all the CSFs. They consist of:

- Highly competitive (which has a score range of 10 down to 7)
- Competitive (with a score range of 6 down to 4)
- Uncompetitive (scoring from 3 down to zero)

For each individual segment, score your own company and each of your main competitors out of ten on each of the CSFs, then multiply the score by the weight, as shown in Table 10.2. This calculation should first be carried out for the start of the planning period, namely Year 0. This enables you to establish a fixed position on the portfolio matrix for your company in each segment against which the forecast outcome of alternative strategies and assumptions for the planning period can be seen when plotted on to the DPM.

Table 10.2   Business strength evaluation (Year 0)

		Market: XYZ		Segment: A			
		Your Company		Competitor A		Competitor B	
CSFs	Weight	Score	Total	Score	Total	Score	Total
1. Price	50	5	2.5	6	3.0	4	2.0
2. Product	25	6	1.5	8	2.0	10	2.5
3. Service	15	8	1.2	4	0.6	6	0.9
4. Image	10	6	0.6	5	0.5	3	0.3
Total	100		5.8		6.1		5.7

From this table it can be seen that:

- This company is not the segment leader
- All competitors score above 5.0

The problem with this and many similar calculations is that rarely will this method discriminate sufficiently well to indicate the relative strengths of a number of segments in a particular company's market portfolio, and many of the SBU's segments would appear on the left of the matrix.

Some method is required to prevent all segments appearing on the left of the matrix. This can be achieved by using a ratio, as in the Boston matrix. This will indicate a company's position relative to the best in the segment.

In the example provided, Competitor A has most strengths in the segment so our organisation needs to make some improvements. To reflect this, our weighted score should be expressed as a ratio of Competitor A (the highest weighted score). Thus,

$$6.7 : 7.8 = 0.86 : 1$$

If we were to plot this on a logarithmic scale on the horizontal axis, this would place our organisation to the right of the dividing line, as shown in Figure 10.1 (we should make the left-hand extreme point '3×' and start the scale on the right at '0.3×').

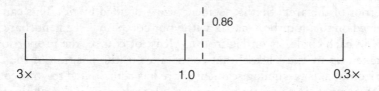

Figure 10.1   Plotting a relative competitive score of 0.86

A scale of '3×' to '0.3×' has been chosen because such a band is likely to encapsulate most extremes of competitive advantage. If it doesn't, just change it to suit your own circumstances (for example, 10× to 0.1×).

■ Producing the Portfolio Matrix

Once you have completed the competitive evaluation for Year 0, you can plot your position for each segment by drawing a vertical line from the relevant point on the horizontal scale, as shown on Figure 10.2, so that it intersects with the appropriate segment's horizontal line (initially from the Year 3 calculations).

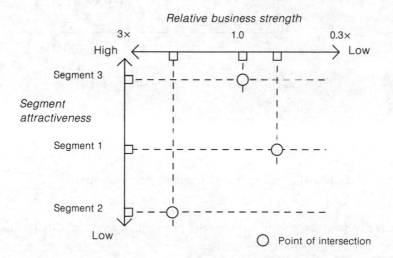

Figure 10.2   Plotting business positions on the portfolio matrix for each segment according to their relative competitive strength

By plotting for each segment the intersection of their scores for both axes, initially using the segment attractiveness ratings for Year 3, along with the relative business strength assessment for the current year (Year 0), circles can be drawn with their area proportional to the forecast size of the segment, as defined in the previous chapter (the radius of the circle, therefore, being the square root of the area: that is, segment size – divided by *pi*). This can then be transferred on to a four box matrix with your company's segment share put as a 'cheese' in each circle, as on Figure 10.3. It is, of course, the proportion of the circle taken up by the 'cheese' that contributes to the position of the circle on the horizontal axis (assuming segment share has contributed to your company's ability to compete in some of the segments). It is the size of the whole circle that contributes to the position of the circle on the vertical axis.

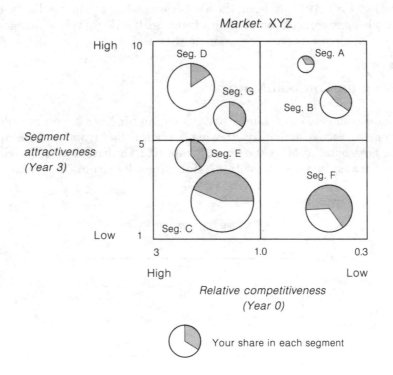

Figure 10.3   The initial segment portfolio matrix

Alternatively, your company's own sales into each segment can be used to determine the size of the circle.

In practice, however, it is advisable to do both and compare them in order to see how closely actual sales match the opportunities.

The purpose of the portfolio matrix is to see how the segments in a market relate to each other in the context of the criteria used. This analysis should indicate whether the portfolio is well balanced or not, and should give a clear indication of any problems.

■ The DPM

It is now possible to start being creative in your use of the matrix and re-draw your portfolio along a number of alternative lines, by, for example:

- Re-scoring your relative business strength for each segment assuming the company continues with the strategies already in place

- Re-scoring your relative business strength for each segment based on some realistic assumptions about your competitors, but assuming your company just stood still

- A combination of the above

By including these new locations of the segments on the original portfolio matrix, the resulting matrix will indicate whether your own position is getting worse or better. If this matrix then also includes the position of the segments in Year 0, you now have a very comprehensive picture of your market, as shown in Figure 10.4.

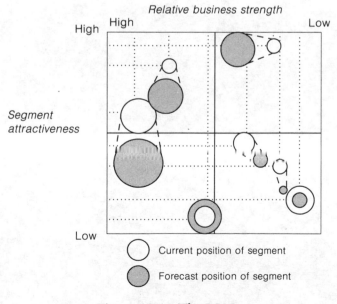

Figure 10.4   The DPM

With this picture of the market in place, consideration should be given to marketing objectives and strategies which are now appropriate to the attractiveness of a segment and the extent to which such opportunities match your capabilities. For the objectives, this involves changing the volumes/values and/or share along with the scores on the horizontal axis (relative strength in a segment) in order to achieve the desired volumes/values. Conceptually, you are picking up the circle and moving it without specifying how this is to be achieved. This is encapsulated in the defined marketing strategies which will change the individual CSF scores.

As the setting of marketing objectives and strategies is obviously the whole point of all the previous diagnosis, the next chapter describes this process in some detail.

Setting Marketing Objectives and Strategies for Identified Segments

■ Summary

Chapter 11 defines what marketing objectives are and explains how to set them. The relationship between marketing objectives and corporate objectives is also shown. To assist in the setting of marketing objectives, there is a section on competitive strategies. This chapter also begins to provide the link between segmentation and marketing planning and describes where and how to start the process of marketing planning, using the method known as 'gap analysis', and discusses new product development as a growth strategy. Finally, there is an explanation of what marketing strategies are and how to set them.

Briefly, *objectives* are what the business unit wants to achieve. They should be *quantitative*, and should be expressed where possible in terms of *values*, *volumes* and *segment* shares. General directional terms such as 'maximise', 'minimise' and 'penetrate' should be avoided unless quantification is included. On the other hand, *strategies* are how you plan to achieve the objectives. Thus, there are objectives and strategies at all levels in marketing, such as advertising objectives and strategies, pricing objectives and strategies, and so on.

Without doubt, setting objectives is the key step in the marketing planning process, for it will by now be clear that, following the analysis that takes place as part of the segmentation process, realistic and achievable objectives should be set for each of the company's major segments. Unless this step is carried out well, everything that follows will lack focus and cohesion. In previous chapters, you have gone to a lot of trouble to select the right targets. The purpose of this chapter is to ensure that you score a bull's-eye on your selected targets!

■ Marketing Objectives: What they are and How they Relate to Corporate Objectives

There are no works on marketing which do not include at least one paragraph on the need for setting objectives. Setting objectives is a mandatory step in the planning process. The literature on the subject, though, is not very explicit, which is surprising when it is considered how vital the setting of marketing objectives is.

An objective will ensure that a company knows what its strategies are expected to accomplish and when a particular strategy has accomplished its purpose. In other words, without objectives, strategy decisions and all that follows will take place in a vacuum.

Following the identification of opportunities and the explicit statement of assumptions about conditions affecting the business, the process of setting objectives should, in theory, be comparatively easy, the actual objectives themselves being a realistic statement of what the company desires to achieve as a result of market-centred analysis, rather than generalised statements born of top management's desire to 'do better next year'. However, objective setting is more complex than at first it would appear.

Most experts agree that the logical approach to the difficult task of setting marketing objectives is to proceed from the broad to the specific. Thus, the starting point would be a statement of the nature of the business, from which would flow the broad company objectives. Next, the broad company objectives would be translated into key result areas, which would be those areas in which success is vital to the firm. At one level, key result areas would include, for example, market penetration and the overall growth rate of sales. At a lower level, 'market penetration' could well be stepped down to 'segment penetration'. The third step would be creation of the sub-objectives necessary to accomplish the broad objectives, such as sales volume goals, geographical expansion, segment extension, product line extension, and so on.

The end result of this process should be objectives which are consistent with the strategic plan, attainable within budget limitations and compatible with the strengths, limitations and economics of other functions within the organisation.

At the top level, management is concerned with long-run profitability which may well extend into market-related objectives; at the next level in the management hierarchy, the concern is for objectives which are defined more specifically and in greater detail, such as increasing sales and segment share, moving into new segments, and so on. These objectives are merely a part of the hierarchy of objectives, in that corporate objectives will only be accomplished if these and other objectives are achieved. At the next level, management is concerned with objectives which are defined even more tightly, such as creating awareness among a specific target segment about a new product, changing a particular customer attitude, and so on. Again, the general marketing objectives will only be accomplished if these and other sub-objectives are achieved. It is clear that sub-objectives *per se*, unless they are an integral part of a broader framework of objectives, are likely to lead to a wasteful misdirection of resources.

For example, a sales increase in itself may be possible, but only at an undue cost. Such a marketing objective is, therefore, only appropriate within the framework of corporate objectives. In such a case, it may well be that an increase in sales in a particular segment will entail additional capital expenditure ahead of the time for which it is planned. If this is the case, it may make more sense to allocate available production capacity to more profitable segments in the short term, allowing sales to decline in another segment. Decisions such as this are likely to be more easily made against a backcloth of explicitly stated broad company objectives relating to all the major disciplines.

Likewise, objectives should be set for advertising, for example, which are wholly consistent with the wider marketing objectives. Objectives set in this way integrate the advertising effort with the other elements in the marketing mix and this leads to a consistent, logical marketing plan.

■ What is a Corporate Objective and What is a Marketing Objective?

A business starts at some time with resources and wants to use those resources to achieve something. What the business wants to achieve is a corporate objective, which describes a desired destination or result. How it is to be achieved is a strategy. In a sense, this means that the only true objective of a company is, by definition, what is stated in the corporate plan as being the principal purpose of its existence. Most often this is expressed in terms of profit, since profit is the means of satisfying shareholders or owners, and because it is the one universally accepted criterion by which efficiency can be evaluated, which will, in turn, lead to efficient resource allocation, economic and technological progressiveness and stability.

This means that stated desires, such as to expand segment share, to create a new image, to achieve an *n* per cent increase in sales, and so on are in fact *strategies* at the corporate level, since they are the means by which a company will achieve its profit objectives. In practice, however, companies tend to operate by means of functional divisions, each with a separate identity, so that what is a strategy in the corporate plan becomes an objective within each department. For example, marketing strategies within the corporate plan become operating objectives within the marketing department, and strategies at the general level within the marketing department themselves become operating objectives at the next level down, so that an intricate web of inter-related objectives and strategies is built up at all levels within the framework of the overall company plan.

The really important point, however, apart from clarifying the difference between objectives and strategies, is that the further down the hierarchical chain one goes, the less likely it is that a stated objective will make a cost-effective contribution to company profits, unless it derives logically and directly from an objective at a higher level.

Corporate objectives and strategies can be simplified in the following way:

- Corporate objective   Desired level of profitability.
- Corporate strategies   Which segments and which products (marketing).
    What kind of facilities (production and distribution).
    Size and character of the staff/labour force (personnel).
    Funding (finance).
    Other corporate strategies such as social responsibility, corporate image, stock market image, employee image and so on.

It is now clear that at the next level down in the organisation (in other words, at the functional level) what products are to be sold into what segments, become *marketing objectives*, while the means of achieving these objectives using the marketing mix are *marketing strategies*. At the next level down there would be, say, *advertising objectives* and *advertising strategies*, with the subsequent *programmes* and *budgets* for achieving the objectives. In this way, a hierarchy of objectives and strategies can be traced back to the initial corporate objective. Figure 11.1 illustrates this point (see p. 132).

■ How to set Marketing Objectives

The Ansoff matrix (H. I. Ansoff, 'Strategies for Diversification', *Harvard Business Review*, September–October 1957, 113–24) can be introduced here as a useful tool for thinking about marketing objectives. It is a concept normally written in terms of 'markets', but for the purposes of this book we will substitute (where appropriate) 'segment' for 'market'.

A firm's competitive situation can be simplified to two dimensions only, products and segments. To put it even more simply, Ansoff's framework is about what is sold (the 'product') and to whom it is sold (the 'segment'). Within this framework, Ansoff identifies four possible courses of action for the firm:

- Selling existing products to existing segments
- Extending existing products to new segments
- Developing new products for existing segments
- Developing new products for new segments

The matrix in Figure 11.2 depicts these concepts.

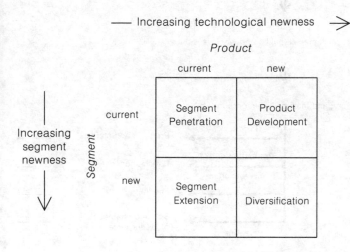

Figure 11.2   The Ansoff matrix

It is clear that the range of possible marketing objectives is very wide, since there will be degrees of technological newness and degrees of segment newness. Nevertheless, Ansoff's matrix provides a logical framework in which marketing objectives can be developed under each of the four main headings above. *In other words, marketing objectives are about products and segments only.* Common-sense will confirm that it is only by selling something to someone that the company's financial goals can be achieved, and that advertising, pricing, service levels and so on, are the means (or strategies) by which it might succeed in doing this. Thus, pricing objectives, sales promotion objectives, advertising objectives, and so on should not be confused with marketing objectives.

Marketing objectives are generally accepted as being quantitative commitments, usually stated either in standards of performance for a given operating period, or conditions to be achieved by given dates. Performance standards are usually stated in terms of sales volume and various measures of profitability. The conditions to be attained are usually a percentage of segment share and various other commitments, such as a percentage of the total number of a given type of retail outlet.

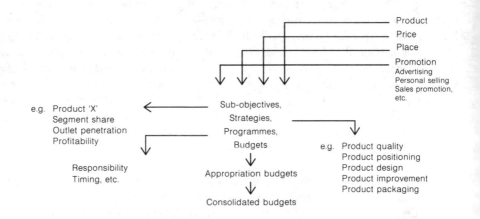

Marketing planning in a
corporate framework

Corporate mission
Define the business and its boundaries
Using considerations such as:
– distinctive competence
– environmental trends
– consumption market trends
– resource market trends
– stakeholder expectations

Corporate objectives
e.g. ROI, ROSHF, image (with stock market, public and employees),
social responsibility, etc.

Corporate strategies
e.g. Involve corporate resources, and must be within corporate
business boundaries

Product ──────────▶ Products and markets ──────
Production and ──────────▶ Physical facilities ──────
distribution
Finance ──────────▶ Funding ──────
Personnel ──────────▶ Size and character ──────
of labour force

Product
Price
Place
Promotion
Advertising
Personal selling
Sales promotion,
etc.

e.g. Product 'X'   ◀──────   Sub-objectives,
Segment share   Strategies,
Outlet penetration   Programmes,
Profitability   Budgets   e.g. Product quality
Product positioning
Responsibility   Product design
Timing, etc.   Appropriation budgets   Product improvement
Product packaging
Consolidated budgets

Figure 11.1   Objectives and strategies in a corporate framework

Source: M. H. B. McDonald, *Marketing Plans – How to Prepare Them: How to Use Them*, 3rd edn (Oxford: Heinemann, 1995).

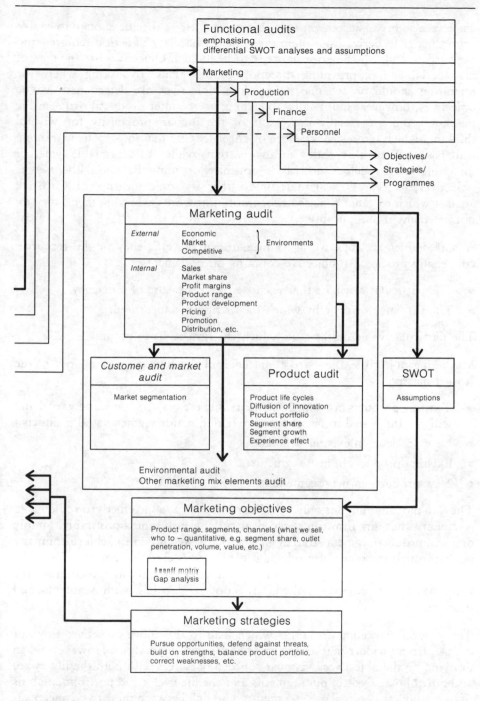

There is also broad agreement that objectives must be specific enough to enable subordinates to derive from them the general character of action required and the yardstick by which performance is to be judged. Objectives are the core of managerial action, providing direction to the plans. By asking where the operation should be at some future date, objectives are determined. Vague objectives, however emotionally appealing, are counter-productive to sensible planning, and are usually the result of the human propensity for wishful thinking, which often smacks more of cheer leading than of serious marketing leadership. What this really means is that while it is arguable whether directional terms such as 'decrease', 'optimise' or 'minimise' should be used as objectives, it seems logical that, unless there is some measure or yardstick against which to gauge a sense of locomotion towards achieving them, they do not serve any useful purpose.

Ansoff defines an objective as 'a measure of the efficiency of the resource-conversion process. An objective contains three elements:

- The particular attribute that is chosen as a measure of efficiency.
- The yardstick or scale by which the attribute is measured.

The particular value on the scale which the firm seeks to attain.'

Marketing objectives, then, are about each of the four main categories of the Ansoff matrix:

- Existing products in existing segments. (These may be many and varied and will certainly need to be set for all existing major segments and products.)
- New products in existing segments.
- Existing products in new segments.
- New products in new segments.

Thus, in the long run, it is only by selling something (a 'product') to someone (a 'segment') that any firm can succeed in staying in business profitably. Simply defined, product/segment strategy means the route chosen to achieve company goals through the range of products it offers to its chosen segments. Thus, the product/segment strategy represents a commitment to a future direction for the firm. Marketing objectives, then, are concerned solely with segments and products.

The general marketing *directions* which lead to the above objectives flow, of course, from product/market life cycle and portfolio analysis. However, when drawing up the objectives, we must concern ourselves with both the life cycles and portfolio analysis of our segments *and* the life cycles and portfolio analysis of our products *in* our chosen segments. The link between these two concepts is illustrated in Figure 11.3. For a full explanation, please refer to M.H.B. McDonald's book, *Marketing Plans*.

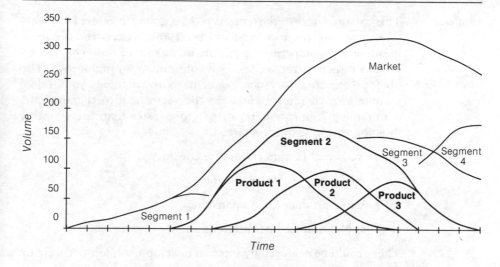

Figure 11.3 Product life cycles within segments

The marketing directions which come out of life cycle and portfolio analysis revolve around the following logical decisions (with a brief guide to the appropriate strategies also listed). Please note that, although we refer to the labels invented by the Boston Consulting Group (for example, 'cash cow'), such labels should not generally be used in connection with the DPM and are used here only for the purpose of explanation. We have suggested more appropriate labels for the DPM in Figure 11.4 and Table 11.1 below.

Maintain   This usually refers to the 'cash cow' type of segment/product (segments that fall in the bottom left-hand box of Figure 9.1) in which the company enjoys a competitive position, and reflects the desire to maintain a competitive and profitable position, even though it is acknowledged these segments/products are not as attractive as other segments/products in terms of achieving the organisation's objectives.

             The emphasis will be on maintaining present earnings in the most profitable segments/products, rather than aggressive growth, while activity in those that are less profitable should be considered for cutting back. Marketing effort should be focused on differentiating products to maintain share of key segments. Discretionary marketing expenditure should be limited, especially when unchallenged by competitors, or when products have matured. Comparative prices should be stabilised, except when a temporary aggressive stance is necessary to defend segment share.

Improve   This usually refers to the 'star' type of segment/product (segments that appear in the top left-hand box) and reflects the desire to improve the competitive position in attractive segments which look as if their attractiveness will continue, or even improve. The obvious objective for such segments is to maintain your sales/volume growth rates at least at the segment growth rate, thus maintaining segment share, or to grow faster than the segment, thus increasing segment share.

Three principal factors should be considered:

(a) possible geographic expansion;

(b) possible product line expansion;

(c) possible product line differentiation.

These could be achieved by internal development, joint venture or acquisition.

The main point is that, in attractive segments, an *aggressive marketing posture is required*, together with a very tight budgeting and control process to ensure that capital resources are efficiently utilised.

Harvest   This usually refers to a particular category of 'dog' type segment/product (segments that appear in the bottom right-hand box, but towards the mid-point vertical line of the matrix) where the company has a moderately good to poor position (as opposed to an unquestionably poor position) and reflects the desire to relinquish competitive position in favour of short-term profit and cash flow, but not necessarily at the risk of losing the business in the short term. These are sometimes referred to as 'cash dogs'.

The reality of low growth should be acknowledged and the temptation to grow sales into these segments/grow sales of those products at the previous high rates of growth should be resisted. They should not be regarded as a 'marketing problem', which will be likely to lead to high advertising, promotion, product development and inventory costs, and therefore to lower profitability. Some of the 'maintain' policies may still be appropriate, but with more of an eye on profit and cash flow.

Finally, the attention of talented managers should be focused on these 'cash dogs'.

Exit   This usually refers to the genuine 'dog' type of segment/product (segments that appear in the bottom right-hand box, but well to the right of the mid-point vertical axis), also sometimes to the 'question mark', and reflects a desire to divest because of a weak competitive position or because the cost of staying in it is prohibitive and the risk associated with improving its position is too high. Generally, immediate divestment is the preferred course of action, unless there is still the opportunity to generate some cash with minimal marketing expenditure.

Enter   This usually refers to the new and most promising emerging segments/products where it has been decided to invest for future segment/product leadership (selected segments that appear in the top right-hand box).

As already stated, however, great care should be taken not to follow slavishly any set of 'rules'. There can be no *automatic* policy for a particular segment or product, and SBU managers should consider three or more options before deciding on 'the best' for recommendation. Above all, SBU managers must evaluate the most attractive opportunities and assess the chances of success in the most realistic manner possible. This applies particularly to new business opportunities. New business opportunities would normally be expected to build on existing strengths, particularly in marketing, which can be subsequently expanded or supplemented.

As already stated, it can help the process if derogatory labels like 'dog', 'cash cow' and so on are avoided, if possible.

A full list of marketing guidelines as a precursor to objective setting is given in Figure 11.4. Table 11.1 sets out a fuller list which includes guidelines for functions other than marketing. One word of warning, however: such general guidelines should not be followed unquestioningly. They are included more as checklists of questions that should be asked about each major product in each major segment *before* setting marketing objectives and strategies.

It is at this stage that the circles in the DPM can be moved to show their relative size and position in three years' time. You can do this to show, first, where they will be if the company takes no action and, second, where you would ideally prefer them to be. These latter positions will, of course, become the marketing objectives. Precisely how this is done was shown in Chapter 10. It is, however, the key stage in the marketing planning process.

■ Competitive Strategies

At this stage of the planning process, it would be helpful to explain recent developments in the field of competitive strategies, since an understanding of the subject is an essential prerequisite to setting appropriate marketing objectives.

Relative business strength

	High	Low
High	*Invest for growth* Defend leadership, gain if possible. Accept moderate short-term profits and negative cash flow. Consider geographic expansion, product line expansion, product differentiation. Upgrade production introduction effort. Aggressive marketing posture, viz. selling, advertising, pricing, sales promotion, service levels, as appropriate.	*Opportunistic* The options are: (i) move it to the left if resources are available to invest in it; (ii) keep a low profile until funds are available; (iii) divest to a buyer able to exploit the opportunity.

Relative market attractiveness

Maintain market position, manage for sustained earnings Maintain position in most successful segments and product lines. Prune less successful product lines. Differentiate products to maintain share of key segments. Limit discretionary marketing expenditure. Stabilise prices, except where a temporary aggressive stance is necessary to maintain segment share.	*'Selective'** Acknowledge low growth. Do not view as a 'marketing' problem. Identify and exploit growth segments. Emphasise product quality to avoid 'commodity' competition. Systematically improve productivity. Assign talented managers.	*Cash* Prune product line aggressively. Maximise cash flow. Minimise marketing expenditure. Maintain or raise prices at the expense of volume.

Low

Figure 11.4   Strategies suggested by portfolio matrix analysis

* The term 'Selective' refers to those segments or products which fall on or near the vertical dividing line in a DPM.

Table 11.1   Other functional guidelines suggested by portfolio matrix analysis

	Invest for growth	Maintain segment position, manage for earnings	Maintain selectively	Manage for cash	Opportunistic development
Segment share	Maintain or increase dominance	Maintain or slightly milk for earnings	Maintain selectively	Forgo share for profit	Invest selectively in share
Products	Differentiate, line expansion	Prune less successful, differentiate for key segments	Emphasise product quality. Differentiate	Aggressively prune	Differentiation, line expansion
Price	Lead. Aggressive pricing for share	Stabilise prices/raise	Maintain or raise	Raise	Aggressive, price for share
Promotion	Aggressive activity	Limit	Maintain selectively	Minimise	Aggressive activity
Distribution	Broaden distribution	Hold wide distribution pattern	Maintain selectively according to segment	Gradually withdraw distribution	Limited coverage
Cost control	Tight control. Go for scale economics	Emphasise cost reduction, viz. variable costs	Tight control	Aggressively reduce both fixed and variable	Tight, but not at expense of entrepreneurship
Production	Expand, invest (organic, acquisition, joint venture)	Maximise capacity utilisation	Increase productivity, for example, specialisation/automation	Free up capacity	Invest
R and D	Expand, invest	Focus on specific projects	Invest selectively	None	Invest
Personnel	Upgrade management in key functional areas	Maintain. Reward efficiency, tighten organisation	Allocate key managers	Cut back organisation	Invest
Investment	Fund growth	Limit fixed investment	Invest selectively	Minimise and divest opportunistically	Fund growth
Working capital	Reduce in process, extend credit	Tighten credit, reduce accounts receivable, increase inventory turn	Reduce	Aggressively reduce	Invest

One of the principal purposes of marketing strategy is for you to be able to choose the customers, hence the segments, you wish to deal with. In this respect, the DPM discussed in Chapter 9 is particularly useful. The main components of competitive strategy are:

- The company
- Customers
- Competitors

Clearly, if we are to succeed, we need to work hard at developing a sustainable competitive advantage. The important word here is 'sustainable', as temporary advantages can be gained in numerous ways, such as from a price reduction or from a clever sales promotion.

Most business people would agree that as segments mature, the only way to grow the business without diversifying is at the expense of competitors, which implies the need to understand in depth the characteristics of each important segment to the company and of the main competitors in it. We briefly referred to the leading thinker in this field in Chapter 10, namely Michael E. Porter of the Harvard Business School, and any reader wishing to explore this vital subject in more depth should refer to his book, *Competitive Strategy: Techniques for Analysing Industries and Competitors* (New York: The Free Press, 1980).

Perhaps the best way to summarise this complex subject would be to tell a story. Imagine three tribes on a small island fighting each other because resources are scarce. One tribe decides to move to a larger adjacent island, sets up camp, and is followed eventually by the other two, who also set up their own separate camps. At first it is a struggle to establish themselves, but eventually they begin to occupy increasing parts of the island; eventually, many years later, they begin to fight again over adjacent land. The more innovative tribal chief – that is, the one who was first to move to the new island – sits down with his senior warriors and ponders what to do, since no one is very keen to move to yet another island. They decide that the only two options are:

- Attack and go relentlessly for the enemy's territory
- Settle for a smaller part of the island and build in it an impregnable fortress.

These two options, namely terrain or impregnable fortress, are, in fact, the same options that face business people as they contemplate competitive strategy. Let's look in turn at each of these options, continuing for a moment longer with the military analogy, and starting with terrain.

Imagine two armies facing each other on a field of battle. One army has fifteen soldiers in it, the other twelve (depicted by circles). Imagine also that they face each other with rifles and all fire one shot at the other at the same time, but they don't all aim at the same soldier! Figure 11.5 depicts the progress of each side in disposing of the other. It will be seen that after only three volleys, the army on the right has only one soldier remaining, while the army on the left, with eight soldiers remaining, is still a viable fighting unit.

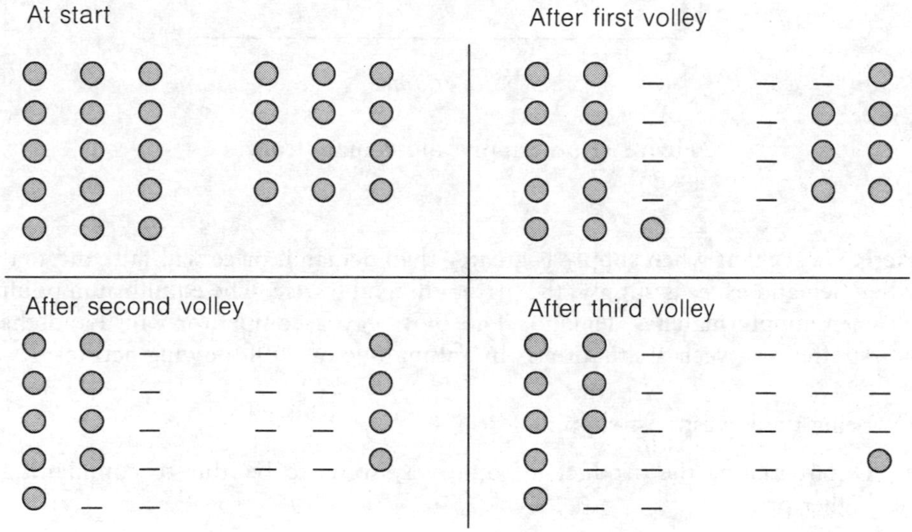

At start | After first volley

After second volley | After third volley

Figure 11.5 The importance of market share

One interesting fact about this story is that the effect observed here is *geometrical* rather than *arithmetical*, and is a perfect demonstration of the effect of size and what happens when all things are equal, except size. The parallel in industry, of course, is segment share. Just look at what used to happen in the computer industry when GE, Rank Xerox, RCA, ICL and others attacked the giant (and once totally impregnable) IBM in its core segments. The larger competitor was able to win the battle. So, all things being equal, a company with a larger segment share than another should win in the long term over a smaller competitor. Or *should* they? Clearly, this is not inevitable, providing the smaller companies take evasive action. Staying with the computer industry, just look at how successful NCR have been with their 'global fortress' strategy (for example, Automatic Teller Machines (ATMs) for the financial market) and Control Data with their scientific controls, each of which focused on particular segments in the overall market *not* dominated by the likes of IBM.

Put yet another way, let us look for a moment at the economists' model of supply and demand shown in Figure 11.6.

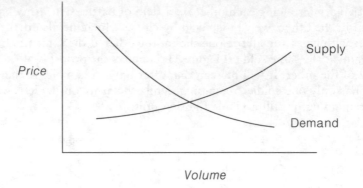

Figure 11.6   Supply and demand curves

Here, we see that when supply is greater than demand, price will fall, and that when demand exceeds supply, the price will tend to rise. The equilibrium point is when supply matches demand. The only way a competitor can avoid the worst effects of such a situation is by taking one of the following actions:

- Being the lowest cost supplier
- Differentiating the product in some way so as to be able to command a higher price

Michael Porter combined these two options into a simple matrix, as shown in Figure 11.7.

It can be seen that Box 1 represents a sound strategy, particularly in commodity-type markets such as bulk chemicals, where differentiation is harder to achieve because of the identical nature of the chemical make-up of the product. In such cases, it is wise to recognise the reality and adopt a productive corporate drive towards being the corporate leader. It is here that the *'experience effect'* becomes especially important.

Very briefly, the experience effect, which also includes the 'learning curve', is a recognition of the fact that the more we do something, the better we are at doing it. Included in the experience effect are such items as better productivity from plant and equipment, product design improvements, process innovations, labour efficiency, work specialisation, and so on. In addition to the experience effect, and not necessarily mutually exclusive, are *economies of scale* that come with growth. For example, capital costs do not increase in direct proportion to capacity, which results in lower depreciation charges per unit of output, lower operating costs in the form of the number of operatives, lower marketing, sales,

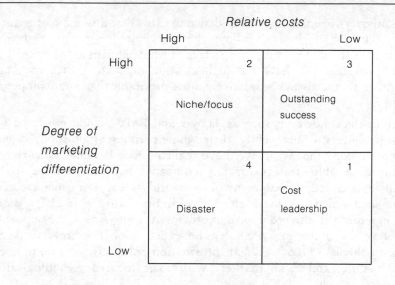

Figure 11.7   Cost versus differentiation matrix

Source: M.E. Porter, *Competitive Advantage – Creating and Sustaining Superior Performance* (New York: The Free Press, 1985).

administration and R & D costs, and lower raw materials and shipping costs. It is generally recognised, however, that cost decline applies more to the value-added elements of cost than to bought-in supplies. In fact, the Boston Consulting Group discovered that costs declined by up to 30 per cent for every cumulative doubling of output. This phenomenon is shown in Figure 11.8.

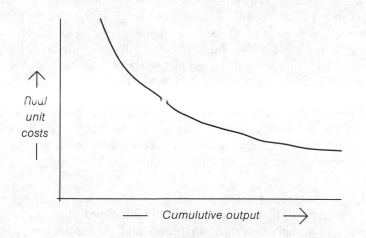

Figure 11.8   The impact on unit costs of the learning curve

There is an overwhelming body of evidence to show that this real cost reduction actually occurs, in which case it follows that the greater your volume, the lower your unit costs should be. Thus, irrespective of what happens to the price of your product, providing you have the highest segment share (hence the biggest volume), you should always be relatively more profitable than your competitors.

Many companies, however, such as Jaguar and BMW, could not hope to be low-cost producers. Consequently, their whole corporate philosophy is geared to differentiation and what we have called 'added value'. Clearly, this represents a sensible strategy for any company that cannot hope to be a world cost beater and, indeed, many of the world's great companies succeed by means of such a focus and locate themselves in Box 2 (in Figure 11.7). Many of these companies also succeed in pushing themselves into Box 3, the outstanding success box, by occupying what can be called 'global fortresses'. A good example of this is AT & T Global Information Solutions, who dominate the world's banking and retail markets with their focused technological and marketing approach.

Companies like McDonalds and GE, however, typify Box 3, where low costs, differentiation and world leadership are combined in their corporate strategies.

Only Box 4 remains. Here we can see that a combination of commodity-type markets and high relative costs will result in disaster sooner or later. A position here is tenable only while demand exceeds supply. When, however, segments in these markets mature, there is little hope for companies who find themselves in this unenviable position.

An important point to remember when thinking about differentiation as a strategy is that you must still be *cost-effective*. It is a myth to assume that sloppy management and high costs are acceptable as long as the product has a good image and lots of added value. Also, in thinking about differentiation, please refer back to the section on benefit analysis in Chapter 6, for it is here that the route to differentiation will be found. It is also clear that there is not much point in offering benefits that are costly for you to provide but which are not highly regarded by customers: in other words, benefits which are not their important CPIs. So consider using a matrix like the one given in Figure 11.9 to classify your benefits. Clearly, you will succeed best by providing as many benefits as possible that fall into the top right-hand box.

ICI is a good example of a company that is proactively changing its global strategy by systematically moving away from bulk chemicals in Box 1 (in Figure 11.7) towards speciality chemicals in Box 2 and then going on to occupy a 'global fortress' position in these specialities (Box 3).

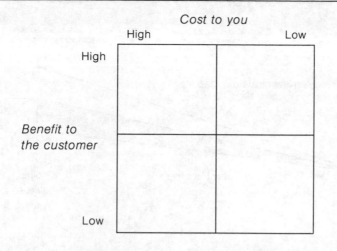

Figure 11.9 Cost/benefit matrix

The main point here, however, is that when setting marketing objectives it is essential for you to have a sound grasp of the position in your segments of yourself and your competitors and to adopt appropriate postures for the several elements of your business, all of which *may* be different. It may be necessary, for example, to accept that part of your product portfolio is in the 'Disaster' box (Box 4). You may well be forced to have some products here: for example, to complete your product range to enable you to offer your more profitable products into your chosen segment(s). The point is that you must adopt an appropriate stance towards these products and set your marketing objectives accordingly, using (where appropriate) the guidelines given in Figure 11.4 and Table 11.1.

Finally, here are some very general guidelines to help you think about competitive strategies.

- Know the terrain on which you are fighting (the market and its segments)
- Know the resources of your enemies (competition analysis)
- Do something with determination that the enemy isn't expecting

■ Where to Start (Gap Analysis)

Figure 11.10 illustrates what is commonly referred to as 'gap analysis'. Essentially, what it says is that if the corporate sales and financial objectives are greater than the current long-range forecasts, there is a gap which has to be filled.

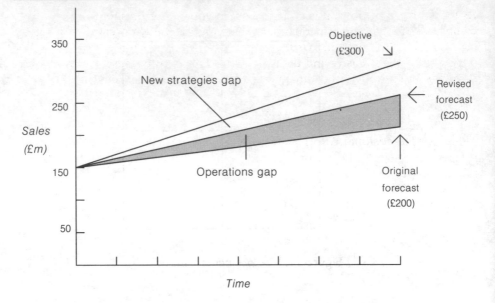

Figure 11.10   Gap analysis

The 'operations gap' can be filled in two ways;

(a)   improved productivity (for example, reduce costs, improve the sales mix, increase price);
(b)   segment penetration (for example, increase usage, increase segment share).

The 'new strategies gap' can be filled in three ways:

(a)   segment extension (for example, find new user groups, enter new segments, geographical expansion);
(b)   product development;
(c)   diversification (for example, selling new products to new segments).

A fourth option, of course, is to reduce the objectives!

If improved productivity is one method by which the expansion gap is to be filled, care must be taken not to use measures such as reducing marketing costs by 20 per cent overall. The portfolio analysis undertaken earlier will indicate that this would be totally inappropriate for some segments (although it may be applicable to some of the products at the later stages of their life cycle sold into these segments) for which increased marketing expenditure may be needed, while for others a 20 per cent reduction in marketing costs may not be sufficient.

As for the other options, it is clear that segment penetration should always be a company's first option, since it makes far more sense to attempt to increase profits and cash flow from *existing* segments and products initially, because this is usually the least costly and the least risky. This is so because, for its present segments and products, a company has developed knowledge and skills which it can use competitively.

For the same reason, it makes more sense in many cases to move along the horizontal axis of the Ansoff matrix for further growth before attempting to find new segments. The reason for this is that it normally takes many years for a company to get to know its segments and to build up a reputation. That reputation and trust, embodied in either the company's name or in its brands, is rarely transferable to new segments, where other companies are already entrenched.

It is essential that you ensure that the method chosen to fill the gap is consistent with the company's capabilities and builds on its strengths. For example, it would normally prove far less profitable for a dry goods grocery manufacturer to introduce frozen foods than to add another dry food product. Likewise, if a product could be sold through existing channels using the existing sales force, this is far less risky than introducing a new product that requires new channels and new selling skills.

Exactly the same applies to the company's production, distribution and people. Whatever new products are developed should be as consistent as possible with the company's known strengths and capabilities. Clearly, the use of existing plant capacity is generally preferable to new processes. Also, the amount of additional investment is important. Technical personnel are highly trained and specialised, and whether this competence can be transferred to a new field must be considered. A product requiring new raw materials may also require new handling and storage techniques, which could prove expensive.

It can now be appreciated why going into new segments with new products (diversification) is the riskiest strategy of all, because *new* resources and *new* management skills have to be developed. This is why the history of commerce is replete with examples of companies which went bankrupt through moving into areas where they had little or no distinctive competence. This is also why many companies that diversified through acquisition during periods of high economic growth have since divested themselves of businesses that were not basically compatible with their own distinctive competence.

The Ansoff matrix, of course, is not a simple four-box matrix, for it will be obvious that there are degrees of technological newness, as well as degrees of segment newness. Figure 11.11 illustrates the point. It also demonstrates more easily why any movement should generally aim to keep a company as close as

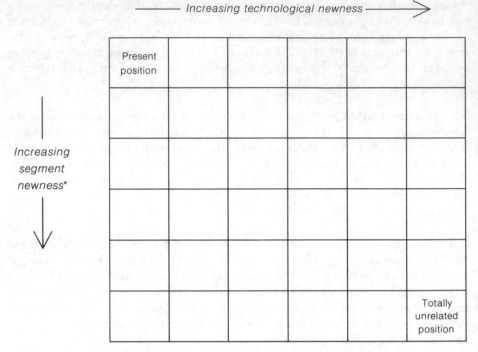

* Which eventually could become new segments in new markets

Figure 11.11   Technological and segment newness

possible to its present position, rather than moving it to a totally unrelated position, except in the most unusual circumstances.

Nevertheless, the life cycle phenomenon will inevitably *force* companies to move along one or more of the Ansoff matrix axes if they are to continue to increase their sales and profits. A key question to be asked, then, is *how* this important decision is to be taken, given the risks involved.

A full list of the possible methods involved in the process of gap analysis is given in Figure 11.12. From this, it will be seen that there is nothing an executive can do to fill the gap that is not included in the list. The precise methodology to implement this concept can be found in M. H. B. McDonald, *Marketing Plans – How to Prepare Them: How to Use Them*, 3rd edn (Oxford: Heinemann, 1995).

At this point, it is important to stress that the 'objectives' point in gap analysis should *not* be an extrapolation, but your own view of what revenue would make this into an excellent business. The word 'excellent' must, of course, be

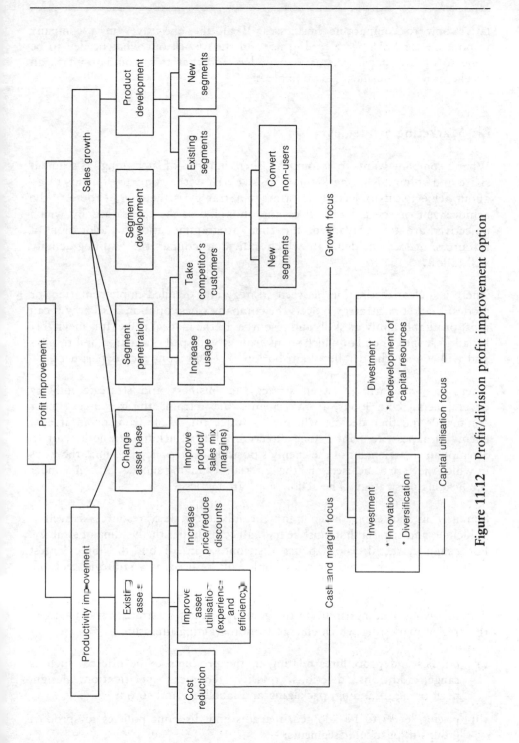

Figure 11.12 Profit/division profit improvement option

lative only to comparable businesses. If all the executives in a company responsible for SBUs were to do this, and then work out what needed to be done to fill any gaps, it is easy to understand that this would result in an excellent overall business performance.

■ Marketing Strategies

What a company wants to accomplish, then, in terms of such things as segment share and volume is a 'marketing objective'. How the company intends to go about achieving its objectives is 'strategy'. Strategy is the overall route to the achievement of specific objectives and should describe the means by which objectives are to be reached, the time programme and the allocation of resources. It does not delineate which individual courses the resulting activity will follow.

There is a clear distinction between strategy and detailed implementation, or tactics. Marketing strategy reflects the company's best opinion as to how it can most profitably apply its skills and resources to the market place. It is inevitably broad in scope. The plan which stems from it will spell out action and timings and will contain the detailed contribution expected from each department.

There is a similarity between strategy in business and strategic military development. One looks at the enemy, the terrain, the resources under command, and then decides whether to attack the whole front or an area of enemy weakness, to feint in one direction while attacking in another, or to attempt an encirclement of the enemy's position. The policy and mix, the ways in which they are to be used, and the criteria for judging success, all come under the heading of strategy. The action steps are tactics.

Similarly, in marketing, the commitment, mix and type of resources as well as guidelines and criteria that must be met, all come under the heading of strategy. For example, the decision to use distributors in all but the three largest segments, in which company salespeople will be used, is a strategic decision. The selection of particular distributors is a tactical decision.

The following headings indicate the general content of strategy statements in the area of marketing which emerge from marketing literature:

(a) policies and procedures relating to the products to be offered, such as range, additions, deletions, quality, technical specification, design, positioning, branding, packaging and labelling, and so on;

(b) pricing levels to be adopted, margins and discount policies for product groups in particular segments;

(c)   the policies for non-personal communication using advertising, direct mail and sales promotion (the creative approach, the type of media, type of displays, the amount to spend, and so on);

(d)   what emphasis is to be placed on personal selling, the sales approach, sales training, and so on;

(e)   the distributive channels to be used and the relative importance of each;

(f)   warehousing, transportation, inventories, service levels, and so on, in relation to distribution.

Thus, marketing strategies are the means by which marketing objectives will be achieved and are generally concerned with the four major elements of the marketing mix as follows:

Product   The general policies for product deletions, modifications, additions, design, packaging, and so on.

Price   The general pricing policies to be followed for product groups in market segments.

Promotion   The general policies for communicating with customers under the relevant headings, such as: advertising, sales force, sales promotion, public relations, exhibitions, direct mail, and so on.

Place   The general policies for channels and customer service levels.

The following list of marketing strategies (in summary form) covers the majority of options open under the headings of the four Ps:

- *Product*   – expand the line
              – acquire new lines/production facilities
              – change performance, quality or features
              – consolidate the line
              – change design
              – standardise design
              – positioning
              – change the product portfolio
              – branding
- *Price*   – change unit price, terms or conditions
              – skimming policies
              – penetration policies
- *Promotion*   – change advertising or promotion
              – change selling

- *Place*
  - change delivery or distribution
  - consolidate distribution
  - change service levels
  - change channels
  - change the degree of forward integration

You should refer to Chapters 7 to 10 of *Marketing Plans – How to Prepare Them: How to Use Them*, by M. H. B. McDonald, 3rd edn (Oxford: Heinemann, 1995), for a much more detailed consideration of promotion, pricing and distribution. These chapters describe what should appear in advertising, sales, pricing and place plans. This detail is intended for those whose principal concern is the preparation of a detailed one-year operational or tactical plan. The relationship between this detail and the strategic plan is in the provision of information to enable the planner to delineate broad strategies under the headings outlined above. In Chapter 5 of the same book, all the product options are covered.

Formulating marketing strategies is one of the most critical and difficult parts of the entire marketing process. It sets the limit of success. Communicated to all management levels, it indicates what strengths are to be developed, what weaknesses are to be remedied, and in what manner. Marketing strategies enable operating decisions to bring the company into the right relationship with the emerging pattern of market opportunities, which previous analysis has shown to offer the highest prospect of success.

It is worth stressing again that the vital phase of setting objectives and strategies is a highly complex process which, if done badly, will probably result in considerable misdirection of resources.

This chapter has confirmed the need for setting clear, definitive objectives for all aspects of the marketing programme, and demonstrated that marketing objectives themselves have to derive logically from corporate objectives. The advantages of this practice are that it allows all concerned with marketing activities to concentrate their particular contribution on achieving the overall marketing objectives, as well as facilitating meaningful and constructive evaluation of all marketing activity.

For the practical purpose of marketing planning, it will be apparent from the observations above (concerning what was referred to as a 'hierarchy of objectives') that overall marketing objectives have to be broken down into sub-objectives which, taken all together, will achieve the overall objectives. By breaking down the overall objectives, the problem of strategy development becomes more manageable, and hence easier.

A two-year study of 35 top industrial companies by McKinsey and Company revealed that leader companies agreed that market/product strategy is the key to the task of keeping shareholders' equity rising. Clearly, then, setting objectives and strategies in relation to market segments and products is a most important step in the marketing planning process.

Once agreement has been reached on the broad marketing objectives and strategies, those responsible for programmes can now proceed to the detailed planning stage, developing the appropriate overall strategy statements into sub-objectives.

Plans constitute the vehicle for getting to the destination along the chosen route, or the detailed execution of the strategy. The term 'plan' is often used synonymously in marketing literature with the terms 'programme' and 'schedule'. A plan containing detailed lists of tasks to be completed, together with responsibilities, timing and cost, is sometimes referred to as an appropriation budget, which is merely a detailing of the actions to be carried out and of the expected sterling results in carrying them out. More about this can be read in Chapters 7 to 10 of *Marketing Plans – How to Prepare them: How to Use them*, which looks at advertising, sales promotion, the sales plan, pricing and distribution plan.

Part II

Segmentation and Organisations

Organisational Issues in Market Segmentation

■ Summary

The structuring of markets into clearly defined segments is undoubtedly a key input for the company's marketing plan. Segmentation not only identifies the customer groups your company should focus its resources into, but also (through the detailed analysis required in a professionally conducted segmentation process) identifies vitally important elements of a successful marketing strategy. Having an organisation which is both supportive of the process and supportive of carrying through the findings into the market place is therefore crucial.

The organisational issues associated with segmentation can best be grouped under two distinct headings:

(a) the company's approach to addressing segmentation; and

(b) the company's approach to implementing the conclusion.

These two areas are, however, closely linked, as the degree of commitment to implementation is directly related to the extent of an organisation's commitment to, and involvement in, its segmentation review. For example, if the review is put into the hands of an 'elite group' who are required to look at segmentation as a 'closed' and confidential study, the implementation of their findings will, at best, be slow and tortuous or, at worst, simply fail.

■ Segmentation as a Company Exercise

Marketing's contribution to business success in manufacturing, the provision of services, distribution or retailing activities lies in its commitment to detailed analysis of future opportunities to meet customer needs, and a wholly professional approach to selling to well-defined market segments those products or services that deliver the sought-after benefits. Achieving revenue budgets and sales forecasts are a function of how good our intelligence services are; how well suited our strategies are; and how well we are led.

■ Support from the Chief Executive and Senior Management

There can be no doubt that unless the chief executive sees the need for a segmentation review, understands the process and shows an active interest in it, it is virtually impossible for a senior marketing executive to implement the conclusions in a meaningful way.

This is particularly so in companies that are organised on the basis of divisional management, for which the marketing executive has no profit responsibility and in which he or she has no line management authority. In such cases, it is comparatively easy for senior operational managers to create 'political' difficulties, the most serious of which is just to ignore the new segments and their requirements entirely.

The vital role that the chief executive and senior management *must* play in segmentation underlines one of the key points in this chapter: that it is *people* who make systems work, and that system design and implementation have to take account of the 'personality' of both the organisation and the people involved, and that these are different in all organisations. A most striking feature is the difference in 'personality' between companies, and the fact that within any one company there is a marked similarity between the attitudes of executives. These attitudes vary from the impersonal, autocratic kind at one extreme to the highly personal, participative kind at the other.

Any system, therefore, has to be designed around the people who have to make it work, and has to take account of the prevailing conditions, attitudes, skills, resource availability and organisational constraints. Since the chief executive and senior management are the key influencers of these factors, without their active support and participation any formalised approach to segmentation is unlikely to work. The worst outcome can be a chief executive and senior management ignoring the plans built out of the segmentation review and continuing to make decisions which appear illogical to those who have participated in the segmentation process and in producing the resulting marketing plan. This quickly destroys any credibility that the emerging plans might have had, leading to the demise of the procedures and to serious levels of frustration throughout the organisation.

Indeed, there is some evidence leading to the belief that chief executives who fail, first, to understand the essential role of marketing in generating profitable revenue in a business and, second, to understand how marketing can be integrated into the other functional areas of the business through marketing planning procedures are a key contributory factor in poor economic performance. There is a depressing preponderance of accountants who live by the rule of 'the bottom line' and who apply universal financial criteria indiscriminately to all products and segments, irrespective of the long-term consequences. There is a similar preponderance of engineers who see marketing as an unworthy activity that is something to do with activities such as television advertising, and who think of their products only in terms of their technical features and functional characteristics, in spite of the overwhelming body of evidence which exists to show that these are only a part of what a customer buys. Not surprisingly, in companies headed by people like this, market-based segmentation reviews and marketing planning are either non-existent or, where they are tried, they fail. This is the most frequently encountered barrier to effective marketing.

■ Size and Diversity

In a large diversified company operating in many markets, a complex combination of market, segment, product and financial plans is possible. For example, what is required at the individual segment level will be different from what is required at headquarters level, while it is clear that the total corporate plan has to be constructed from the individual building blocks. Furthermore, the function of marketing itself may be further functionalised for the purpose of planning, such as market research, market management, segment management, product management, advertising, selling, distribution and so on.

Clearly, in a large diversified group, irrespective of any organisational issues, anything other than a systematic approach to the issues addressed in marketing is unlikely to enable the necessary control to be exercised over the public 'face' of the corporation. As size and diversity grow, so the degree of formalisation in its marketing processes must also increase. This can be simplified in the form of a matrix, as shown in Figure 12.1.

Size is without doubt the biggest determinant of the two in the type of marketing systems required.

In small companies, there is rarely much diversity of markets, and top management has an in-depth knowledge of the key determinants of success and failure. While in such companies the central control mechanism is the sales forecast and budget, top managers are able to explain the rationale lying behind the numbers; they have a very clear view of their comparative strengths and weaknesses; and they are able to explain the company's marketing strategy without difficulty. This understanding and familiarity with the strategy is shared with key operating subordinates by means of personal, face-to-face dialogue throughout the year. Subordinates are operating within a logical framework of ideas, which they understand. There is a shared understanding between top and middle management of the industry and prevailing business

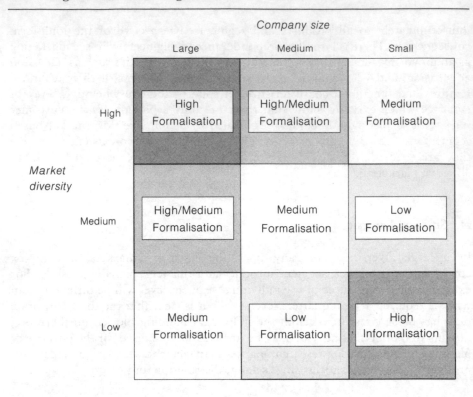

Figure 12.1   The influence of size and diversity on the need for formalisation in marketing.

conditions. In such cases, since either the owner or a director is usually also deeply involved in the day-to-day management of the business, the need to rely on informational inputs from subordinates is considerably less than in larger companies. Consequently, there is less need for written procedures about understanding markets, SWOT analyses, marketing objectives and strategies, as these are carried out by senior management, often informally at meetings and in face-to-face discussions with subordinates, the results of which are the basis of forecasts and budgets. Written documents in respect of the target segments and their price, advertising and selling strategies, for example, are very brief, but those managers responsible for those aspects of the business know what part they are expected to play in achieving the company's objectives. Such companies are, therefore, operating according to a set of structured procedures, but in a relatively informal way.

On the other hand, many small companies that have a poor understanding of the marketing concept and in which the top manager leaves his or her strategy implicit, suffer many serious operational problems.

These operational problems become progressively worse as the size of company increases. As the number and levels of management increase, it becomes progressively more difficult for top management to enjoy an in-depth knowledge of industry and business conditions by informal, face-to-face means. In the absence of written procedures and a structured framework, the different levels of operating management become increasingly less able to react in a rational way to day-to-day pressures.

From the point of view of management control, the least complex environment in which to work is an undiversified company. For the purposes of this discussion, 'undiversified' is taken to mean companies with homogeneous customer groups or limited product lines. For example, a diverse range of products could be sold into only one market such as, say, the motor industry, with this being the only 'market' in which segmentation is required. Alternatively, hydraulic hoses could be sold to many diverse markets, but it is only the benefits being sought from hydraulic hoses the segmentation work is required to consider. However, the need for institutionalised marketing processes will still increase with size and the resulting complexity of the management task. For example, an oil company will operate in many diverse markets around the world, through many different kinds of marketing systems, and with varying levels of segment share and segment growth. In most respects, therefore, the control function for headquarters management is just as difficult and complex as that in a major diversified conglomerate. The major difference is the greater level of in-depth knowledge which top management has about the key determinants of success and failure underlying the market or product world-wide, because of its homogeneity.

As a result of this homogeneity of market or product, it is usually possible for headquarters to impose world-wide policies on operating units in respect of things such as certain aspects of advertising, public relations, packaging, pricing, trade marks, product development and so on, whereas in the headquarters of a diversified conglomerate, overall policies of this kind tend to be impracticable and meaningless.

The view is often expressed that having common marketing processes in companies comprising many heterogeneous units is less helpful and confuses rather than improves much in handling between operating units and headquarters. However, the truth is that conglomerates often consist of several smaller multinationals, some diversified and some not, and that the actual task of marketing rests on the lowest level in an organisation at which there is general management profit responsibility. Forecasting and budgeting systems by themselves rarely encourage anything but a short-term, parochial view of the business at these levels, and in the absence of the kind of procedures described in this book, and found in books devoted to the process of marketing planning, higher levels of management do not have a sufficiently rational basis on which to set long-term marketing objectives.

Exactly the same principles apply at the several levels of control in a diversified multinational conglomerate, in that at the highest level of control there has to be some rational basis on which to make decisions about the portfolio of investments, and research has shown that the most successful companies are those with standard marketing procedures to aid this process. In such companies there is a hierarchy of audits, segments, SWOT analyses, assumptions, objectives, strategies and marketing programmes, with increasingly more detail required in the procedures at the lowest levels in the organisation. The precise details of each step vary according to circumstances, but the eventual output of the process is in a universally consistent form.

The basis on which the whole system rests is the information input requirements at the highest level of command. The marketing objectives and strategies necessary to exploit the chosen segments are frequently synthesised into a multi-disciplinary corporate plan at the next general management profit-responsible level, until at the highest level of command the corporate plan consists largely of financial information and summaries of the major operational activities. This is an important point, for there is rarely a consolidated operational marketing plan at conglomerate headquarters. This often exists only at the lowest level of general management profit responsibility, and even here it is sometimes incorporated into the corporate plan, particularly in capital goods companies, where engineering, manufacturing and technical services are major factors in commercial success.

To summarise, the smaller the company, the more informal and personal the procedures for segmentation and marketing planning. As company size and diversity increase, so the need for institutionalised procedures increases.

The really important issue in any system is the degree to which it enables *control* to be exercised over the key determinants of success and failure. A formally designed system seeks to find the right balance between the flexibility of operating units to react to changes in local market conditions and centralised control. The main role of headquarters is to harness the company's strengths on a world-wide basis and to ensure that lower-level decisions do not cause problems in other areas and lead to wasteful duplication. At the same time, however, it must not stifle creativity.

There would be little disagreement that in today's abrasive, turbulent and highly competitive environment, it is those firms which succeed in extracting entrepreneurial ideas and creative marketing programmes from systems that are necessarily yet acceptably formalised, which will succeed in the long run. Much innovative flair can so easily get stifled by systems.

Injecting new enthusiasm into the periodic reviews of the market is often best achieved by the involvement of senior managers, from the chief executive down through the hierarchy. Essentially what takes place is a personalised presentation of the findings in the review of the market and its segments, together with the proposed marketing objectives and strategies and outline budgets for the strategic planning period. These are discussed, and amended where necessary, and agreed in various synthesised formats at the hierarchical levels in the organisation *before* any detailed operational planning takes place. It is at such meetings that managers are called upon to justify their views, which tends to force them to be bolder and more creative than they would have been had they been allowed merely to send in their proposals. Obviously, much depends even here on the degree to which managers take a critical stance, and this will be much greater when the chief executive himself takes an active part in the process. *Every hour of time devoted at this stage by the chief executive has a multiplier effect throughout the remainder of the process.* And let it be remembered we are not, repeat not, talking about budgets at this juncture in anything other than outline form.

Although the segmentation task and the development of the findings into marketing objectives and strategies is less complicated in small, undiversified companies, and there is less need for formalised procedures than in large, diversified companies, experience has shown that exactly the same framework should be used in all circumstances, and that this approach brings similar benefits to all.

In a multinational conglomerate, headquarters management is able to assess major trends in markets and products around the world, and is thus able to develop strategies for investment, expansion, diversification and divestment on a global basis. For their part, subsidiary management can develop appropriate strategies with a sense of locomotion towards the achievement of coherent overall goals.

This is achieved by means of synthesised information flows from the bottom upwards, which facilitates useful comparison of performance around the world, and the diffusion of valuable information, skills, experiences and systems from the top downwards. The procedures which facilitate the provision of such information and knowledge transfers also encourage operational management to think strategically about their own areas of responsibility, instead of managing only for the short term.

It is abundantly clear that it is through the complete process of segmentation, marketing planning and planning skills that such benefits are achieved, and that discussions such as those about the standardisation *process* are largely irrelevant. Any standardisation that may be possible will become clear only if a company can successfully develop a system for identifying the needs of each market and each segment in which it operates, and for organising resources to satisfy those needs in such a way that best resource utilisation results world-wide.

■ **Planning for the Segmentation Process**

A recipe for failure in segmentation is to assume that the process appearing in this book can be implemented immediately and taken all the way through to its conclusions in a matter of days, or even weeks. If the outcome of the review is best put into effect by incorporating it into a complete marketing planning system, then we are talking about years, with research indicating that a period of around three years is required in a major company before a complete marketing planning system can be implemented according to its design.

Failure, or partial failure, then, is often the result of not developing a timetable for introducing a new system, to take account of the following:

● The need to communicate why segmentation and reviews of segmentation are necessary

● The need to recruit top management support and participation

● The need to test the process out on a limited basis to demonstrate its effectiveness and value

● The need for training programmes, or workshops, to train line management in its use

● Complete lack of data and information in some parts of the world, or data and information built either around products or around past 'segments'

● Shortage of resources

Above all, a resolute sense of purpose and dedication is required, tempered by patience and a willingness to appreciate the inevitable problems which will be encountered in implementing the conclusions.

This is all closely linked to the next issue companies need to get right in the segmentation process: line management support.

■ **Line Management Support**

Hostility, lack of skills, lack of data and information, lack of resources, and an inadequate organisational structure, all add up to a failure to obtain the willing participation of operational managers.

New processes inevitably require considerable explanation of the procedures involved and the accompanying pro-formas, flow charts and so on. Often these devices arrive on the desk of a busy line manager in the form of a book or a manual, without any previous explanation or discussion. The immediate reaction often appears to be fear of failing to understand it, let alone comply with it, followed by anger and finally rejection. Headquarters becomes the remote 'ivory tower', divorced from the reality of the market place.

This is often exacerbated by line management's absorption in the present operating and reward system, which is geared to the achievement of *current* results, while the segmentation process, and its translation into operational requirements through the marketing planning process, is geared towards establishing the future revenue sources for the company. Also, because of the trend in recent years towards the frequent movement of executives around organisations, there is less interest in spending time on future business gains from which someone else is likely to benefit.

The solutions to the problems which could stand in the way of line management support require a good deal of patience, common-sense, ingenuity and flexibility on the part of both headquarters and operating management. This is closely connected with the need to consider resource availability and the prevailing organisation structure. The problem of lack of reliable data and information can only be solved by devoting time and money to its solution and, where available resources are scarce, it is unlikely that the information demands of headquarters can be met.

It is for this reason that some kind of appropriate headquarters organisation has to be found for the collection and dissemination of valuable information, and that training has to be provided on ways of solving this problem.

Again, these issues are complicated by the varying degrees of size and complexity of companies. It is surprising to see the extent to which organisational structures cater inadequately for marketing as a function. In small companies, there is often no one other than the sales manager, who spends all his or her time engaged either in personal selling or in managing the sales force. Unless the chief executive is marketing-oriented, detailed extensive studies of markets to determine the most appropriate segments for the business will just not be done.

In medium-sized and large companies, particularly those that are divisionalised, there is rarely any provision at Board level for marketing as a discipline. Sometimes there is a commercial director with line management responsibility for the operating divisions, but apart from sales managers at divisional level, or a marketing manager at head office level, marketing as a function is not particularly well catered for. Where there is a marketing manager, that person tends to be somewhat isolated from the mainstream activities.

The most successful organisations are those with a fully integrated marketing function, whether it is line management responsible for sales, or a staff function, with operating units being a microcosm of the head office organisation.

■   **Integrating the Segmentation Process into a Marketing Planning System and into a Total Corporate Planning System**

Segmentation as a stand-alone process will end up being an intellectually challenging, but theoretical, exercise if the process and conclusions are not incorporated into a marketing planning system.

In turn, it is difficult to initiate an effective marketing planning system in the absence of a parallel corporate planning system. This is yet another facet of the separation of operational planning from strategic planning for, unless similar processes and time scales to those being used in the marketing planning system are also being used by other major functions (such as distribution, production, finance and personnel), the sort of trade-offs and compromises that have to be made in any company between what is wanted and what is practicable and affordable will not take place in a rational way. These trade-offs have to be made on the basis of the fullest possible understanding of the reality of the company's multi-functional strengths and weaknesses, and opportunities and threats.

One of the problems of systems in which there is either a separation of the strategic corporate planning process, or in which marketing planning is the only formalised system, is the lack of participation by key functions of the company, such as engineering or production. Where these are key determinants of success, as in capital goods companies, a separate marketing planning system is virtually ineffective.

Where marketing, however, is a major activity, as in fast-moving industrial goods companies, it is possible to initiate a separate marketing planning system. The indications are that when this happens successfully, similar systems for other functional areas of the business quickly follow suit because of the benefits which are observed by the chief executive.

■   **Cross-Functional Involvement**

The very nature of the segmentation process brings with it the temptation to delegate the process in its entirety to the market research manager, or to the marketing planning manager or, in the absence of a marketing planning manager, to the corporate planning function. This divorcing of the process from operations is likely to result in a strong reluctance by line management to accept the conclusions, especially if they represent a change from current thinking, as well as a resentment of the rigorous process it involves and of the people who follow it.

It also has to be said that such an approach is unlikely to produce the best results. Those staff in contact with the market place bring practical experience to the process. Staff from other areas of the company bring a different perspective to the issues addressed in the process, as well as a further resource for creative thinking.

The detailed work required for segmentation does not, however, suit a committee environment. As suggested in our opening chapter, a core team of two or three individuals needs to be established, whose job it is to carry out the detailed work, commission externally contracted agencies as required or agree such briefs with the relevant section of the company, use the cross-functional steering group as a sounding board, and raise topics with other members of staff as appropriate.

This raises the question again of the key role of the chief executive in both the segmentation process and marketing planning as a whole. Without both the chief executive's support and understanding of the very serious implications of initiating an effective segmentation review, everyone else's efforts will be largely ineffective.

■ Successful Implementation of Segmented Marketing

As was pointed out at the beginning of this chapter, it is impossible to divorce implementation from the process of arriving at the concluding segments. Of critical importance here are:

(a) the support of the chief executive and senior management;

(b) a feeling of 'ownership' of the conclusions by the company's key operating units generated by their involvement in the process;

(c) an institutionalised marketing planning process which can take the results of the segmentation review and develop it into both a strategic three-year plan and a one-year marketing programme.

In addition, to operate effectively in the selected segments, the company's activities should be organised around them. If this cannot be achieved, the company's market share goals and financial objectives are unlikely to be reached.

This consideration of 'internal compatibility' is so important that it should be borne in mind whilst following the segmentation process. It is also one of the criteria used to assess the suitability of a concluding segment, along with size, differentiation and reachability.

Marketing departments can, of course, operate within the new segmentation structure on their own and develop advertising and promotional programmes accordingly (an implementation strategy referred to as 'Bolt-on Segmentation' (Jenkins and McDonald, 1994; see Chapter 1) because of its high level of customer focus, but low level of organisational integration). This approach will not, however, be as successful as one which has both a high level of customer focus *and* a high level of organisational integration, or 'Strategic Segmentation' as it is called by Jenkins and McDonald (Chapter 1).

Organisational integration can be looked at on three levels, the strategic, the managerial and the tactical.

■   **Strategic Integration through the Mission Statement**

Many organisations find their different departments, and sometimes even different groups in the same department, pulling in different directions. This often has disastrous results, simply because the organisation has not defined the boundaries of the business and the way it wishes to do business in its mission or purpose statement.

Take the example of a high-technology company. One group of directors felt the company should be emphasising technology, while another group felt technology was less important than marketing. With such confusion at the top of the company, it is not hard to imagine the chaos further down.

A different example concerns a hosiery buyer for a department store group. She believed her mission was to maximise profit, whereas research showed that women shopped in department stores for items other than hosiery. They did, however, expect hosiery to be on sale, even though that was rarely the purpose of their visit. This buyer, in trying to maximise profit, limited the number of brands, colours and sizes on sale, with the result that many women visitors to the store were disappointed and did not return. So it can be seen that in this case, by maximising her own profit, she was sub-optimising the total profit of the group. In this case, the role of her section was more of a *service* role than a profit-maximising role.

Here we can see two levels of mission. One is a *corporate* mission statement, the other is a lower-level, or *purpose*, statement. But there is yet another level, as shown in the following summary:

Type 1   'Motherhood', usually found inside annual reports designed to 'stroke' shareholders. Otherwise no practical use.

Type 2   The real thing. A meaningful statement, unique to the organisation concerned, which 'impacts' on the behaviour of the executives at all levels.

Type 3   This is a 'purpose' statement (or lower-level mission statement). It is appropriate at the strategic business unit, departmental or product group level of the organisation.

The mission statement should in itself consist of brief statements which cover the following points:

- *Role or contribution of the unit*
  For example, profit generator, service department, opportunity seeker.

- *Definition of business*
  Preferably in terms of the *benefits* you provide or the *needs* you satisfy. Do not be too specific (for example, 'we sell milking machinery') or too general (for example, 'we are in the engineering business').

- *Distinctive competence*
  These are the essential skills/capabilities/resources that underpin whatever success has been achieved to date. This statement should be brief, consisting of one particular item or the possession of a number of skills that apply only to your organisation or specific SBU. A statement that could equally apply to any competitor cannot, by definition, be a *distinctive* competence and is therefore unsatisfactory.

- *Indications for future direction*
  A brief statement of the principal things you will do, and those you would give serious consideration to (for example, move into a new segment). In some instances it may also be appropriate to cover what you will *never* do.

It is particularly in the 'business definition' and 'indications for the future' areas that the conclusions drawn from the segmentation review will have an influence.

■ Managerial integration

In addition to adopting an organisational structure built around the segmentation structure, as discussed earlier, it will be necessary to provide management information in a form that supports the new segmentation focus. It has to be said, however, that changing organisational structures and management information systems are not tasks that can be achieved overnight. Both will take time, and it may take a great deal of determination to prevent the difficulties that will be encountered becoming a justification for throwing out the segmentation conclusions. Evolution, as opposed to revolution, may need to be the order of the day, and the process of evolution will be slower the more the 'new order' challenges the status quo and the distribution of power.

■ Tactical Integration

Here we are concerned with the ability of the organisation at the operational level to be effective in the segment.

The advertising and promotions department needs to be able to target their activities into the selected segments. Single approach solutions will have to be dropped in favour of differentiated solutions, some of which may have to employ techniques currently unfamiliar to the department.

The sales force will need to be trained both in distinguishing between the different segments, and in the appropriate benefits to be highlighted during sales meetings. Alternatively, of course, it may be possible to re-organise the sales group around the segments.

Differential pricing will need to be supported and understood within the organisation, as the days of the single pricing policy will most likely have disappeared. This will be particularly difficult for the sales force, but they will be helped by being given carefully targeted products/services, supported by clear and distinctive promotional campaigns.

Distribution will also need to adapt, both in terms of the availability levels and channels required by the segments.

■ The Human Face in Segmentation

The personal dimension in segmentation is clearly very important: without the belief and commitment of the employees to this method of looking at the market, the segmentation process is all but sunk. But the 'personal' side of the segments themselves can help win the support and enthusiasm of staff and, in doing so, encourage them to change any previously entrenched ways.

A number of companies have turned to cartoonists in order to give a human face to their segments and put their segments on first name terms. This has the additional advantage of emphasising that each segment is, in fact, a collection of living, breathing human beings who, just like the company's employees, look for the offer that best meets their needs. If in doing this they find themselves having to switch brands, then that is exactly what the segments will do.

This 'personalising' of segments was certainly put to good effect in ICI Fertilizers when a new marketing plan was rolled out at the end of their extensive segmentation project. After internally researching the needs of the target market (the company's employees) and testing alternative 'offers', the seven segments which emerged from the project were named Martin, David, Oliver, Brian, George, Arthur and Joe. All seven of them were captured as cartoon characters, with each drawing carefully tested amongst the target market in terms of its ability to portray the profile of the segment it was meant to represent. The cartoon depictions of Brian, George and Joe appear below.

Drawings by Arthur Shell

Part III

The Epilogue

The Contribution of Segmentation to Business Planning: A Case Study of the Rise, Fall and Recovery of ICI Fertilizers

■ **Summary**

For this final chapter, we look at the important contribution made by segmentation to a business plan that proved to be a critical turning point for a UK manufacturing company, which had enjoyed enormous success and prosperity but, within a very short time, found itself fighting for survival.

To ensure the part played by segmentation is seen in context, the case study starts well before the segmentation project was even commissioned.

■ **Background**

ICI Fertilizers (ICIF), formerly part of ICI Agricultural Division, is an operating company in ICI plc. ICIF's business is best described as 'crop nutrition', its main product lines supplementing the principal soil nutrients used up by today's intensive agricultural practices.

The elements most likely to be depleted in the soil are nitrogen (N), phosphate (P) and potash (K), collectively known as NPK. While, of course, there are other nutrients which occasionally become deficient in certain soils or for special crops, production of fertilisers containing just one element or various combinations of nitrogen, phosphate and potash has been the main function of the fertiliser industry.

'Chemical fertilisers' have an advantage over 'organic manures' because they are much more concentrated and thereby more efficient. In addition, they can be 'tailor-made' to suit specific soil conditions.

At ICIF, the manufacturing processes for nitrogen, phosphate and potash are as follows:

- Phosphate fertilisers: phosphate rock is imported, mainly from Senegal, where it is mined on a large scale. In this raw state it is insoluble in water, even if finely ground. By treating it with sulphuric acid, it finishes up as superphosphate, which is soluble and can be produced in granular form.

- Potash: originally potash was imported, but now most of it is mined at Boulby near Whitby in North Yorkshire. This material is ready to use and can be incorporated into compound fertilisers without any further treatment.

- Nitrogen: although 80 per cent of the air around us is nitrogen, most crops cannot take advantage of it until it has been converted into nitrate by either bacteria or a chemical process.

The chemical process involves combining nitrogen and hydrogen under high pressure and temperature in the presence of a catalyst. This produces ammonia, a gas, which, under pressure, becomes a liquid.

The source of hydrogen, a key raw material, can be from any fossil fuel such as suitably treated coal, naphtha or from natural gas. Ammonia is the first stage in the production of nitrogen fertiliser. In the second production process ammonia is reacted with nitric acid to produce ammonium nitrate.

Finally, ammonium nitrate is solidified into prills (small pellets), containing 34.5 per cent nitrogen, in which form it is sold as a straight nitrogen fertiliser. It may also be granulated along with phosphate and potash to produce the required compound ratio.

Therefore, taking the production of NPK as a whole, phosphate and potash present little in the way of manufacturing problems, any technology involved being low level. On the other hand, the nitrogen production, needing as it does the ammonia plant, represents high levels of investment and technical competence.

It should be pointed out that, during the manufacture of ammonia, there are several useful by-products which are subsequently sold. They include nitrous oxide (anaesthetics) and carbon dioxide (in liquefied form used in soft drinks, beer and as a heat exchange medium for nuclear reactors, in solid form used in refrigerated transport and food processing). In addition, a number of other products are also sold which, although not by-products, are closely associated with the technology of ammonia production. Among these are methanol (plastics and synthetic resins), nitrate of soda (glass, explosives and flares), nitric acid, sulphuric acid, urea (resins, adhesives, plastics and as a fertiliser in its own right), pentaerythritol (resins for paints, varnishes and printing inks) and sodium nitrite (dyestuffs, heat treatment, pharmaceutical products, anti-corrosion, meat preservation).

However, the production of these products cannot be described as the Company's main mission. They are only mentioned here for completeness.

■ 1917–87

In 1917, the Government bought a site in Billingham on the north bank of the River Tees for a factory to make synthetic ammonia, 'Synthonia', as a first stage for producing the chemicals for munitions. After the war, in 1919, Brunner Mond and Company took over the site to make fertiliser from ammonia using the same process as originally intended in the government plan.

It wasn't until 1923 that the first ammonia plant started production, and by the following year the first 'straight' nitrogen fertiliser (that is, containing no phosphate or potash), sulphate of ammonia, was manufactured.

In 1928, another straight nitrogen fertiliser, 'Nitrochalk', was produced especially for grassland.

By 1930, the first concentrated complete fertiliser (CCF) was produced. This was the first compound of nitrogen, phosphate and potash. During the next three decades, the company experienced steady growth and accumulated considerable expertise; indeed, it led the way in the process, design and control of ammonia plants. In addition, its knowledge about catalysts and their manufacture became extensive.

The interruption of the war years, 1940–45, saw the Company's expertise being applied to producing aviation spirit from coal. In order to reduce the risks of bomb damage threatening output, the Company was directed to disperse production. As a result, relatively small factories were set up at Heysham, Dowlais Prudhoe and Mossend. These additional facilities were converted to fertiliser production after the war, but have now all closed.

This enforced foray into new technology was a determining factor in ICI developing its post-war interests in plastics, petro chemicals and agriculture (plant protection). All of these fields of work were eventually harnessed into substantial operating divisions within the Group.

Until the 1960s, the hydrogen essential to the production process was obtained by 'gasifying' local coal from the Durham coalfield. However, there was a vociferous and increasing concern about environmental pollution which arose from using coal. This, coupled with the run-down of the Durham mines, was instrumental in causing the Company to switch its hydrocarbon fuel source from coal to naphtha. The Company developed a commanding lead in the new technology associated with using naphtha and licensed the process all around the world. Finally, the Company converted to its present source of hydrogen, North Sea gas. This took place in the early 1970s and, although not recognised at the time, this step was to prove to be one of the most significant steps in the Company's history (for reasons that became clear later).

The 1960s was an expansionist period for the Company. The goal was to be really big in ammonia, both in the UK and export markets.

Three very large ammonia plants of revolutionary design were bought from the USA, and new fertiliser production capacity was also built at Billingham. In addition, the Company built a manufacturing unit at Severnside (Bristol), which contained two ammonia plants and ancillary fertiliser equipment. Offshoots were also being sponsored in India, Malaysia, Australia, South Africa and Canada, all eventually becoming autonomous operations.

Yet, even with this increased level of activity, the 1960s decade was not a particularly profitable one, mainly because of over-capacity in the industry and the relatively poor profitability of UK farming. The UK agricultural and international fertiliser markets were depressed for much of the period. In addition, the Company had a protracted and expensive struggle to make the new ammonia plants work. In 1969–71, profits were close to zero.

A profound upturn in Company fortunes followed the 1973 oil crisis, which had such a disastrous effect on most of the rest of manufacturing industry. As the price of oil soared, so did the production costs of ICI's competitors who used this as the source of hydrogen in their production processes.

In comparison, the virtually fixed-price gas contract negotiated earlier by ICI began to yield rich dividends, and effectively gave the Company a tremendous cost advantage for this essential processing ingredient throughout the 1970s and into the 1980s. Not surprisingly, safeguarding the gas contract from political attack became a cornerstone of policy.

This advantage in manufacturing costs was exploited in the market place and the Company became increasingly dominant. By 1980 it had 80–90 per cent of ammonia production in the UK (there was competition from only one other ammonia plant) and was certainly the largest producer in Europe, outside what was then referred to as the Eastern Bloc. From this position of strength, the Company pursued a policy of holding prices high and maximising profits, rather than seeking increased market share, and dictating how much of the product its distributors and farmer customers could take, and when.

Even so, in nitrogen fertiliser terms, the Company had the lion's share of the UK market: some 60 per cent, compared with the 25 per cent share of Fisons, the nearest competitor.

All of this contributed to the fertiliser business becoming the veritable jewel in the crown of ICI. In 1981, ICIF contributed over a third of Group profits and its future looked very bright.

Such was the level of confidence within the Company that it dictated to the industry on prices and increasingly geared its output to what constituted the most economic production runs at the plants. The Company's perspective had become very inward looking, and its over-confidence began to generate complacency. A discerning eye might have spotted some warning signals; nothing too obvious at first, but nevertheless worthy of attention. The danger was not from within the Company, *but from outside in the market place*.

■ **The Fertiliser Market**

To describe the UK fertiliser market over the years to 1980 is tantamount to chronicling the fortunes of two companies, ICIF and Fisons.

Fisons was a long established company and highly respected in the trade. The Company was reputed to have a marketing ear 'close to the ground' and, as a result, carried a wider range of fertilisers than ICIF. A significant difference in their history, however, compared with ICIF, was that in the early 1960s a corporate decision was made not to be involved in basic ammonia production. Instead, Fisons chose to buy ammonia from other suppliers. This decision was coincident with ICIF's expansionist phase and it was seen to be mutually acceptable for ICIF to build and commission an ammonia plant dedicated to supplying the Fisons main site at Immingham, near Grimsby on Humberside.

From this time onwards, the two companies' destinies were somewhat inter-linked. Whenever ICIF chose to increase prices, Fisons invariably followed. It was a strategy that suited the two fertiliser giants, and their growing dominance had the effect of removing some twenty or so small fertiliser manufacturers from the competitive arena. The smaller companies just did not have the advantage of the economies of scale of production and distribution afforded to the market leaders.

Thus by 1980, as mentioned above, ICIF had some 60 per cent share of the UK market and Fisons 25 per cent, the remainder being met by a number of small manufacturers, or by imports.

■ **Imports**

Just as it suited ICIF to have the number two competitor in the home market partially dependent upon it for basic raw materials and operating very much in ICIF's shadow, so it suited the Company to keep imports to a minimum: not an easy task.

However, their major competitors on mainland Europe were just as concerned to protect their own home markets. Thus, the European market operated under an uneasy truce, and major producers did not see it as being in their interest to disturb the status quo. The risk of massive retaliation for violating the unspoken code of conduct was too high a price to pay. There was some economic logic in this, since fertilisers are low-cost, bulky products and therefore expensive to transport.

■ Changes in the Market Place

Traditionally, fertiliser had been supplied in 50kg bags, and for a long time these suited the needs of the market place. However, as farms became more mechanised and less dependent on muscle power, a demand for fertiliser bags to be palletised started to emerge.

At first, only minor suppliers responded to this need. There was a reluctance on the part of the major producers to switch to this form of packaging because of the additional costs which would be incurred at their plants. Not surprisingly, therefore, ICIF turned its back on this particular concept, and Fisons followed suit.

Another innovation in packaging was the introduction of 'shrink-wrapping' of pallets. Again, while this seemed to strike a chord in the market place, the two giants still resisted making any response to this development until forced to do so because of the lead given by small manufacturers.

Clearly, farmers were now becoming interested in semi-bulk packaging.

It was Fisons and some other small producers who eventually took the initiative by introducing a half-tonne 'Top Lift' bag, a tough but floppy plastic bag with a sturdy loop for lifting at the top. It was ideal for many farmers, who could use any tractor with a front end loading arm to position it over the hopper of the spreading vehicle. The unloading could be accomplished by pulling a draw cord and allowing its contents to fall into the hopper. So popular was this packaging that Fisons soon brought out a larger one-tonne 'Top Lift' bag to add to its range.

ICIF had to respond to the threat that Fisons and other smaller companies now posed. Its hitherto seemingly unassailable market share was now under threat. At first sight another form of top lift bag might have sufficed to restore the differential between the two companies, but there were snags.

The rather shapeless and bulky top lift bags could not be stacked more than two high. Above this height, the bags became very unstable. This was no worry for a farmer who would not be holding very much stock, but for ICIF (with its throughput of some 2 million tonnes per annum of fertiliser) the overall effect would be to reduce the warehouse storage capacity several fold. The prospect of investing in new storage, and its subsequent impact on production costs, turned the Company against the top lift bag, yet it somehow had to respond to the new and increasing demand in the market for bulk deliveries.

When it came, in 1984, ICIF's response was in keeping with its production engineering traditions. It was called the 'Dumpy' bag, and it held 750kg. More sophisticated than the 'Top Lift' bag, the 'Dumpy' was basically a squat cylindrical bag sitting in a wooden cradle, not unlike a simplified form of the pallet idea that had been rejected earlier. The cradle and bag shape ensured that the 'Dumpy' met its main design criteria: it could be stacked high enough to make good use of the existing storage facilities at ICIF and it lent itself to transportation by lorry. The cradle was also designed to accommodate the arms of a fork lift truck and was cheap enough to be considered disposable.

However, using a fork lift truck in a warehouse is a different proposition from using one on a farm, and the advantages of the 'Dumpy' could only be exploited to the full by farmers with good pallet handling facilities. Unfortunately, such farmers were in the minority.

For these reasons, the 'Dumpy' never completely matched the competitive advantage of the 'Top Lift' bag, and ICIF failed to keep pace with the growth in this semi-bulk delivery market. Although initial sales were promising, repeat business fell short of expectation and eventually the Company was forced to introduce an additional range of top lift products in 1986.

Despite Fisons' success with 'Top Lift', it had been progressively weakened by its lack of ammonia capacity and its poor production assets had been debilitated by the need to supply cash to Fisons' growing pharmaceutical business. By 1980, it was clear that the end was in sight, but for monopoly reasons ICI's hands were tied. In 1982, Fisons' fertiliser interest was bought for some £40 million by Norsk Hydro, a Norwegian state-owned company which had grown rich from North Sea oil, reputedly earning a surplus of approximately £400 million per year, and £80 million was earmarked for updating and improving the former Fisons' production facilities.

It was soon evident that Norsk Hydro was buying its position in the European fertiliser market. In addition to its investment in the UK, Norsk acquired the premier fertiliser producer in Sweden (Supra) and the second largest in Germany (Brunsbuttle), France (Cofaz) and Holland (NSM).

In contrast, ICIF appeared to have no European strategy. Indeed, it could even have pre-empted the purchase of NSM, since as a 25 per cent shareholder it had first refusal. It chose, instead, to turn its back on continental involvement.

Meanwhile, UKF (which had bought the Shell Fertilisers' complex at Ince, Cheshire, in 1975) became increasingly competitive in the market place. By a combined strategy of increasing capacity and enterprising marketing, they quietly acquired something like a 20 per cent market share in straight nitrogen fertilisers and about 15 per cent in compounds, while ICIF's attentions were directed towards Norsk. In addition to Norsk Hydro and UKF buying into the UK market, Kemira Oy, the Finnish state fertiliser company, acquired a 4 per cent market share by purchasing in 1982 a small company, L & K Fertilisers; they embarked upon an expansionist strategy aiming to give them national coverage and a stated 10 per cent market share objective.

As if this were not enough, substantial imports reappeared on the UK fertiliser scene. Since most of these imports originated from the Eastern Bloc, the pricing was not subject to conventional economic rationale and, in effect, the material was being dumped at prices with which ICIF could not compete.

Not all the pressure came purely from competitors, however. The problems surrounding surplus production of many agricultural products in the European Community resulted in lower prices and a decline in farm incomes. The hitherto buoyant European fertiliser market went into decline. There was again considerable over-capacity of fertiliser production in Europe.

The delicate, gentlemanly restraints regarding exporting to a competitor's country were now severely tested by a new economic reality and were found to be wanting.

From ICIF's viewpoint, this was something of a disaster, because their earlier strategy of dominating the market and keeping prices high made the UK an extremely attractive market for continental producers with surplus capacity, and indeed for manufacturers from even further afield.

To put this new development into perspective, between 1982 and 1987 ICIF lost something like 15 per cent of their market share in straight nitrogen fertilisers as follows:

- Norsk Hydro: 1 per cent
- UKF: 3 per cent
- Imports: 11 per cent

All of the above factors, uncomfortable as they were, might have been weathered because ICIF had such a tremendous advantage over its competitors due to the 'cost plus' gas contract that had been negotiated in the early 1970s; however, in 1983, this contract was re-negotiated in advance of the old contract reaching completion.

■ New Gas Contract

The basis of the initial contract was for ICIF to be provided with gas on a 'cost plus' formula. A key determinant in the contract price was the fact that the gas could be extracted relatively easily from the accessible Lincolnshire gas field, which was just off-shore.

As this reservoir of natural energy became depleted, a new source had to be found. This proved to be the Ninian field, well out in the North Sea, with all the attendant costs. Gas at 1970s prices was now out of the question.

Despite hard re-negotiations, ICIF ended up paying a series of annual stepped increases for gas over a five-year period. Each increase was equivalent to adding £20 million to the Company's raw materials costs, though this was far better than having to pay the increase in one horrendous jump.

At the very time that ICIF's main advantage was being eroded in this way, the vagaries of world economics led to a fall in oil prices, which in turn benefited competitors who used that source of hydrogen for their ammonia plants. Although such a benefit might be a transitory phenomenon only, lasting perhaps one or two years, it can be quite significant in terms of providing a launch pad for winning a few points' market share. Inevitably, a proportion of customers will remain loyal to their new supplier and so the transition can have repercussions in the longer term.

Indeed, so critical is the hydrocarbon 'raw material' to fertiliser production that, unlike the UK, many governments subsidise the energy prices that their domestic manufacturers pay. Again, this is an important factor when taking into account a company's competitive position, since the majority of ICIF's competitors are state companies.

■ The Impact of Local Blenders

The rich, flat landscape of East Anglia lent itself to mechanised farming. Field sizes could be optimised without any interfering topographical features, and farmers were quick to seize the economic advantages that larger field sizes and mechanisation gave them. In turn, the demand for fertilisers increased dramatically in this area as crop yields improved.

As in any market with a record of growth, it does not take long before the entrepreneur, with ears tuned in to the customers' wavelength, discovers unmet needs and new opportunities in the market place. So it was with fertilisers.

The relatively low technology for producing phosphate and potash fertilisers meant that someone with very little capital could set up a small 'manufacturing' plant. The raw materials, phosphates and potash, could be imported by the ship-load to the East Anglian ports. All that remained for the manufacturer to do was to blend these raw materials in proportions sought by the market place and 'bag' them up. The equipment required for doing this was not sophisticated, being rather like a cement mixer, and even second-hand production facilities were easy to obtain. The unskilled, often casual, labour necessary for this work and all the ancillary jobs could be readily found. Thus, start up costs were negligible.

Not surprisingly, a number of 'blenders' (as they are called) set up small businesses in old barns, converted hangars and similar readily available buildings. Typically, the blenders only distributed on a local basis, probably within a 50-mile radius of the plant. To exceed this distance would cause the small company considerable logistical problems.

However, the blenders' modest scale of operation, with its low fixed costs, meant that they could make a tonne of compound for some £30 less than ICIF.

The impact of blenders was easy to see. Nationally, ICIF's share of the compound fertiliser market was about 22 per cent. In East Anglia it was only 8–10 per cent and in Essex it was even less, at around 5 per cent. In these two localities, it was estimated that blenders had something like 50 per cent of the market.

While blenders were only involved in phosphate and potash fertilisers, ICIF were not over-concerned. The Company did not see this as a real threat; it was just a locally irritating, but explainable phenomenon.

However, the activities of the small local suppliers did have the effect of stimulating the already very price-conscious farmers of the region to be on the look-out for ever better bargains.

The more enterprising blenders were also quick to latch on to the over-capacity for nitrogen fertilisers in Europe. They found it an easy process to import straight nitrogen from mainland Europe, primarily through Antwerp. Without having to invest in new equipment, these blenders now had the capacity to offer nitrogen, phosphate and potash compound fertilisers as well as straight nitrogen. Thus, collectively, blenders had become significant competitors to ICIF, albeit on a confined, local basis.

The lower prices offered by blenders, combined with the weakening international market, put so much pressure on ICIF's pricing structure that eventually, in mid-1986, it was found to be impossible for the Company to stick to its previous policy of umbrella pricing. Prices were lowered to a level necessary to compete with imports. This step, combined with the higher gas contract, had the effect of transforming the Company into a loss maker once more.

■ Seasonal Demand and Discounts

The use of fertilisers is highly seasonal. Thus the need to equate monthly sales with monthly output from fertiliser plants has made it necessary for manufacturers to offer seasonal prices to encourage an even off-take of production.

However, with the international market becoming increasingly volatile, during the 1980s the out-of-season purchaser was frequently penalised, rather than rewarded, for planning ahead. This being the case, farmers began to delay making commitments on future purchases and instead bought at the time of usage in order to take advantage of the best 'bargains' available at that moment.

As would be expected, this shift in the purchasing pattern caused something of a logistics problem at the production end. 'A nightmare' was how one company spokesman described this particular development.

■ ICIF's Marketing Organisation

Historically, sales and marketing were seen as two separate functions and this was embodied in the original organisation structure, which had the respective heads of the two groups reporting directly to the Board.

Increasingly, this separation was proving to be unhelpful and was often a weakness when the Company needed to respond to new circumstances. For example, responsibility for pricing policy tended to fluctuate between marketing, sales (effectively the regional sales managers) and the Board.

The Board would insist on the need to have sales at a 'cost-plus' recovery or not at all. Yet, whenever stocks accumulated at the plants, they had to be moved. The regional sales managers duly obliged by taking large orders at low prices.

Within this 'stop-go' situation, the marketing department was somewhere in the middle. The market was confused, and sometimes felt betrayed.

In late 1985, the organisation structure was changed with the objective of getting a much better integration of the sales and marketing functions within the fertiliser business: they now reported to one General Manager. In addition, the new structure addressed itself to the problem of establishing better co-ordination with the autonomous distribution channels.

■ Distribution Channels

Sales to the ultimate consumer, the farmer, are made via a wholesale route using agricultural merchants as distributors. In all, there were approximately 400 distributors in the mid-1980s.

These distributors range from large private companies, operating nationally, down to individual traders. In between are a number of small and medium-sized companies (some of which are co-operatives) whose sales are essentially regional in nature.

To maintain a service to its wholesalers, ICIF had 70 local depots throughout the UK. The Company's sales force (of approximately 100 technical representatives) at that time were responsible for maintaining contact with distributors and influencing them to stock ICIF products. They also provided a technical service to farmers and encouraged them to use the local ICIF distributor.

However, large individual farmers and many local groups of farmers were seeking to by-pass the traditional wholesale system and deal direct with the manufacturers.

An added complication came from the Pareto 80/20 rule when distributors were measured against throughput. In fact, one distributor accounted for nearly 20 per cent of ICIF's sales. So, increasingly, the bargaining position of major distributors was becoming more powerful, with the net effect being a downward pressure on wholesale prices.

In an attempt to counter 'distributor power', as well as retaining as much of the available margin in-house as possible, the Company had two separate retail sales organisations, selling direct to farmers under their own brand names. Both were secured through previous acquisitions, with 'Britag' selling solid fertilisers and 'Chafer' selling liquids. Some 100 sales representatives were employed in this part of the organisation.

However, the only way the direct sales operations can take business away from major distributors, and keep them in their place, is to be more competitive on pricing. This also had the effect of pushing down prices or reducing sales of ICIF's leading branded products.

■ Missed Opportunities

In addition to ICIF being slow to recognise opportunities for palletising and semi-bulk delivery systems, opportunities were missed in special compound fertilisers. The Company, mainly for reasons of its technology and the relative advantage this gave over its competitors, had always been mainly concerned with nitrogen fertilisers. Phosphate and potash compounds were something like poor relations, and treated as accessories to improve the range of use (and thus production throughput) of the nitrogen fertilisers.

Perhaps the Company was right to adopt this philosophy. Certainly, the straight nitrogen market showed the more spectacular growth pattern, growing by roughly 7 per cent per annum until 1983–84, as shown in Figure 13.1.

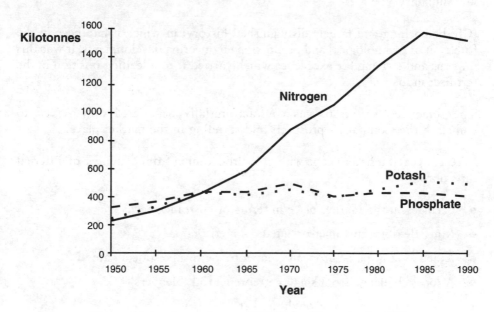

Figure 13.1   Annual use of NPK fertilisers in the UK

Source: The Fertiliser Manufacturers Association, *UK Consumption of Inorganic Fertilisers (1952–92).*

However, while the market for compounds overall was growing at perhaps a modest 0–2 per cent per annum, within this sector the demand for some individual compounds was growing quite rapidly. For example, a compound of 25 per cent nitrogen, 5 per cent phosphate and 5 per cent potash, used extensively on grassland, became very popular.

Both UKF and Norsk Hydro/Fisons spotted this opportunity, while ICIF didn't. By 1987 the total market for this compound was estimated at 350 000 tonnes and the relative sales of the three companies tell their own story: UKF 120 000 tonnes; Norsk Hydro 100 000 tonnes; ICIF 25 000 tonnes.

Another growth sector was for zero nitrogen fertilisers which are used with Autumn sown winter wheat. Typically, the formula for these will be 0–5 per cent nitrogen, 24 per cent phosphate and 24 per cent potash. These are low-margin products to ICIF, but not to the blenders referred to earlier. ICIF's position in this market fluctuated, although towards the end of this period it decided to become more competitive in this sector, believing that lost sales in compounds also resulted in lost sales in straight nitrogen fertilisers.

■ Summary

ICIF had a long and largely distinguished history, in which it had been in the forefront of technological and production engineering developments. It was this impetus and striving for excellence which carried it to a leading position in the fertiliser industry.

The somewhat fortuitous gas contract initially negotiated only served to embellish the Company's prospects and standing in the market place.

In recent years, it had to cope with pressures coming from a number of different directions:

- Changes in the market place in terms of customer needs
- More flexible, customer-oriented competitors
- A new, giant, pan-European competitor with investment capital
- A local challenge from small entrepreneurial 'blenders'
- Adjustment to a zero-growth market
- An increase in imports
- A large price increase in its key raw material, gas, which did not affect competitors in the same way

All of these factors had their effect on the Company's profits:

1981:   £120 million
1985:   £72 million (£55 million of which was made in the first six months)
1986:   Break-even

Notwithstanding this, the Company was still the market leader in terms of share and had considerable assets in terms of facilities, expertise and staff. Coupled with this was a determination to fight back and recover much of the lost ground.

■ 1987–89

ICIF fought back on a number of fronts: in its manufacturing technology and capacity; through its organisational structure; and in its sales and marketing strategies. This enabled the Company to retain its market-leadership in the UK fertiliser market, though its share in straight nitrogen fertilisers, its primary product, had fallen from a high of 50 per cent down to 30 per cent. Norsk Hydro was the number two supplier and Kemira was in third position (assisted by its acquisition of UKF), having retained their combined straight nitrogen market share at 32 per cent. Blenders were collectively still an effective competitor. No major producer had the flexibility and closeness to customers that characterised these small 'producers'. However, blenders also exhibited other characteristics of small firms, in that many started up only to end in failure. Even so, as one failed another started up elsewhere. The picture was, therefore, fragmented and transitory but, overall, the aggregate effect of blenders – while not increasing – still made an impact on the Company's sales, particularly in East Anglia.

In the European fertiliser market, Norsk Hydro retained its market leadership, with Kemira effectively number two. ICIF remained some way down the European 'league' table.

■ Manufacturing Facilities

Production capacity at ICIF was trimmed to get it more in line with demand, which had declined quite significantly since the mid-1980s. As a result, plants were closed at Barton and Beverley, calcium ammonium nitrate production at Billingham was closed and the compound production facility at Severnside was closed in the Summer of 1989. In addition, old ammonia-producing equipment at Severnside was replaced by a new, more energy-efficient ammonia plant commissioned in early 1989. Nitrate production at Leith also ceased, but the nitric acid and compound plants continued to function there.

At the same time, however, Norsk Hydro had built a new ammonium nitrate facility at Immingham. The commissioning of the new plant was celebrated by the launch of a new branded fertiliser called 'ExtraN'. With its 34.5 per cent nitrogen concentration, ExtraN became a direct competitor for ICIF's 'Nitram', a product which had remained virtually unchanged for over 25 years. The only perceptible difference between the products was the prill size. To be strictly accurate, ExtraN is made as granules. ExtraN's larger size was claimed to be more acceptable to users and was marketed as having 'extra spread width'. ICIF claimed that the larger granule was technically inferior and was not so conducive to even distribution. Despite this technical counter-attack, farmers claimed to prefer the larger size.

A particular success at the close of this period was the turn-round in the Company's profits slide. After approximately two years in the 'red', the Company returned to the 'black' in 1989, achieved essentially by reducing costs, improving efficiency and increasing market prices, rather than by increasing sales volume.

This turn-round was no small achievement, taking into account the volatile industry conditions in which the Company had to perform.

■ The Gas Contract

The once highly favourable gas contract became history. Gas became purchased at commercial rates through negotiated, short-term contracts. Even so, the volatility of relative gas prices in the UK and mainland Europe could still be significant. For example, a 1p per therm difference could make an impact on the bottom line by as much as £3.5 million, and during 1989 the Company was at a significant disadvantage compared with the Dutch tariff.

■ Imports

In this second period of the Company's history, fertiliser prices tended to be higher in the UK than in much of mainland Europe. This meant that, although fertiliser is bulky and costly to transport over great distances, sales margins achievable in the UK made it a viable proposition for some foreign producers to export. As a result, imports had been gradually increasing and now accounted for well over one-third of the UK straight nitrogen market. It is interesting to note that most imports were in the form of urea, a technically inferior nitrogen fertiliser according to ICIF, but one which was becoming increasingly popular with the final users. Of more particular concern to ICIF was the more recent arrival in the UK of quality ammonium nitrate.

■ The Marketing Initiative

One of the Board directors took an interest in marketing and attended a public course at one of the UK's leading business schools, Cranfield University School of Management. The most immediate result of this was the adoption of a company-specific education and training programme run by the Marketing faculty at Cranfield for all the key staff of ICIF and its subsidiaries. This was quickly followed by the commissioning of some preliminary market research amongst both the distributors (agricultural merchants) and final users (farmers), and the recruitment of someone totally new to the chemical business, but with a strong background in marketing. This appointment precipitated a complete re-assessment of the UK market, starting at its very roots, the final user. In 1988 ICIF began to re-learn its business.

Despite initial pressure from senior management to move straight to a product strategy, distribution strategy and advertising strategy for the Company, it was soon agreed that to arrive at any effective marketing strategies a structure for the market first needed to be developed and accepted. Target customer groups would then need to be identified and accepted, along with an assessment of the resources required to become successful in the target groups. A 'segmentation' project got underway.

■ Segmentation

In the past, the traditional way the Company segmented the market was by splitting it between the products used (Nitram or compounds), further split (at times) between arable and grass. In some cases, the Company's view of segmentation further broke the market down by the crop being grown in the arable market or by the type of stock being kept in the grassland market.

In early 1988, a structure for the final users of fertilisers had been put together solely from taking account of *their* approach and attitudes towards the purchase of fertilisers along with *their* farming style. No account was taken of how the Company viewed the market.

The key stages of the process gone through to reach this segmentation were as follows:

- Group discussions with farmer groups from around the country, across farming practice and with different manufacturing loyalties, were conducted by an independent consultant, with the sponsoring company (ICIF) kept confidential.

- The important issues were identified and a questionnaire developed, then tested with farmers to ensure it would cover the areas required. The questionnaire was then amended and the final questionnaire completed using face-to-face interviews. Again, these were conducted by an independent group of field researchers, with the sponsoring company's name not being revealed.

- Data were analysed and an initial view of segmentation made based on farmer attitudes to fertilisers and their farming style. Four segments were identified, but some farmers fell into 'grey' areas and weren't satisfactorily categorised in the four-segment structure. The two major features accounting for this uncertainty were price and brand.

● The first segmentation structure was tested in the market with consumers and the grey areas explored by repeating the whole process again, but this time with a more detailed look at price sensitivity and the components of brand. To enable this more detailed discussion to take place, members of each group were recruited from the same initial segment.

● Final analysis was undertaken, which led to a seven-segment structure being made. Then, for each segment, a profile (attitudes, motivations and needs), SWOT analysis, critical success factors and offer (product, price, promotion, place) was drawn up *without* any reference to ICIF's offers available in the market.

● A preliminary Marketing Plan for ICIF was drawn up matching ICIF's capabilities with the needs of each segment.

□ *Segmentation Summary*

A summary of the segments appears in Figure 13.2 and in Table 13.1.

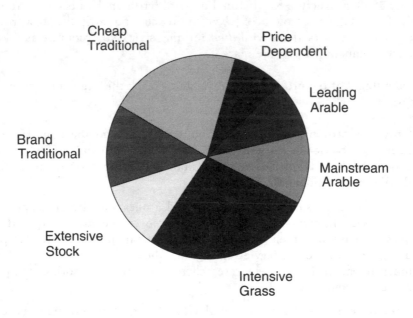

Figure 13.2   Segments in the UK fertiliser market

Table 13.1   A brief summary of the segments in the UK fertiliser market

Farmer Segment	Profile	Trend
Leading Arable	Profit driven. Innovative. Produces for a market (as opposed to impressing the neighbouring farmers). Has the latest equipment. Prefers complicated approaches (because what is being done is not simple!). Sources product from anywhere. Can handle a range of qualities.	Growing in number and affected by the first environmental legislation. This had yet to reflect in demand.
Mainstream Arable	Prefers branded products. Adopts proven approaches. Requires quality. Becoming increasingly confident in their merchant's recommendations. Attracted to practical approaches.	Declining in number and buying straight nitrogen products increasingly on recommendation from merchants. Environment becoming an issue.
Intensive Grassland	Focus is on intensive dairy farming. Looks for quality practical approaches. Local technical support. Merchant oriented. Requires product development. Will spend money to impress neighbours (show off).	Static/slightly declining in numbers. Tending to see straight nitrogen as a commodity, therefore increasingly price sensitive. Milk quota restrictions and the impact of 'mad cow' disease (BSE – Bovine Spongiform Encephalitis) on sales becoming concerns.
Extensive Stock	Quality practical approaches. Local technical support. Local proof required on new ideas. Paced product development. Right merchant the key to a sale.	Stable segment, but could be affected by tightening of subsidies. Could also be affected by BSE.
Mixed: Brand Traditional	Established approaches preferred (the good old ways). Doesn't want any changes to the current offers. Established brands give security. Prefers simple approaches. Local availability of product required.	Slowly declining in number.
Mixed: Cheap Traditional	Looks for low-cost approaches. Established approaches preferred. Dislikes manufacturers' branded products. Simple approaches. Quality not important. Chooses the cheapest.	Growing at the expense of Brand Traditional.
Grassland and Arable: Price Dependent	Price. Price. Price. Price.	Growing. The only option left, particularly for frustrated Leading Arable and Intensive Grassland farmers. Also some Mainstream Arable.

☐ *Segments in a Portfolio Matrix*

When the requirements of each segment were matched up to the capabilities of
ICIF, and the attractiveness of each segment to ICIF was determined, a segment
portfolio matrix was arrived at, as shown in Figure 13.3.

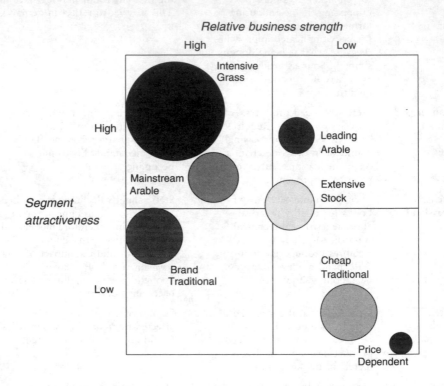

Figure 13.3   ICIF's segment portfolio matrix

For segments in which the Company believed it was strong, the opposite had
proved to be the case. One segment was also waiting for specific offers to be
made to it and was ripe for development.

■   **Marketing Strategy: The First Changes**

☐ *New Products*

With the exception of ExtraN, mentioned earlier, the only heavily promoted
new products to come on to the fertiliser market during this period were from
ICIF.

In the Autumn of 1988, its first new heavily promoted fertiliser products since 1975 were launched. These were designed for a newly-identified market segment, the Intensive Grassland farmer. This segment had, of course existed for some time; only its recognition by ICIF can be said to be new, especially in a marketing sense. These new products were given brand names, 'Turn Out' and 'First Cut'. As well as providing the obvious benefits, these products were, in addition, characterised by their efficient use of ammonium nitrate. Thus, these fertilisers were more environmentally 'friendly' because they reduced the risk of polluting rivers and other water supplies.

The most interesting fact about these new products was that this was the first time products had been given names reflecting their usage (after market research) rather than reflecting their chemical analysis. The specific design and subsequent targeting on a clearly defined market segment made both of these products immediate successes with, at that time, no obvious rivals. Sales of these products in the launch season were in excess of £8 million.

As might be expected, the Company's expertise in new product launches was somewhat 'rusty' after such a long period. Nevertheless, 'Turn Out' and 'First Cut' rapidly became established and produced considerable 'on-the-job' learning for all those who were involved in the project.

This was quickly followed by the launch of a new Arable range of compounds (strictly speaking, an old range re-packaged) which, for the first time, were presented as a flexible range under the brand name 'Crop Start'. These fertilisers were just phosphate and potash fertilisers for use in the Autumn; the deliberate omission of nitrogen again has an environmental story and recognises that nitrogen is usually readily available in the soil in the Autumn from natural processes.

However, the linkage which had been assumed to exist between the purchase of Nitram and compounds had proved to be unfounded in a number of segments.

□ *Packaging*

The market continued to show a preference for semi bulk packaging and so the trend for larger pack sizes continued.

Although the original 'Dumpy' bag had its faults, it did prove to be popular with those users who had bottom loading equipment.

Its successor, 'Dumpy 2', also a 750kg container, had the facility of top or bottom lifting: that is, using the front end loading arm of a tractor or fork lift truck. It was, therefore, extremely versatile and competed favourably with competitor alternatives. Its 'squatter' profile also improved its storage ability on the farm (which had been a problem with Dumpy 1).

The 50kg bags remained a popular size and were palletised and 'shrink-wrapped'. A recent innovation in this field was the use of coloured shrink film on which was printed the product's name. It is interesting to note that the market still prefers 50kg bags.

□ *Advertising*

Advertising had been very much a 'committee' affair, with the committee being made up of ICIF representatives from sales and marketing. Visuals and copy were approved by the committee, with no reference to the consumer. Each product also had its own campaign, often changed each year, and there was no overall ICIF campaign for its products.

In 1988, a proposed advertising campaign for the Company's mainline product, Nitram, was tested opposite the consumer along with some alternative advertisements. The proposed campaign failed badly, as it was seen as too clever and complicated, but by including alternative advertisements in the research, a more effective campaign was developed and used. No internal committee played any part in advertising for this campaign (and subsequent ones). This consumer-based approach was carried through to the advertising for the two new products ('Turn Out' and 'First Cut'), and resulted in recall levels above 60 per cent during their first three months. Advertising for these products also had a similar look to the Nitram advertisements, thus forming the basis of an ICIF campaign.

□ *Distribution*

An activity which also occupied much of this period was that of rationalising the distributor network.

From something in the order of 350, a sharper and altogether more professional network of just 68 approved distributors was set up. Those chosen were selected with improved customer service in mind, so that the eternal 'trade-off' of service levels versus distribution costs could be better balanced. Britag remained as one of the distributors, as did SAI in Scotland.

It was expected that the number of distributors would continue to be reduced, by about 5–10 per year, over the next few years. Such changes in the distribution network necessitated a re-think about the role of the sales organisation.

□ *New Sales Organisation*

Heading the field sales organisation was a national sales manager to whom reported seven business managers (six in England and Wales, one in Scotland).

Each business manager had a number of account managers reporting to him, along with technical representatives and distributor support representatives.

Each business manager also controlled a distributor training manager, who played a training and development role for the approved distributors.

The whole ethos of the new sales organisation was to generate sales by working with and through the chosen distributors and could be described as follows:

Business Manager　　Responsible for the business performance in a defined geographical area.

Account Manager　　Responsible for the business performance of specified distributors, being the distributor's first-line contact with ICIF.

Technical　　Provided the distribution sales representatives with the
Representatives　　agronomic story behind the products and services ICIF provides. They also acted as technical trainers for the distributors in their area and went to farms with or on behalf of the distributor to sort out technical queries or to provide technical advice in support of a sale. A danger, however, was that ICIF's traditional agronomic expertise and approaches could well lead to over-kill and few sales.

A summary of the sales organisation appears in Figure 13.4.

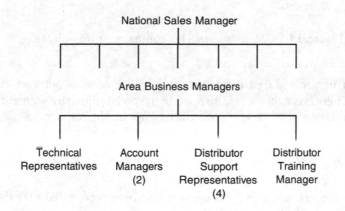

Figure 13.4　The sales organisation

This new sales organisation was achieved with an overall reduction of about 25 staff from the sales force.

☐ *Organisational Structure*

In order to simplify the organisational structure, clarify jobs and responsibilities, and provide less 'top-down' management, on 1 December 1988 a new structure for the commercial section was introduced, as shown in Figure 13.5.

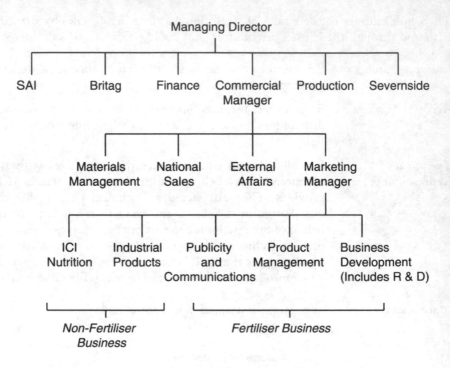

Figure 13.5   Structure of the commercial organisation

This new structure reduced confusion and improved communications within the group. There were, however, no specific responsibilities by segment, but the most appropriate way of tackling this omission with the resources available was a hot topic between the business development and product management groups.

☐ *Business Teams*

Even before the organisational changes, it had been recognised that there were benefits to be derived from setting up cross-functional teams charged with running distinctive product ranges as independent businesses, including the more effective exploitation of the products.

As a result, four Business Teams were set up to focus on ammonium nitrate, Spring compounds, Autumn compounds and calcium ammonium nitrate.

The leaders of each of these teams met with selected Board members on a regular basis as the Fertiliser Business Team, which made recommendations about policy and operational issues to the full Board.

These business teams went some way towards improving cross-functional communication and tapping a broader range of the Company's brain-power. Useful though this was, it might be concluded that the business teams were doing no more than might be expected from an integrated marketing function.

It is also interesting to note that the focus was on product, as opposed to market.

■   **Concerns on the Horizon in 1989**

☐ *'1992: An Opportunity or a Threat?'*

The European fertiliser market had always been susceptible to structural changes as individual governments changed their agricultural policies. The removal of trade barriers at the end of 1992 should, in theory, have made little difference to the 1989 situation because there were, in effect, already no barriers.

☐ *European Legislation*

Perhaps more worrying than the 'new order' of 1993 was the way that EC legislation was already having an increasing influence in the member countries. There was a relentless inevitability that Euro-laws would gradually take over and set new and comprehensive standards, designed mainly to protect water supplies from nitrate contamination.

Although fertiliser manufacturers argued that nitrate levels in soils had risen mainly through natural processes (for example, because more grassland had been converted to arable use, particularly during the last war), and from the burning and ploughing in of stubble, they were not winning the day. As a result, legislation was expected in several areas, such as:

- Restrictions on the use of fertilisers within specified distances of rivers and boreholes, in order to prevent contamination of water supplies.

- Restrictions on the number of cattle that can be kept per acre. (This can have implications about how land might be converted to other uses in the future.)

- The introduction of tighter milk quotas introduced earlier in the decade, which, on their introduction, led to rationalisation of production and, for the survivors, a very profitable dairy sector. The next move, in addition to the possible tightening of milk quotas, could be grain quotas.

On the whole, the UK had more relaxed standards than those being proposed in Europe, but the public interest in 'green' issues was seen as being a contributing factor which ensured the UK would fall into line with the new legislation.

Some farmers were already anticipating some of these changes and this, along with financial pressures in the arable sector, had resulted in a recent decline of the fertiliser market.

☐ *Phosphate and Potash Fertilisers*

These were still very much also-rans when compared with nitrates and often only used when soil correction was required. Their relatively low usage in the UK had not put them under the 'microscope' of the environmental lobby in the same way as nitrates. This could be a factor which provided some commercial possibilities. However, phosphate and potash fertilisers do carry in-built environmental problems (for example, recent studies have shown a build up of phosphates in Dutch soil).

■ **1990**

Fully attuned to the market place, the ICIF Board now required a full strategic business plan, based on utilising the Company's current resources, to cover the period mid-1990 to mid-1993. This plan was quickly to prove a watershed in the affairs of the Company, in a most unexpected way. What follows are some of the marketing issues which, in addition to the segmentation work, further contributed to the shape and nature of that plan.

■ **Background Analysis**

☐ *Forecast of Demand and Supply*

In Europe it was forecast that the demand for calcium ammonium nitrates and straight ammonium nitrates would fall by about 20 per cent by 1992. This would be due to the combined influence of legislation, more efficient use of the product and its substitution by urea solutions (both forecast to grow).

Even though manufacturing capacity had been reduced, there was still a considerable excess. In addition, the relatively high fertiliser prices in Europe were attracting imports, mainly from the Eastern Bloc (approximately 4 per cent of the market).

With respect to the UK, domestic nitrogen fertiliser capacity was below demand, but imports more than bridged the gap, making it difficult for manufacturers to maximise their output. Nitrogen fertiliser demand was forecast to fall by about 7 per cent by 1993.

☐ *Competitors' Activity*

Kemira seemed to have a strategy similar to ICIF, in that they were differentiating their products by quality and brand, having successfully adopted the higher-quality image of UKF. They also launched new products to compete directly with Turn Out and First Cut, but a delayed response had given ICIF the competitive advantage they had sought.

Norsk Hydro concentrated on improving the quality and branding of their straight nitrogen fertiliser. In compounds, they appeared to be rationalising their range and cutting out uneconomic production units or processes. Thus, they could still maintain their overall volume, but at lower cost.

Both Kemira and Norsk Hydro priced below ICIF in order to support their strategies of maximising volume sales and hence filling their production capacities. In addition, both had established distributor networks which operated in a similar way to ICIF's. Blenders continued to concentrate on the arable market with phosphate/potash fertilisers, or phosphate/potash with a low level of Nitrogen included, along with commodity compounds.

☐ *ICIF's Products*

The ICIF products which sold in the greatest volume were all in the later stages of their life cycles, either in the saturation or decline phase. Turn Out and First Cut (ICIF's two new brands) were at the beginning of the growth phase. A summary of the Company's product portfolio appears in Figure 13.6.

Although not all of the products appear in the portfolio matrix, they all tended to fall within the same general area.

☐ *ICIF's Strategy by Market Segment since 1989*

Leading Arable	No new products or services had been developed for this segment.
Mainstream Arable	The sales force had been withdrawn from calling on farmers. Contact was only through distributors, which would weaken loyalty in this segment to the ICIF brand.
Intensive Grassland	The withdrawal of the sales force was expected to have the same impact as with Mainstream Arable. In the past no new products or services had been targeted at this segment. It was a growth area for Turn Out and First Cut.

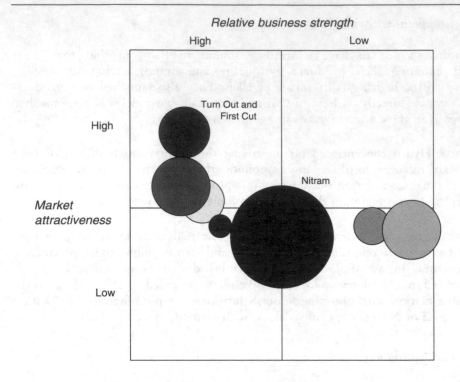

Figure 13.6   The fertiliser product portfolio of ICIF

Extensive Stock	ICIF had a good image in this segment, but withdrawal of the sales force and the move to distributors might weaken it. There were no new products or services. There was increasing use of Turn Out by sheep farmers.
Mixed: Brand Traditional	Withdrawal of farm visits by the sales force was weakening this segment's loyalty to the ICIF brand.
Mixed: Cheap Traditional	Although sales were continuing to this segment, no special activity was targeted at it.
Grassland and Arable: Price Dependent	Sales also continued into this segment, but, again, no special activity was targeted at it.

☐ *Distribution*

The current practice was for the product to be available within 24 hours, and at 'farm gate' pricing. To achieve this, ICIF effectively took on the costs of distribution and storage. The latter was required because of uneven usage patterns and the need for constant production levels. This approach cost just under £28 million in the last operating year. No other major competitor had such an approach.

■ Marketing Strategy

The overall mission for the Company was to continue to generate a positive cash balance from its trading. Furthermore, it needed to establish a basis for ensuring that there would be sustained profitability in future years.

In line with this thinking, the mission of the fertiliser business in ICIF was stated as:

'To *maximise the profit contribution to the Group by selling our own manufactured high Nitrogen fertilisers.*'

The strategy for achieving this involved a number of activities:

- Focusing only on those UK segments where cost leadership was possible

- Developing a product range for those segments which not only met the farmers' needs, but also made good use of the existing production facilities and for which ICIF was a credible supplier

- Minimising the costs of distribution by effective development of trade channels

- Maintaining high plant utilisation by exporting to the rest of Europe those products which returned acceptable margins

- Eliminating the re-selling of purchased products unless they were essential to providing a full product range to the targeted segments

In short, this strategy was aimed at focusing on key segments in the home territory, developing strengths in new ones in order to retain overall sales volumes, and putting pressure on Norsk Hydro and Kemira in Europe in an attempt to force some of the reduction in the UK market on to them.

However, at the heart of this strategy was the need for plant capacity to have a high utilisation. Unless this was achieved, it would be impossible for the Company to achieve cost leadership, as is clear in Figure 13.7.

The break-even point was around 650 000 tonnes of production. The higher the volume above this level, the more advantageous the net margin became, and the better the Company's scope for manoeuvre.

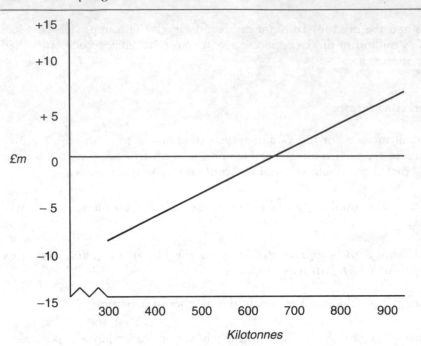

Figure 13.7   Relationship between plant utilisation and net margins

☐ *Product Strategy*

Straight Nitrogen Fertilisers

The objective was to maintain a 45 per cent share of the solids market available to Norsk Hydro, Kemira and ICIF.

A larger Nitram prill needed to be developed to compete with Norsk Hydro's granulated ExtraN. The current 'prilled' version was not perceived as having the same quality. However, converting to a granulation plant would cost in the order of £10 million. An alternative, and less costly, development was pursued which would perceptibly increase the size of the prill, although not increase it to quite the size of the ExtraN granule.

Calcium ammonium nitrate sales could be maintained using the Nitrochalk brand. Bulk calcium ammonium nitrate sales to blenders were to be increased. This business produced good margins and gained ICIF a foothold in the blender market. However, only blenders supplying to the arable market were to be considered, otherwise this strategy would be tantamount to the Company shooting itself in the foot by undermining its own markets.

Autumn Compounds	The objective was to exit from this market. For ICIF, these were unprofitable and did not pull through other product sales. Local blenders were better placed to meet the needs of this market.
Spring Compounds	The objective was to concentrate production capacity into compounds requiring high levels of nitrogen, as these produced the highest gross margins. The portfolio of compounds also needed to be such as to minimise production and distribution costs.

The manufacture of products for Scotland was to be based at Leith, whereas those for England and Wales would come from Billingham. This would rationalise aspects of production and improve the distribution logistics.

Research and product development was to focus on the Intensive Grassland segment. Three new products were to be launched in the Autumn of 1991, including a development based on Nitram, plus a development of Turn Out.

☐ *Pricing Strategy*

The overall positioning of ICIF as a leading, quality manufacturer with value-for-money products meant that price levels could never be reduced to a level which made them appear cheap.

Even so, newly-introduced products had to be aggressively priced in order to gain penetration and win market share quickly.

Those products at the mature end of the life cycle needed to be priced relative to competition, in order to maintain market share and production volume.

Where strong branding could be developed, prices were inclined to be less sensitive to competing formulae.

The pricing strategy for Europe needed to be geared to volume objectives. Here there were advantages, since ICIF was a relatively small player and there was little branding on the Continent.

☐ *Packaging Strategy*

It was intended to drop the Dumpy and explore how to introduce intermediate bulk packaging more in line with market requirements.

☐ *Promotion Strategy*

The overall strategy was to re-open the dialogue with farmers via direct marketing, while also building up close ties with selected distributors.

It would also be necessary to train the farmer-contact personnel of distributors, especially in the segments where the relationship with the farmer was critical.

ICIF's own Company farms were to be kept, because market research had confirmed that they played an important role in the image of the Company, particularly in the practical testing of new products.

☐ *Service Strategy*

Services were only of value to ICIF if:

● They differentiated the product
● They brought the 'product package' up to a level of competing products
● They attracted extra margins for the product
● They pulled through a greater sales volume of product
● Their costs could be recovered in product sales or from fees

Of the main services on offer from ICIF, the soil nitrogen testing service certainly led to sales of Nitram and for this reason would be continued, free of charge, though it needed to be simplified and more suited to its users.

Additional margins generated by the soil-sampling service, a service expected from major suppliers of fertilisers, were tenuous. This service would therefore have to be self-financing.

Despite the focus on the Grassland sector, the two specific services for this sector were dropped. They did not meet the required criteria.

The remaining ICIF services would be designed to help distributors differentiate themselves from their competitors. This was to be done by providing preferential terms, such as a lower fee or fast response.

☐ *Environmental Strategy*

An industry-wide strategy was essential, because the environmental issues were affecting all businesses adversely in terms of:

(a) the market size, which was reducing;
(b) the products which could be sold and the way in which they were sold;
(c) the image of the agricultural sector.

Notwithstanding this, ICIF still had to have environmentally responsible products and practices. Therefore, technical information needed to be provided with products so that they would be used correctly.

It was possible to turn environmentalism into an opportunity by insisting that nitrogen fertilisers should only be used after nitrogen testing of soil. Exporters of fertilisers to the UK would not be able to respond to such a requirement easily.

☐ *R&D Strategy*

The key R&D activities were to centre on new high nitrogen products for grassland, which could be economic and produce grass in greater quantity, or to a higher and more consistent quality, without damaging the environment.

Improvement in existing products would also be required, as would technical 'updating' of the remaining services on offer.

☐ *Distribution*

It was intended to consolidate around the present distribution pattern, recognising that the channels used would vary according to geographic areas.

☐ *Segment Strategy*

This is summarised in Table 13.2.

■ **Threats**

☐ *Possible Competitor Response*

It was likely that Norsk Hydro and Kemira would respond to ICIF's UK strategy by putting pressure on prices. The extent of this pressure would depend on two issues:

(a) how much ICIF's European strategy convinced Norsk Hydro and Kemira that ICIF would be a threat to their overall business; and

(b) how successful ICIF was in reducing its cost base, by filling its ammonium nitrate capacity with non-UK destined product.

Since it was in nobody's interest to get involved in a price war in a declining market, some sabre-rattling might have been expected as an initial response from the major competitors. However, the more likely result would have been that UK straight nitrogen prices declined slightly or, at best, remained static.

Table 13.2 ICIF's segment strategy, 1990–93

Segment	Objective	Products	Price	Promotion	Place	Product Development
Leading Arable	Bottom out declining share to 7%	Mainly Nitram	Prevailing market price for quality ammonium nitrate product	Sales to work with selected distributors	Through selected distributors. Direct to buying groups	None for solid fertilisers. Some specialist liquids
Mainstream Arable	Hold share to 33% for Nitram	1. Nitram 2. Spring compounds	Nitram price to shadow Hydro and Kemira. Compounds priced for volume sales	Retain brand awareness. Promote 'N-Sure'	Through limited number of specified distributors	As above
Intensive Grassland	Retain 30% share. Increase sales of compounds	1. Nitram 2. Turn Out 3. First Cut 4. Kaynitro	Nitram at market price. Compounds at highest price for volume sales	Full support. Develop 'umbrella' brand. Use ICI farms and soil sampling	Selected key distributors dealt with by Account Managers	Develop a specific straight nitrogen product. Enhance First Cut and Turn Out
Extensive Stock	Increase share of Nitram to 30%, and Spring compounds to 30%	1. Nitram 2. Spring compounds 3. Launch version of Turn Out	Nitram and Spring compounds to be priced in line with volume objectives	Full promotional support	As above	Grazing and cutting compounds including sulphur
Mixed: Brand Traditional	Maintain share – Nitram 40%, Spring compounds 30%	1. Nitram 2. Spring compounds	As above	No specifically targeted activity	As above	None specifically
Mixed: Cheap Traditional	Hold share – Nitram 12%, Spring compounds 20%	1. Nitram 2. Spring compounds	Nitram near market price to achieve volumes. Spring compounds at top end of range	As above	As above	None specifically
Price Dependent	Residual sales only					

In Europe, it was considered unlikely that home producers would drop their prices in response to ICIF's exports, since they would be selling at market price. However, they might strive to maintain their capacity volumes by exporting to the UK in retaliation. Even so, ICIF would be in a stronger position to resist imports in its key market segments. Also, a 'pre-emptive' push for sales on the Continent should be successful in the short term, and could provide ICIF with a bridge-head on which to build.

The ICIF focus on the profitable Grassland segment would not go unnoticed and would be likely to attract 'me-too' products from Norsk Hydro and from the blenders, in addition to the response already seen from Kemira. However, ICIF had a lead in this segment and there was still growth potential, especially if ICIF could continue to develop new products ahead of the field.

☐ *Other Possible Threats*

- The UK market might decline faster than predicted because of any of the following:

  - Higher levels of imports than forecast
  - Legislation restricting the use of nitrogen
  - Other legislation with a 'knock-on' effect reducing the use of nitrogen (for example, limits on the number of cattle per acre of land)

  If this were to happen, it might become necessary to adopt a fall-back strategy (see below).

- BSE leading to a slaughter programme to remove all possible links with the virus. This would have the effect of reducing demand for fertiliser while stocks were being re-built.

- Unseasonal weather conditions (which seemed to be becoming more frequent) could intervene to affect fertiliser use.

Other than the possible competitor response reaching damaging levels, none of these threats deterred ICIF from following their proposed strategy.

■ **Alternative Strategy**

If Norsk Hydro and Kemira continued to price their way into the UK straight nitrogen market, ICIF would have to switch from a strategy of holding market share and expanding in key segments to one of maximising its cash flow potential.

In effect, this would mean scaling down to a one-plant operation and achieving the massive cost reductions that would come from a smaller and much simpler

In effect, this would mean scaling down to a one-plant operation and achieving the massive cost reductions that would come from a smaller and much simpler business. Such a step would also lead to a dramatic reduction in what the Company could offer, or indeed tackle. For example, it could mean pulling out of Europe and/or several market segments, or it could mean dropping Nitram sales for other compounds. Product development could be curtailed, and the distributor network would shrink.

ICIF could buy in fertilisers to make up some lost sales, but the logistics of doing this and the margins involved would need to be calculated carefully to ensure that this would be a profitable route.

In fact, it would not be possible to be specific about the one-plant option, except to say that its acceptance could produce a high return on investment in the short term, but in the long term ICIF would probably be too small a player to survive in an industry dominated by larger and literally more resourceful competitors.

■ And then . . .

The glimpses that have been provided about the issues and the thinking that went into the strategic marketing plan for 1990 to 1993 demonstrate that the Company's response to its situation was not taken lightly. Considerable effort went into this plan, as well as into the other areas covered by the business plan, which, in effect, was a plan to rescue the Company's ailing fortunes and to build a foundation for continued success in the future.

For reasons of confidentiality, volume sales and profit margins have been omitted from this case study. Nevertheless, an interested reader will have understood the rationale and thrust behind this marketing plan.

When put before the Board of ICIF in May 1990, the proposed plan was accepted as reflecting the best possible use of the resources the Company had. All that remained was for the plan to gain the approval of the Main Board of ICI plc.

At the Main Board meeting, held in July 1990, it was decided that ICIF's plan, although optimising assets, did not hold the prospect of delivering consistent and satisfactory levels of return in future years. As a consequence of this, it was agreed to sell the business to Kemira, which had for some time expressed an interest and had already submitted an attractive bid. A public statement to this effect was issued by the Company.

All that remained was to verify that such a business transaction did not fall foul of the legislation surrounding monopolies and mergers. Thus, the issue was tabled for a meeting of the Monopolies and Mergers Commission (MMC) in September 1990. The decision at this meeting was that the MMC would have to submit their deliberations on the sale in a written report to the Minister of Trade and Industry by the end of 1990.

In the event, ICI faced something of a setback when, in early 1991, the Minister for Trade and Industry refused to approve the £75 million sale of its fertiliser business to Kemira. Had the sale gone ahead, it would have increased the Finnish state-owned group's share of the UK fertiliser market from something like 18 per cent to approximately 50 per cent. This factor, coupled with the Minister's avowed policy of preventing British companies from being controlled by foreign nationalised industries, no doubt weighed heavily in favour of this decision.

However, since the only other possible buyer would be Norsk Hydro (51 per cent owned by the Norwegian Government), ICI's options were severely limited.

■ Postscript

The segmentation project of 1988 provided ICIF with a fresh insight into its market and enabled the Company to arrive at an extremely realistic view of its prospects and the way ahead. The final decision to pull out of the fertiliser business did not, however, come as a complete surprise to many who worked in ICIF.

However, ICIF lives on.

After the rejection of the Kemira bid, the Board of ICIF proposed an alternative plan to the ICI Board which slimmed the business down even further than had been proposed in the 1990/93 Marketing Plan, but at the same time increased the returns from the Company.

This resulted in a very different ICIF re-emerging in the UK market: an ICIF focused on a very limited product range which includes Turn Out and First Cut, and the recently launched Nitram successor Graze More, along with some other solid stable mates, including Nitram. Profitability has not only returned but has been maintained, although at levels much lower than those seen in the Company's heyday, but certainly at a level commensurate with its lower turnover.

Appendix 1: Customer Classification Systems

Social Grading

Source: D. Monk, extract from *Interviewers' Guide on Social Grading*, from JICNARS, *Social Grading on National Research Surveys*, 1978.

Guide to Grade 'A' households (Upper middle class)

Informants from Grade 'A' households constitute about 3 per cent of the total. The head of the household is a successful business or professional person, senior civil servant, or has considerable private means. A young person in some of these occupations who has not fully established himself or herself may still be found in Grade 'B' though he or she eventually should reach Grade 'A'.

In country or suburban areas, 'A' grade households usually live in large detached houses or in expensive flats. In towns, they may live in expensive flats or town houses in the better parts of town. Some examples, which are by no means exhaustive, are given below.

☐ *Examples of Occupations of the Head of the Household*

Professional and semi-professional

Church of England dignitaries (bishop and above) and those of other denominations.

Physician, surgeon, specialist.

Established doctor, dentist (if a principal or partner in a large practice).

Established solicitor, barrister (own practice or partner in a large practice).

Matron of a large teaching hospital.

Headmaster of a public or grammar school or of any large school or college (750 pupils or more).

Architect, chartered accountant, surveyor, actuary, fully qualified and either principal or partner in a large practice. Also if working as a very senior (at or near Board level) executive in a very large (200+) organisation.

Senior civil servant, for example, Permanent Secretary, Deputy Secretary, Under Secretary, Assistant Secretary, Principal.

Local Government chief officers.

Senior Local Government Officer (for example, Town Clerk, County Planning Officer, Borough Surveyor).

University Professor.

Editor of a newspaper or magazine; senior journalist on national or very large provincial publication.

Commercial airline pilot (captain or first officer).

Captain of large merchant vessel (5000 tons or more and/or 25+ crew).

Senior professional executives: that is, professionally qualified people working as very senior executives or administrators (at or near Board level in very large (200+) establishments), for example, Chief Engineer, Company Surveyor, Chief Accountant, Curator, Artistic Director, Chief Designer and so on.

Librarian, qualified, in charge of a really major library.

Business and industry

Senior buyers for leading wholesale or retail establishments.

Self-employed owners of businesses with 25 or more employees.

Self-employed farmers with 10 or more employees.

Board (Directors) or near Board level managers in large organisations (with 200 or more employees).

Managers in sole charge of branches or outlying establishments with 200 or more employees at the branch (for example, factory managers, managers of very large retail establishments, depots, hotels and so on).

Stockbroker or jobber (principal or partner in the firm).

Insurance underwriter.

Advertising, research, public relations executives (and others offering professional or semi-professional services in specialised agencies) if at Board level or principals or partners in agencies or practices with 25 or more employees.

Bank branch managers; managers of branches of other financial institutions (for example, building society, insurance company, finance house) with 25 or more employees at the branch.

Police and Fire Brigade

Superintendent, Chief Constable.

CID Superintendent and Chief Superintendent.

Chief Fire Officer.

Armed Forces

Army: Lieutenant Colonel and above.

Navy: Commander and above.

RAF: Wing Commander and above.

Non-earners

People living in comfort on investments or private income.

Retired people where the head of the household before retirement would have been 'A' grade.

■ Guide to Grade 'B' households (Middle class)

Grade 'B' informants account for about 12 per cent of the total. In general, the heads of 'B' Grade households will be quite senior people but not at the very top of their profession or business. They are quite well-off, but their style of life is generally respectable rather than rich or luxurious. Non-earners will be living on private pensions or on fairly modest private means.

□ *Examples of Occupations of the Head of the Household*

Professional and semi-professional

Vicars, rectors, parsons, parish priests and ministers; clergymen above these ranks but below Bishop.

Headteachers of secondary, primary or preparatory schools with fewer than 750 pupils; qualified teachers aged 28 and over in public, secondary or grammar schools.

Civil servant: higher and senior and Chief Executive Officers, Executive Officers. Recently qualified assistant principal.

Local government: senior officers (9 grades).

University lecturers, readers; technical college lecturers.

Established journalist for provincial and local papers, trade and technical publications; less senior journalist for national press.

Matron of a smaller hospital (non-teaching); sister tutor in large hospital or teaching hospital.

Qualified pharmacist.

Qualified accountants, surveyors, architects, solicitors and so on, who do not have their own practices but are employed as executives not senior enough to be graded 'A'.

Newly qualified professional men/women of all sorts who have not yet established themselves (that is less than 3 years from qualification).

Librarian, qualified, in charge of a library or branch library.

Business and industry

Self-employed owners of business with 5–24 employees in skilled or non-manual trades (for example, shopkeepers, plumbing contractors, electrical contractors and so on).

Self-employed farmers with 2–9 employees.

Managers of large farms, stewards, bailiffs and so on.

Bank clerks with special responsibilities (for example, chief clerk, teller and so on.).

Insurance clerk with professional qualifications and/or special responsibilities in large branch or head office.

Manager of a retail or wholesale establishment with 25–199 employees at the establishment.

Some relatively senior managers or executives in commerce and industry.

General Foreman, Clerk of Works (that is, with other foremen under him or her).

Chief buyers for wholesale or retail establishments.

Area sales managers or senior representatives (especially if technically professionally qualified).

Executives with professional or technical qualifications who are not senior enough to be graded 'A' (for example, department managers).

Technicians with degree or equivalent qualifications, especially in high-technology industries such as electronics, computers, aircraft, chemicals, nuclear energy and so on.

Police and Fire Brigade

Chief Inspector, Inspector

Assistant Chief Officer.

Divisional Officer.

Armed Forces

Army: Captain, Major.

Navy: Lieutenant, Lieutenant-Commander.

RAF: Flight Lieutenant, Squadron Leader.

Non-Earners

People with private income living in a less luxurious way than 'A' grade people. Retired people who, before retirement, would have been 'B' grade people.

■ **Guide to Grade 'C1' households (Lower middle class)**

Grade 'C1' constitutes about 23 per cent of total informants. In general it is made up of the families of small trades-people and non-manual workers who carry out less important administrative, supervisory and clerical jobs, namely those who are sometimes called 'white-collar' workers.

□ *Examples of Occupations of the Head of the Household*

Professional and semi-professional

Curates in the Church of England; ministers of 'fringe' free churches; monks and nuns of any denomination, except those with special responsibilities.

Teachers, other than those graded 'B'.

Student nurses; staff nurses; sisters in smaller hospitals; midwives; dispensers; radiographers.

Bank clerk, insurance clerk with no special qualifications or responsibilities.

Insurance agent (door to door collector).

Civil servant: clerical grades.

Local government: clerical, junior administrative, professional and technical grades.

Articled clerk.

Library assistant (not fully qualified).

Student (on grant).

Business and industry

Self-employed owners of small business (1–4 employees) in non-manual or skilled trades (for example, shopkeepers, electrical contractors, builders and so on).

Self-employed farmers with only one employee.

Manager of a retail or wholesale establishment with 1–24 employees.

Some relatively junior managers in industry and commerce.

Clerks, typists, office machine operators, punch operators.

Telephonists, telegraphists.

Buyers (except very senior buyers).

Representatives, salesmen (except those graded 'B').

Technicians/engineers and so on, with professional/technical qualifications below degree standard.

Foremen in charge of 25 or more employees, mainly supervisory work (other than a few very senior foremen coded 'B').

Draughtsman.

Driving instructor.

Police and Fire Brigade

Station Sergeant, Sergeant, Detective Sergeant.

Station Officer and Sub-Station Officer, Leading Fireman.

Armed Forces

Army: Sergeant, Sergeant Major, Warrant Officer, 2nd Lieutenant, Lieutenant.

Navy: Petty Officer, Chief Petty Officer, Sub-Lieutenant.

RAF: Sergeant, Flight Sergeant, Warrant Officer, Pilot Officer, Flying Officer.

Non-Earners

Retired people who, before retirement, would have been 'C1' grade and have pensions other than state pensions or have private means of a very modest nature.

■ **Guide to Grade 'C2' households (The skilled working class)**

Grade 'C2' consists in the main of skilled manual workers and their families. It constitutes about 32 per cent of informants. When in doubt as to whether the head of the household is skilled or unskilled, check whether that person has served an apprenticeship; this may be a guide, though not all skilled workers have served an apprenticeship.

□ *Examples of Occupations of the Head of the Household*

General

Foreman (responsible for up to 24 employees), Deputy (mining) Charge Hand, Overlooker, Overseer, whose work is mainly manual (these may be found in nearly all trades and industries, including farming and agriculture).

Agriculture

Agricultural workers with special skill or responsibilities (for example, head cowman, chief shepherd).

Building Industry (including Construction and Woodworkers)

Most adult male skilled workers or craftsmen including: bricklayer, carpenter, plasterer, glazier, plumber, painter.

Coal Mining

Skilled underground workers, including: coal cutter, filler, getter, hewer, miner, putter.

Metal Manufacturing, Shipbuilding and Repairing, Engineering, Furnace, Forge, Foundry and Rolling Mills

Most adult male workers including: furnaceman (except coal, gas and coke ovens), moulder, smelter, blacksmith, coppersmith.

Plater, riveter, shipwright.

Fitter, grinder, millwright, setter, toolmaker, turner.

Vehicle builder, welder.

Electrical fitter, electrician, lineman.

Skilled labourer (docks and Admiralty only).

Rubber

Most adult skilled workers.

Textiles, Clothing and Leather

Skilled workers in rayon or nylon production.

Skilled knitters (hosiery or other knitted goods), weaver, bleacher, dryer, drawer-in.

Boot and shoemaker.

Cutter and fitter (tailoring).

Furniture and Upholstery

Most adult male skilled workers including carpenter, joiner, cabinet maker.

Paper and Printing Trades

Most adult male skilled workers including machine man, finisher (paper and board manufacturer).

Compositor, linotype operator, typesetter, electrotyper, stereotyper, process engraver.

Transport

A few only of the better paid workers such as: all heavy and long distance vehicle drivers, engine driver and fireman; bus drivers, bus inspectors, signalmen, train drivers, shunters; passenger and goods guards; AA patrolman, ambulance drivers; Post Office sorters and high grade postman; stevedore.

Distributive Trades

Proprietors and managers of small shops with no employees.
Shop assistants with responsibilities.

Glass and Ceramics

Most adult workers including: formers, finishers and decorators, furnacemen and kilnmen.

Electrical and Electronics

Including radio and radar mechanics, telephone installers and linesmen, electrical and electronic fitters.

Agriculture: Farming, Forestry and Fishing

Skilled and specialised workers.

Food and Drink

Baker.
Pastrycook.
Brewer.
Maltster.

Police and Fire Brigade

Prison Officer.
Constable.
Fireman.
CID Detective Constable.

Security Officers

For example, Securicor.

Miscellaneous

Self-employed unskilled workers with 1–4 employees: for example, chimney sweep, window cleaner, taxi driver (London).

Self-employed skilled manual workers with no employees.

Coach builder, plumber.

Dental mechanic and technician.

Armed Forces

Army: Lance Corporal, Corporal.

Navy: AB Seaman, Leading Seaman.

RAF: Aircraftsman, Leading and Senior.

Non-earners

Retired people who before retirement would have been in 'C2' grade and have pensions other than state pensions or have private means.

■ **Guide to Grade 'D' households (The semi-skilled and unskilled working class)**

Grade 'D' consists entirely of manual workers, generally semi-skilled or unskilled. This grade accounts for 21 per cent of families.

□ *Examples of Occupations of the Head of the Household*

General

Most semi-skilled and unskilled workers.

Labourers and mates of the occupations listed in 'C2' grade.

All apprentices to skilled trades.

Agriculture: Farming, Forestry and Fishing

The majority of male agricultural workers, other than those with special skills or responsibilities, including: tractor or other agricultural machine driver, ditcher, hedger, farm labourer; forestry worker, timber man; fisherman; gardeners and self-employed market gardeners with no employees.

Coal Mining and Quarrying

Surface workers except those with special responsibilities.
Unskilled underground workers.

Textiles and Clothing Manufacture

Most manual workers including the following: woolsorter, blender, carder, comber, spinner, doubler, twister, textile printer.
Machinist (clothing manufacturer).

Food, Drink and Tobacco

The majority of adult workers, including the following: dough mixer, oven man; bottler, opener; stripper, cutter (tobacco).

Transport

Bus conductor, railway porter (including leading porter).
Ticket collector (railway).
Cleaner.
Traffic warden.

Distributive Trades

Shop assistant without special training or responsibility.

Gas, Coke and Chemical

Most adult workers including furnacemen and chemical production process workers.

Plastics

Most adult workers.

Glass and Ceramics

Production process workers.

Electrical and Electronics

Assemblers.

Miscellaneous

Caretaker, warehouseman, park keeper, storekeeper, postman, works police-man, domestic servant, woman factory worker, waitress, laundry worker.

All goods delivery including milk and bread roundsmen.

Meter readers.

Self-employed manual workers with no employees: for example, window cleaner, chimney sweep, taxi driver (provinces).

Armed Forces

Army: Private or equivalent.

Navy: Ordinary Seaman.

RAF: Aircraftsman.

Non-earners

Retired people who before retirement would have been in 'D' grade and have pensions other than state pensions, or have other private means.

■ Guide to Grade 'E' households (Those at lowest levels of subsistence)

Grade E consists of old age pensioners, widows and their families, casual workers and those who, through sickness or unemployment, are dependent on social security schemes, or have very small private means. They constitute about 9 per cent of all informants. Individual income of the head of the household (disregarding additions such as supplementary benefits) will be only slightly, if at all, above the basic flat-rate social security benefit.

Only those informants will be graded as 'E' whose head of the households is 'E' and where no other member of the family is in fact the chief wage earner.

□ *Examples of Occupations of the Head of the Household.*

Earners

Casual labourers

Part-time clerical and other workers.

Non-earners

Old age pensioners.

Widow (with state widow's pension).

Those dependent on sickness, unemployment and supplementary benefits for over two months who are without benefits related to earnings.

Disabled pensioners.

Private means, private pension, disability pension compensation, and so on, amounting to little, if any, above the basic flat-rate social security benefit.

■ Examples of Occupations under Industries

□ *Social Grade*

I Farmers, Foresters, Fishermen

D   Agricultural workers, unskilled.
C2   Skilled agricultural workers.
D   Agricultural machinery drivers.
D   Gardeners with no qualifications.
D   Foresters and woodmen with no qualifications.
D   Fishermen (employed).
C1   Agricultural workers (junior technically qualified).
B   Grieve (Scotland only) farm manager, bailiff, steward (of large farms or estate).

II Miners and Quarrymen

C2   Coal mine: face workers.
C2   Coal mine: underground workers (skilled).
D   Coal mine: underground workers (unskilled).
D   Coal miners (majority of workers above ground).

III Gas, Coke and Chemicals Makers

D   Furnacemen, coal, gas and coke ovens.
D   Chemical production process workers.

IV Glass and Ceramics Makers

C2   Ceramic formers.
C2   Glass formers, finishers and decorators.
C2   Furnacemen, kilnmen, glass and ceramic.
C2   Ceramics' decorators and finishers.
C2   Ceramics' decorators doing hand painting.
D   Glass and ceramics production process workers.

V   Furnace, Forge, Foundry, Rolling Mill Workers

C2   Furnacemen: metal.

C2   Rolling, tube mill operators, metal drawers.

C2   Moulders and coremakers (foundry).

C2   Smiths, forgemen.

D   Metal making and treating workers.

D   Fettlers, metal dressers.

VI   Electrical and Electronic Workers

C2   Radio and radar mechanics.

C2   Installers and repairmen, telephone.

C2   Linesmen, cable jointers.

C2   Electricians.

C2   Electrical and electronic fitters.

D   Assemblers (electrical and electronic).

C2   Electrical engineers (manual).

D   Mates to above workers.

VII   Engineering and Allied Trades Workers

C2   Sheet metal workers.

C2   Constructional engineers: riggers.

C2   Metal plate workers: riveters.

C2   Gas, electric welders, cutters: braziers.

C2   Machine tool setters, setter-operators.

D   Machine tool operators.

C2   Tool makers, tool room fitters.

C2   Fitters, machine erectors and so on.

C2   Engineers (manual).

C2   Electro-platers, dip platers and related workers.

C2   Plumbers, lead burners, pipe fitters.

D   Press workers and stampers.

C2   Metal workers (skilled).

C2   Watch and chronometer makers and repairers.

C2   Precision instrument makers and repairers.

C2   Goldsmiths, silversmiths, jewellery makers.

C2   Coach, carriage, wagon builders and repairers.

D   Other metal making, working; jewellery and electrical production process workers (unskilled).

VIII   Woodworkers

C2   Carpenters and joiners.

C2   Cabinet makers.

C2   Sawyers and wood working machinists.

C2   Coopers, hoop makers and benders.

C2   Pattern makers.

C2   Woodworkers.

D   Mates to above workers.

IX   Leather Workers

C2   Tanners: leather, fur dressers, fellmongers.

C2   Shoemakers.

C2   Shoe repairers.

C2   Cutters, lasters, sewers, footwear and related workers.

C2   Leather product makers.

D   Mates to above workers.

X   Textile Workers

D   Fibre preparers.

D   Spinners, doublers, winders, reelers.

C2   Warpers, sizers.

C2   Drawers-in.

C2   Weavers.

D   Weavers: jute, flax, hemp (Scotland only).

C2   Knitters.

C2   Bleachers and finishers of textiles.

C2   Dyers of textiles.

C2   Textile fabrics and related product makers and examiners.

D   Textile fabrics (etc.) production process workers.

D   Winders and reelers.

C2   Rope, twine and net makers.

XI   Clothing Workers

C2   Tailors: cutters and fitters.

C2   Upholsterers and related workers.

D   Sewers and embroiderers, textile and light leather products.

XII   Food, Drink and Tobacco Workers

C2   Bakers and pastry cooks.

C2   Butchers and meat cutters.

C2   Brewers, wine makers and related workers.

D   Food processors.

D   Tobacco preparers and product makers.

XIII   Paper and Printing Workers

C2   Makers of paper and paperboard.

C2   Paper products makers.

C2   Compositors.

C2   Printing press operators.

C2   Printers (so described).

C2   Printing workers.

D   Mates to above workers.

XIV   Makers of Other Products

C2   Workers in rubber.

D   Workers in plastics.

C2   Craftsmen.

D   Other production process workers.

D   Mates to above workers.

XV   Construction Workers

C2   Bricklayers, tile setters.

C2   Masons, stone cutters, slate workers.

C2   Plasterers, cement finishers, terrazzo workers.

D   Mates to above workers.

XVI Painters and Decorators

D Aerographers, paint sprayers.
C2 Painters, decorators.
D Mates to above workers.

XVII Drivers of Stationary Engines, Cranes, and so on

D Boiler firemen.
C2 Crane and hoist operators: slingers.
C2 Operators of earth moving and other construction machinery.
D Stationary engine, materials handling plant operators: oilers and greasers.

XVIII Labourers

D Railway lengthmen.
D Labourers and unskilled workers.
D Chemical and allied trades.
D Engineering and allied trades.
D Foundries in engineering and allied trades.
D Textiles.
D Coke ovens and gas works.
D Glass and ceramics.
D Building and contracting.
D All other labourers.

XIX Transport and Communications Workers

B Deck, engineering officers and pilots, ships.
D Deck and engine room rating, barge and boatmen.
A Aircraft pilots, navigators and flight engineers.
C2 Drivers, motormen, firemen, railway engine
C2 Railway guards (passenger and goods).
C2 Drivers of buses, coaches, trams.
C2 Drivers of road goods vehicles (heavy or long distance).
D Drivers of road goods vehicles (local and light).
C2 Shunters, pointmen.
C1 Telephone operators.
C1 Telegraph and radio operators.
D Postmen.

C2   Sorters and higher grade postmen.

D   Messengers.

D   Bus and tram conductors.

D   Porters, railway.

D   Ticket collectors, railway.

C2   Bus Inspector.

C2   Stevedores.

D   Dock labourers.

C2   Skilled labourers (Dock and Admiralty only).

D   Lorry drivers' mates, van guards.

D   Unskilled workers in transport and communication occupations.

XX   Warehousemen, Storekeepers, Packers, Bottlers

D   Warehousemen, storekeepers.

D   Assistant warehousemen, assistant storekeepers.

D   Packers, labellers, and related workers.

XXI   Clerical Workers

C1   Typists.

C1   Shorthand writers, secretaries.

C1   Clerks, cashiers, office machine operators.

XXII   Sales Workers

C1   Salesmen, representatives (unless professionally qualified).

C1   Shop assistants with qualifications and training.

C2   Shop assistants with special responsibilities.

D   Shop assistants without special responsibilities and training.

D   Roundsmen (bread, milk, laundry, soft drinks).

D   Street vendors, hawkers.

XXIII   Service, Sport and Recreation Workers

C2   Security guards.

D   Barmen, barmaids.

D   Housekeepers.

D   Stewards.

D   Waiters, counter hands.

C2   Cooks.

D   Kitchen hands.

D   Maids, valets and related service workers.

D   Caretakers, office keepers.

D   Chimney sweeps (employed).

D   Charwomen, office cleaners.

D   Window cleaners (employed).

C2   Hairdressers, beauticians if apprenticeship served.

D   Hairdressers, beauticians if serving apprenticeship.

D   Hospital or ward orderlies.

D   Launderers, dry cleaners and pressers.

C2   Ambulance men.

XXIV   Administrators and Managers

A   Ministers of the Crown; MPs: senior government officials.

A   Local authority senior officers.

XXV   Professional, Technical Workers, Artists

A   Medical practitioners (qualified with own practice).

B   Junior medical practitioners (recently qualified).

A   Dental practitioners (qualified with own practice).

B   Junior practitioners.

A, B, C1
     Authors, journalists and related workers. Stage managers, actors, entertainers, musicians. Painters, sculptors and related creative artists.

     The grade of these and similar cases, for example sportsmen, obviously depends on their success, and your grading must depend on this.

■ Classification of Occupations

Source: J. H. Goldthorpe, D. Lockwood, F. Bechhofer and J. Platt, *The Affluent Worker: Industrial Attitudes and Behaviour* (Cambridge University Press, 1968).

The occupational classification set out below was constructed on the basis of previous efforts by British sociologists, notably that of Hall and Cardog Jones (and is sometimes referred to as the 'Hall–Jones' classification).

In allocating occupations to classes, we followed the general rule of choosing the 'lower' alternative in all bordering cases where our information was incomplete or ambiguous. The examples given below are selected in order to give some idea of the range of occupation included in particular categories as well as 'typical' occupations.

	Occupational Status Level	Example	Registrar-General's Social Class Equivalent
1(a)	Higher professional, managerial and other white-collar employees.	Chartered accountant, business executive, senior civil servant, graduate teacher.	I
1(b)	Large industrial or commercial employers, landed proprietors.		
2(a)	Intermediate professional, managerial and other white-collar employees.	Pharmacists, non-graduate teachers, departmental manager, bank cashier.	II
2(b)	Medium industrial or commercial employers, substantial farmers.		
3(a)	Lower professional, managerial and other white-collar employees.	Chiropodist, bar manager, commercial traveller, draughtsman, accounts or wages clerk.	III Non-manual
3(b)	Small industrial or commercial employers, small farmers.	Jobbing builder, taxi owner-driver, tobacconist.	
4(a)	Supervisory, inspectional, minor official and service employees.	Foreman, meter-reader, shop assistant, door-to-door salesman.	III Manual or non-manual
4(b)	Self-employed men (no employees or expensive capital equipment).	Window cleaner, jobbing gardener.	
5	Skilled manual workers (with apprenticeship or equivalent).		III
6	Other relatively skilled manual workers.	Unapprenticed mechanics and fitters, skilled miners, painters and decorators, public service vehicle drivers.	III Manual or IV
7	Semi-skilled manual workers.	Machine operator, assembler, storeman.	IV
8	Unskilled manual workers.	Farm labourer, builder's labourer, dustmen.	V

■ Life Cycle (An Over-view)

Source: G. Gubar and W. D. Wells, 'Life Cycle Concepts in Marketing Research', *Journal of Marketing Research* (November 1966).

Bachelor-stage young single people not living at home	*Newly married couples, young, no children*	*Full nest I (youngest child under six)*	*Full nest II (youngest child six or over six)*
Few financial burdens.	Better off financially than they will be in the near future.	Home purchases at peak, liquid assets low.	Financial position better.
Fashion opinion leaders.		Dissatisfied with financial position and amount of money saved.	Some wives work.
Recreation orientation.	Highest purchase rate and highest average purchase of durables.		Less influenced by advertising.
BUY: basic kitchen equipment, basic furniture, cars, equipment for the mating game, vacation.	BUY: cars, refrigerators, stoves, sensible and durable furniture, vacations.	Interested in new products. Like advertised products. BUY: washers, dryers, television, baby food, chest rubs and cough medicine, vitamins, dolls, wagons, skates.	Buy larger sized packages, multi-unit deals. BUY: many foods, cleaning materials, bicycles, music lessons, pianos.

continued overleaf

Full nest III (older married couples with dependent children)	*Empty Nest I (older married couples, no children living with them, head in labour force*	*Empty Nest II (older married couples, no children living at home, head retired)*	*Solitary survivor, in labor force*	*Solitary survivor, retired*
Financial position still better.	Home ownership at peak.	Drastic cut in income.	Income still good but likely to sell home.	Same medical and products needs as other retired group, drastic cut in income.
More wives work.	More satisfied with financial position and money saved.	Keep home. BUY: medical appliances, medical care, products which aid health, sleep and digestion.		Special need for attention, affection and security.
Some children get jobs.				
Hard to influence with advertising.	Interested in travel, recreation, self-education.			
High average purchase of durables.	Make gifts and contributions.			
BUY: new more tasteful furniture, autotravel, non-necessary appliances, boats, dental services, magazines.	Not interested in new products. BUY: vacations, luxuries, home improvements.			

■ Registrar-General's 'Social Class'

Source: 'Classification of Occupations', and each year's *'Census Report of Great Britain'*, Office of Population, Censuses and Surveys (Crown Copyright).

Occupied* Males and Females aged 16 and over	% of Total		
	1971[†]	1981	1991
Class I: Professional, Administrative	3.7	3.9	4.7

Examples: company directors and secretaries, bankers, shipowners and managers, stock brokers, insurance underwriters, clergymen, lawyers, doctors, scientists, administrative class of civil service, officers of armed forces, professional engineers (civil, electrical and so on).

Class II: Intermediate	17.4	22.0	27.8

Owners and managers: farmers, land agents, dock and harbour officials, local authority, administration, commercial managers, hotel managers, proprietors of retail shops.

Professional: teachers, trained nurses, medical auxiliaries, social welfare workers, artists, civil service executive class.

Class III: Skilled Workers	50.1	48.5[‡]	45.0
(N = Non-manual, M = Manual).	N = 21.6	N = 23.0	N = 23.3
Four main sub-groups: (a) foreman, under	M = 28.5	M = 25.5	M = 21.7

managers and overlookers; (b) clerks, typists; (c) skilled craftsmen; (d) salesmen, shop assistants.

Class IV: Intermediate	20.8	18.9	16.2

Semi-skilled machine minders, labourers assisting craftsmen (provided there is some degree of skill).

Class V: Unskilled Labour	8.0	6.7	6.3

Railway porters, builders' labourers, dock labourers, lift attendants, watchmen, charwomen.

* Excludes armed forces, those on government schemes and those whose occupation is inadequately described or not stated.

[†] The population sample appearing in the 1971 census included those aged 15 and over.

[‡] For the 1980 'Social Class' changes, see list overleaf:

Class I Professional occupations

General administrators, national government (Assistant Secretary and above). Judges, solicitors, accountants, management consultants, clergymen, doctors, dentists, opticians, vets, scientists, engineers, architects, town planners, mathematicians.

Class II Intermediate occupations

Personnel and industrial relations officers, authors, marketing, advertising, PR executives, sales managers, actors, entertainers, proprietors and managers of hotels, pubs and so on, company secretaries, brokers, taxation experts, computer programmers, teachers, nurses, farmers, police officers (inspectors and above), prison officers (chief officers and above). National government (HEO to Senior Principal level). Local government officers (administration and executive functions).

Class III (N) Skilled occupations: Non-manual

Market and street traders, typists, secretaries, driving instructors, hairdressers and barbers, managers and proprietors, restaurateurs, sales representatives, scrap dealers, supervisors of: clerks, telephone operators, tracers, shop assistants, police sergeants.

Class III (M) Skilled occupations: Manual

Repairers (shoes, watches, television, radio); production workers for various industries, plumbers, welders, fitter/mechanics, painters, building workers, gardeners, service workers, foremen/supervisors, bus inspectors.

Class IV Partly-skilled occupations

Street traders and assistants, security guards, materials processing handlers. Sewers, making and repairing of plastics, other (excluding metal and electrical), machine tool operators, construction workers, waiters/waitresses, bar staff, domestic assistants, bus conductors.

Class V Unskilled occupations

Messengers, dustmen, cleaners, drivers mates, stevedores, dockers, railway stationmen, labourers and unskilled workers in textiles, gas works, chemicals and so on.

Appendix 2: Standard Industrial Classifications

■ UK

0000 Agriculture, Forestry and Fishing

0100 Agriculture and Horticulture

0100 Agriculture and Horticulture (General); Agricultural and Horticultural Services; Arable Farming and Livestock Production; Horticulture

0200 Forestry

0300 Fishing

0300 Commercial Sea Fishing and General Fishing; Commercial Fishing in Inland Waters

1000 Energy and Water Supply Industries

1100 Coal Extraction and Manufacture of Solid Fuels

1113 Deep Coal Mines

1114 Open Coal Working

1115 Manufacture of Solid Fuels

1200 Coke Ovens

1300 Extraction of Mineral Oil and Natural Gas

1400 Mineral Oil Processing

1401 Mineral Oil Refining

1402 Other Treatment of Petroleum Products Excluding Petrochemical Manufacture

1500 Nuclear Fuel Production

1600 Production and Distribution of Electricity, Gas and Other Forms of Energy

1610 Production and Distribution of Electricity

1620 Public Gas Supply

1630 Production and Distribution of Other Forms of Energy

1700 Water Supply Industry

2000   **Extraction of Minerals and Ores Other Than Fuels; Manufacture of Metals, Mineral Products and Chemicals**

2100   *Extraction and Preparation of Metalliferous Ores*

2200   *Metal Manufacturing*

2210   Iron and Steel Industry

2220   Steel Tubes

2230   Drawing, Cold Rolling and Cold Forming of Steel

2234   Drawing and Manufacture of Steel Wire and Steel Wire Products

2235   Other Drawing Cold Rolling and Cold Forming of Steel

2240   Non-Ferrous Metals Industry

2245   Aluminium and Aluminium Alloys

2246   Copper, Brass and Other Copper Alloys

2247   Other Non-Ferrous Metals and Their Alloys

2300   *Extraction of Minerals Not Elsewhere Specified*

2310   Extraction of Stone, Clay, Sand and Gravel

2330   Salt Extraction and Refining

2390   Extraction of Other Minerals Not Elsewhere Specified

2400   *Manufacture of Non-Metallic Mineral Products*

2410   Structural Clay Products

2420   Cement, Lime and Plaster

2430   Building Products of Concrete, Cement or Plaster

2436   Ready Mixed Concrete

2437   Other Building Products of Concrete, Cement or Plaster

2440   Asbestos Goods

2450   Working of Stone and Other Non-Metallic Minerals Not Elsewhere Specified

2460   Abrasive Products

2470   Glass and Glassware

2471   Flat Glass

2478   Glass Containers

2479   Other Glass Products

2480   Refractory and Ceramic Goods

2481   Refractory Goods

2489   Ceramic Goods

2500   *Chemical Industry*

2510   Basic Industrial Chemicals

2511 Inorganic Chemicals Except Industrial Gases

2512 Basic Organic Chemicals Except Specialised Pharmaceutical Chemicals

2513 Fertilisers

2514 Synthetic Resins and Plastic Materials

2515 Synthetic Rubber

2516 Dye Stuffs and Pigments

2551 Paints, Varnishes and Painters Fillings

2552 Printing Ink

2560 Specialised Chemical Products Mainly for Industrial and Agricultural Purposes

2562 Formulated Adhesives and Sealants

2563 Chemical Treatment of Oils and Fats

2564 Essential Oils and Flavouring Materials

2565 Explosives

2567 Miscellaneous Chemical Products for Industrial Use

2568 Formulated Pesticides

2569 Adhesive Film, Cloth and Foil

2570 Pharmaceutical Products

2580 Soap and Toilet Preparations

2581 Soap and Synthetic Detergents

2582 Perfumes, Cosmetics and Toilet Preparations

2590 Specialised Chemical Products Mainly for Household and Office Use

2591 Photographic Materials and Chemicals

2599 Chemical Products Not Elsewhere Specified

2600 *Production of Man-Made Fibres*

3000 Metal Goods, Engineering and Vehicle Industries

3100 *Manufacture of Metal Goods Not Elsewhere Specified*

3111 Ferrous Metal Foundries

3112 Non-Ferrous Metal Foundries

3120 Forging, Pressing and Stamping

3130 Non-Precision Chains

3137 Bolts, Nuts, Washers, Rivets, Springs and so on

3138 Heat and Surface Treatment of Metals, Including Sintering

3142 Metal Doors, Windows and so on.

3160 Hand Tools and Finished Metal Goods

3161   Hand Tools and Implements

3162   Cutlery, Spoons, Forks and Similar Tableware: Razors

3163   Metal Storage Vessels (Mainly Non-Industrial)

3164   Packaging Products of Metal (Cans and Boxes)

3165   Domestic Heating and Cooking Appliances (Non-Electrical)

3166   Metal Furniture and Safes

3167   Domestic and Similar Utensils of Metal

3169   Finished Metal Products, Needles, Pins, Smallwares, Mountings for Furniture

3200   Mechanical Engineering

3201   Industrial Plant and Steelwork

3204   Fabricated Constructional Steelwork

3205   Boilers and Process Plant Fabrications

3210   Agricultural Machinery and Tractors

3211   Agricultural Machinery

3212   Wheeled Tractors

3220   Metal-Working Machine Tools and Engineers Tools

3221   Metal-Working Machine Tools

3222   Engineers' Small Tools

3230   Textile Machinery and Accessories

3240   Machinery for the Food, Chemical and Related Industries; Process Engineering Contractors

3244   Food, Drink and Tobacco Processing Machinery; Packaging and Bottling Machinery

3245   Chemical Industry Machinery; Furnaces and Kilns; Gas, Water and Waste Treatment Plant

3246   Process Engineering Contractors

3250   Mining Machinery, Construction and Mechanical Handling Equipment

3251   Mining Machinery

3254   Construction and Earth Moving Equipment

3255   Mechanical Lifting and Handling Equipment

3260   Mechanical Power Transmission Equipment

3261   Precision Chains

3262   Ball, Needle and Roller Bearings

3270   Machinery for Printing, Paper, Wood, Leather, Rubber, Glass and Related Industries; Laundry and Dry Cleaning Machinery

3275 Machinery for Woodworking, Rubber and Plastics Working, Leatherwork, Footwear Making and Repairing, Paper Making, Glass and Brick Making and Similar Machinery; Laundry and Dry Cleaning Machinery

3276 Printing, Bookbinding and Papergoods Machinery

3280 Other Machinery and Mechanical Equipment

3281 Internal Combustion Engines

3283 Compressors and Fluid Power Equipment

3284 Refrigerating Machinery, Space Heating, Ventilating and Air Conditioning Equipment

3285 Scales, Weighing Machinery and Portable Power Tools

3286 Other Industrial and Commercial Machinery

3287 Pumps

3288 Industrial Valves

3289 Mechanical, Marine and Precision Engineering Not Elsewhere Specified

3290 Ordnance, Small Arms and Ammunition

3300 *Manufacture of Office Machinery and Data Processing Equipment*

3301 Office Machinery

3302 Electronic Data Processing Equipment

3400 *Electrical and Electronic Engineering*

3410 Insulated Wires and Cables

3420 Basic Electrical Equipment

3430 Electrical Equipment for Industrial Use, and Batteries and Accumulators

3432 Batteries and Accumulators

3433 Alarms and Signalling Equipment

3434 Electrical Equipment for Motor Vehicles, Cycles and Aircraft

3435 Electrical Equipment for Industrial Use Not Elsewhere Specified

3440 Telecommunications Equipment, Electrical Measuring Equipment, Electronic Capital Goods and Passive Electronic Components

3441 Telegraph and Telephone Apparatus and Equipment

3442 Electrical Instruments and Control Systems

3443 Radio and Electronic Capital Goods

3444 Components Other than Active Components Mainly for Electronic Equipment

3450 Other Electronic Equipment

3452 Gramophone Records and Pre-recorded Tapes

3453 Active Components and Electronic Sub-Assemblies

3454 Electronic Consumer Goods and Other Electronic Equipment Not Elsewhere Specified

3460   Domestic-Type Electrical Appliances

3470   Electric Lamps and Other Electric Lighting Equipment

3480   Electrical Equipment Installation

3500   *Manufacture of Motor Vehicles and Parts Thereof*

3510   Motor Vehicles and their Engines

3520   Motor Vehicle Bodies, Trailers and Caravans

3521   Motor Vehicle Bodies

3522   Trailers and Semi-Trailers

3523   Caravans

3530   Motor Vehicle Parts

3600   *Manufacture of Other Transport Equipment*

3610   Shipbuilding and Repairing

3620   Railway and Tramway Vehicles

3630   Cycles and Motor Cycles

3633   Motor Cycles and Parts

3634   Pedal Cycles and Parts

3640   Aerospace Equipment Manufacturing and Repairing

3650   Other Vehicles

3700   *Instrument Engineering*

3710   Measuring, Checking and Precision Instruments and Apparatus

3720   Medical and Surgical Equipment and Orthopaedic Appliances

3730   Optical Precision Instruments and Photographic Equipment

3731   Spectacles and Unmounted Lenses

3732   Optical Precision Instruments

3733   Photographic and Cinemagraphic Equipment

3740   Clocks, Watches and Other Timing Devices

4000   Other Manufacturing Industries

4100   *Food Manufacturing Industries*

4110   Organic, Oils and Fats (Other Than Crude Animal Fats)

4115   Margarine and Compound Cooking Fats

4116   Processing Organic Oils and Fats (Other Than Crude Animal Fat Production)

4120   Slaughtering of Animals and Production of Meat and By-Products

4121   Slaughter Houses

4122   Bacon Curing and Meat Processing

4123   Poultry Slaughter and Processing

4126   Animal By-Product Processing

4130   Preparation of Milk and Milk Products

4140   Processing of Fruit and Vegetables

4150   Fish Processing

4160   Grain Milling

4180   Starch

4190   Bread, Biscuits and Flour Confectionery

4196   Bread and Flour Confectionery

4197   Biscuits and Crispbread

4200   *Sugar, Confectionery, Animal Feeds, Drink and Tobacco Manufacturing Industries*

4210   Ice Cream, Cocoa, Chocolate and Sugar Confectionery

4213   Ice Cream

4214   Cocoa, Chocolate and Sugar Confectionery

4220   Animal Feeding Stuffs

4221   Compound Animal Feeds

4222   Pet Foods and Non-Compound Animal Feeds

4230   Miscellaneous Foods

4240   Spirit Distilling and Compounding

4260   Wines, Cider and Perry

4270   Brewing and Malting

4280   Soft Drinks

4290   Tobacco Industry

4300   *Textile Industry*

4310   Woollen and Worsted Industry

4320   Cotton and Silk Industries

4321   Spinning and Doubling on the Cotton System

4322   Weaving of Cotton, Silk and Man-Made Fibres

4330   Throwing, Texturing and so on, of Continuous Filament Yarn

4340   Spinning and Weaving Flax, Hemp and Ramie

4350   Jute and Polypropylene Yarns and Fabrics

4360   Hosiery and Other Knitted Goods

4363   Hosiery and Other Weft Goods and Fabrics

4364   Warp Knitted Goods

4370   Textile Finishing

4380	Carpets and Other Textile Floor Coverings
4384	Pile Carpets and Carpeting and Rugs (Woven-Tufted)
4385	Other Carpets, Carpeting, Rugs and Matting (Needles and Bonded Hard Fibre)
4390	Miscellaneous Textiles
4395	Lace
4396	Rope, Twine and Net
4398	Narrow Fabrics (Braided Elastics – Ribbons, Braids and Trimmings)
4399	Other Miscellaneous Textiles (Felt-Kapok and Vegetable Down)
4400	*Manufacture of Leather and Leather Goods*
4410	Leather and Fellmongery
4420	Leather Goods
4500	*Footwear and Clothing Industries*
4510	Footwear
4530	Clothing, Hats and Gloves
4531	Weatherproof Outer Wear
4532	Men's and Boys' Tailored Outer Wear
4533	Women's and Girls' Tailored Outer Wear
4534	Working Clothing and Mens' and Boys' Jeans
4535	Men's and Boys' Shirts, Underwear and Nightwear
4536	Women's and Girls' Light Outerwear, Lingerie and Infants' Wear
4537	Hats, Caps and Millinery
4538	Gloves
4539	Other Dress Industries
4550	Household Textiles and Other made up Textiles
4555	Soft Furnishings
4556	Canvas Goods, Sacks and Other made up Textiles
4557	Household Textiles
4560	Fur Goods
4600	*Timber and Wooden Furniture Industries*
4610	Sawmilling, Planing, and so on, of Wood
4620	Manufacture of Semi-Finished Wood Products and Treatment of Wood
4630	Builder's Carpentry and Joinery
4640	Wooden Containers
4650	Other Wooden Articles (Except Furniture)
4660	Articles of Cork and Plaiting Materials, Brushes and Brooms

4663 Brushes and Brooms

4664 Articles of Cork and Basket Ware, Wicker Work and Other Plaiting Materials

4670 Wooden and Upholstered Furniture and Shop and Office Fittings

4671 Wooden and Upholstered Furniture

4672 Shop and Office Fitting

4700 Manufacture of Paper and Paper Products; Printing and Publishing

4710 Pulp, Paper and Board; Pulp; Newsprint; Writing and Printing Papers; Wrapping and Packaging Papers; Household, Toilet Papers and Tissues; Industrial; Corrugated; Building Board Including Bituminised; Other Boards

4720 Conversion of Paper and Board

4721 Wall Coverings

4722 Household and Personal Hygiene Products of Paper

4723 Stationery (Note Paper, Binders and so on)

4724 Packaging Products of Paper and Pulp (Sacks and Bags, Other)

4725 Packaging Products of Board (Fibre Board Packing Cases, Rigid Boxes, Cartons)

4728 Other Paper and Board Products (Papier Mache or Wood Pulp Not Elsewhere Specified)

4750 Printing and Publishing

4751 Printing and Publishing of Newspapers

4752 Printing and Publishing of Periodicals

4753 Printing and Publishing of Books

4754 Other Printing and Publishing (Security Printing, for example, Bank Notes, Stamps, Tickets, Greeting Cards; Bookbinding, Etching, Engraving, Printing on Metal)

4800 Processing of Rubber and Plastics

4810 Rubber Products

4811 Rubber Tyres and Inner Tubes

4812 Other Rubber Products - Hose and Tubing, Belting, Reclaimed Rubber

4820 Retreading and Specialist Repairing of Rubber Tyres

4830 Processing of Plastics

4831 Plastic Coated Fabric

4832 Plastics Semi-Manufactures

4833 Plastic Floorcoverings

4834 Plastic Building Products

4835 Plastic Packaging Products

4836 Plastic Products Not Elsewhere Specified
4900 *Other Manufacturing Industries*
4910 Jewellery and Coins
4920 Musical Instruments
4930 Photographic and Cinematographic Processing Laboratories
4940 Toys and Sports Goods
4941 Toys and Games
4942 Sports Goods
4950 Miscellaneous Manufacturing Industries
4954 Miscellaneous Stationers' Goods (Pens and Pencils, Inks, Office Accessories)
4959 Other Manufacturers (Ivory, Meerschaum, Bone, Horn, Tortoise-shell and Smokers' Requisites, Taxidermist)

5000 Construction: General Construction and Demolition Work

5000 General Construction and Demolition Work
5001 Property Developers
5002 Municipal and Service Building Contractors
5003 Concrete Work
5004 Structural Steel Work
5005 Excavation and Foundation Work
5006 Wreckage and Demolition
5010 Construction and Repair of Buildings
5011 Domestic House Builders
5012 Residential Construction – Hotels, Flats and so on
5013 Industrial Building Contractors
5014 Scaffolding Erection
5020 Civil Engineering
5021 Street and Paving Construction
5022 Bridge, Tunnel and Flyover Construction
5023 Water, Sewer, Pipe Line and Power Line Construction and Installation
5024 Heavy Construction and Civil Engineering
5030 Installation of Fixtures and Fittings
5031 Plumbing, Heating and Air Conditioning
5032 Electrical Contracting
5040 Building Completion Work
5041 Painting and Decorating

5042 Plastering

5043 Floorlaying

5044 Roofing Contractors

5045 Glass and Glazing Work

5046 Special Trade Contractors

6000 Distribution, Hotels and Catering: Repairs

6100 Wholesale Distribution: Except Dealing in Scrap and Waste Materials

6110 Wholesale Distribution of Agricultural Raw Materials, Live Animals, Textile Raw Materials and Semi-Manufactures

6120 Wholesale Distribution of Fuels, Ores, Metals and Industrial Materials

6130 Wholesale Distribution of Timbers and Building Materials

6140 Wholesale Distribution of Machinery, Industrial Equipment and Vehicles

6148 Wholesale Distribution of Motor Vehicles and Parts and Accessories

6149 Wholesale Distribution of Machinery, Industrial Equipment and Transport Equipment Other Than Motor Vehicles

6150 Wholesale Distribution of Household Goods, Hardware and Ironmongery

6160 Wholesale Distribution of Textiles, Clothing, Footwear and Leather Goods

6170 Wholesale Distribution of Food, Drink and Tobacco

6180 Wholesale Distribution of Pharmaceutical Medical and Other Chemist Goods

6190 Wholesale Distribution of Other Non-Food Goods: Paper; Board; Stationery, Books, Periodicals, Newspapers, Photographic, Optical Goods, Watches and Clocks, Jewellery, Toys, Sports Goods, Cycles, Perambulators

6200 Dealing in Scrap and Waste Materials

6210 Dealing in Scrap Metals: Ferrous and Non-Ferrous Scrap Metals

6220 Dealing in Other Scrap Materials or General Dealers

6300 Commission Agents and Commodity Brokers

6400 Retail Distribution: Food, CTN, Off-Licences, Chemists, Leather, Clothing, Footwear, Home Furnishings and Household Goods

6410 Food Retailing

6420 Confectioners, Tobacconists and Newsagents; Off Licences

6430 Dispensing and Other Chemists

6450 Retail Distribution of Clothing

6460   Retail Distribution of Footwear and Leather Goods

6470   Retail Distribution of Furnishing Fabrics and Household Textiles

6480   Retail Distribution of Household Goods, Hardware and Ironmongery

6500   *Other Retail Distribution: Cars, Fuel, Books, Mixed Retailing and so on*

6510   Retail Distribution of Motor Vehicles and Parts

6520   Filling Stations: Motor Fuel and Lubricants

6530   Retail Distribution of Books, Stationery and Office Supplies

6540   Other Specialised Retail Distribution (Non-Food)

6560   Mixed Retail Businesses

6600   *Hotels and Catering*

6610   Restaurants, Snack Bars, Cafes and Other Eating Places

6611   Licensed and Unlicensed Eating Places: No Accommodation

6612   Take-Away Food Shops

6620   Public Houses and Bars

6630   Night Clubs and Licensed Clubs

6640   Catering Contractors; Other Canteens and Messes

6650   Hotel Trade

6670   Other Tourist or Short-Stay Accommodation

6700   *Repair of Consumer Goods and Vehicles*

6710   Repair and Servicing of Motor Vehicles

6720   Repair of Footwear and Leather Goods

6730   Repair of Other Consumer Goods

7000   **Transport and Communication**

7100   *Railways*

7200   *Other Inland Transport*

7210   Urban Railways; Bus, Motor Coach and Tramway Services

7220   Other Road Passenger Transport

7230   Road Haulage

7260   Transport not Elsewhere Specified: Pipe Line Transport; Other Transport by Land; Inland Water Transport

7400   *Sea Transport: Deep Sea Routes; Short Sea Routes; Domestic and Coastal Routes; Shore Bases*

7500   *Air Transport*

7600   *Supporting Services to Transport*

7610   Supporting Services to; Inland Transport; Land Transport; Inland Water Transport

7630   Supporting Services to Sea Transport

7640   Supporting Services to Air Transport

7700   *Miscellaneous Transport Services and Storage Not Elsewhere Specified*

7900   *Postal and Telecom Services*

7901   Postal Services

7902   Telecommunications

8000   Banking, Finance, Insurance, Business Services and Leasing

8100   Banking and Finance

8140   Banking and Bill-Discounting; Central Banking Authorities; Banks and Discount Houses; Savings Banks

8150   Other Financial Institutions: Granting of Credit; Investment in Securities

8200   Insurance, Except for Compulsory Social Security

8300   Business Services

8310   Activities Auxiliary to Banking and Finance

8320   Activities Auxiliary to Insurance

8340   House and Estate Agents

8350   Legal Services

8360   Accountants, Auditors, Tax Experts

8370   Professional and Technical Services Not Elsewhere Specified: Architects, Surveyors and Consulting Engineers; Technical Services

8380   Advertising

8390   Business Services

8394   Computer Services

8395   Business Services Not Elsewhere Specified: Management Consultants; Market Research and Public Relations Consultants; Document Copying, Duplicating and Tabulating; Miscellaneous Business Services

8396   Central Offices Not Allocable Elsewhere

8400   Renting of Movables

8410   Hiring out Agricultural and Horticultural Equipment

8420   Hiring out Construction Machinery and Equipment

8430   Hiring out Office Machinery and Furniture

8460   Hiring out Consumer Goods: Television and Radio Hire; Other Consumer Goods, for example, Photographic Equipment, Musical Instruments, Crockery

8480   Hiring out Transport Equipment

8490   Hiring out Other Movables

8500   Owning and Dealing in Real Estate

9000   Other Services

9100   *Public Administration, National Defence and Compulsory Social Security*

9110   National and Local Government Services Not Elsewhere Specified

9120   Justice

9130   Police

9140   Fire Services

9150   National Defence

9190   Social Security

9200   *Sanitary Services*

9210   Refuse Disposal, Sanitation and Similar Services

9211   Refuse Disposal, Street Cleaning, Fumigation and so on

9212   Sewage Disposal

9230   Cleaning Services

9300   *Education*

9310   Higher Education

9320   School Education (Nursery, Primary, Secondary)

9330   Education Not Elsewhere Specified

9360   Driving and Flying Schools

9400   *Research and Development*

9500   *Medical and Other Health Services; Veterinary Services*

9510   Hospitals, Nursing Homes and so on

9520   Other Medical Care Institutions

9530   Medical Practices

9540   Dental Practices

9550   Agency and Private Midwives, Nurses and so on

9560   Practices and Hospitals Run By, or Under the Supervision Of, Registered Veterinarians

9600   *Other Services Provided to the General Public*

9610   Social and Charitable Community Services

9630   Professional and Scientific Organisations; Business Organisations; Trade Unions

9660   Religious and Similar Organisations

9690   Tourist Offices; Other Community Services

9700   *Recreational Services and Other Cultural Services*

9710   Film Production, Distribution and Exhibition

9740   Radio and Television Services, Theatres and so on

9760   Authors, Music Composers and Other Own Account Artists Not Elsewhere Specified

9770   Libraries, Museums, Art Galleries and so on

9790   Sport and Other Recreational Services

9800   *Personal Services*

9810   Laundries and Drycleaning

9811   Laundries

9812   Drycleaning and Allied Services

9820   Hairdressing and Beauty Parlours

9890   Photographic and Other Personal Services

9900   *Domestic Services*

0000   *Diplomatic Representation, International Organisations and Allied Armed Forces*

■ USA

000   **Agriculture, Forestry and Fishing**

010   *Agricultural Production – Crops*

011   Cash Grains Including Rice and Soya Beans

013   Field Crops Excluding Cash Grains

016   Vegetables

017   Fruits and Tree Nuts

018   Horticultural Specialists Including Food Crops Grown Under Cover and Floriculture

019   General Farms, Primarily Crop

020   *Agricultural Production – Livestock*

021   Livestock, Excluding Dairy and Poultry

024   Dairy Farms

025   Poultry and Eggs

027   Animal Specialties Not Elsewhere Specified

029   General Farms, Primarily Livestock

070   *Agricultural Services*

071   Soil Preparation Services

072   Crop Services

074   Veterinary Services

075   Livestock and Animal Specialty Services, Excluding Veterinary

076   Farm Labour and Management Services
078   Landscape, Lawn, Garden, Ornamental Shrub and Tree Services
080   *Forestry*
081   Timber Tracts
082   Forest Nurseries and Gathering of Forest Products
084   Gathering of Forest Products Not Elsewhere Specified
085   Forestry Services
090   *Fishing, Hunting and Trapping*
091   Marine Products
092   Fish Hatcheries and Reserves
097   Hunting, Trapping and Game Propagation

100   Mining

100   *Metal Mining*
101   Iron Ores
102   Copper Ores
103   Lead and Zinc Ores
104   Gold and Silver Ores
105   Bauxite and Other Aluminium Ores
106   Ferroalloy Ores, Excluding Vanadium
108   Metal Mining Services
109   Metal Ores Not Elsewhere Specified
110   *Anthracite Mining*
111   Anthracite Mining and Services
120   *Bituminous Coal and Lignite Mining*
121   Bituminous Coal and Lignite Mining and Services
130   *Oil and Gas Extraction*
131   Crude Petroleum and Natural Gas
132   Natural Gas Liquids
138   Oil and Gas Drilling and Field Services
140   *Mining, Quarrying Non-Metallic Minerals Excluding Fuels*
141   Dimension Stone
142   Crushed and Broken Stone Not Elsewhere Specified
144   Sand and Gravel
145   Clay, Ceramic and Refractory Minerals
147   Chemical and Fertiliser Minerals

148   Non-Metallic Mineral Services Excluding Fuel
149   Non-Metallic Minerals, Not Elsewhere Specified

150   Construction

150   Building Construction – General Contractors
152   Domestic House Builders and Residential Construction – Hotels, Flats and so on
153   Operative Builders
154   Industrial, Municipal and Service Building Contractors
160   Construction, Excluding Buildings, General Contractors
161   Street and Paving Construction
162   Heavy Construction and Civil Engineering
170   Construction – Special Trade Contractors
171   Plumbing, Heating and Air Conditioning
172   Painting and Decorating
173   Electrical Contracting
174   Masonry, Stonework, Plastering, Marble, Tile and Mosaic Work
175   Carpentry and Floorlaying
176   Roofing Contractors
177   Concrete Work
178   Water Well Drilling
179   Special Trade Contractors Not Elsewhere Specified

200   Manufacturing

200   Food and Kindred Products
201   Production of Meat and Meat Products Including Poultry and Egg Processing
202   Dairy Products
203   Canned, Dried, Dehydrated, Pickled and Frozen Fruit and Vegetable Products; Frozen Specialities Not Elsewhere Specified
204   Products From Grain and Rice Milling; Pet Food and Animal Feeds
205   Bread and Bakery Products
206   Sugar, Chocolate, Confectionery and Cocoa Products
207   Cottonseed, Soya Bean and Vegetable Oil Mills; Animal and Marine Fats and Oils
208   Malt and Malt Beverages, Spirits, Soft Drinks, Carbonated Waters and Flavourings

209   Food Preparations, Not Elsewhere Specified

210   *Tobacco Products*

211   Cigarettes

212   Cigars

213   Tobacco (Chewing and Smoking) and Snuff

214   Tobacco Stemming and Redrying

220   *Textile Mill Products*

221   Broad Woven Fabric Mills, Cotton

222   Broad Woven Fabric Mills, Man-Made Fibre, Silk

223   Broad Woven Fabric Mills, (Including Dyeing and Finishing)

224   Narrow Fabrics: Cotton, Wool, Silk, and Man-Made Fibre

225   Hosiery and Knitting Mills

226   Finishers of Textiles

227   Carpets and Rugs

228   Yarn Spinning, Texturising, Throwing, Twisting and Winding Mills; Thread Mills

229   Textile Goods Not Elsewhere Specified Including Processed Waste and Recovered Fibres and Flock; Rope Twine and Net

230   *Apparel and Other Finished Fabric Product Manufacturers*

231   Men's and Boys' Suits, Coats and Overcoats

232   Men's and Boys' Clothing Not Elsewhere Specified

233   Women's and Girls' Outerwear

234   Women's, Girls' and Babies' Underwear and Nightwear; Corsets and Allied Garments

235   Millinery, Hats and Caps

236   Girls' and Babies' Outerwear

237   Fur Goods

238   Apparel and Accessories Not Elsewhere Specified

239   House Furnishings, Textile Bags, Canvas and Related Products; Pleating, Stitching and Tucking for the Trade; Automotive Trimmings, Apparel Findings and Related Products; Fabricated Textile Products Not Elsewhere Specified

240   *Timber and Wood Products, Excluding Furniture*

241   Forestry Camps and Forestry Contractors

242   Sawmills, Planing Mills and Flooring Mills; Special Products Sawmills Not Elsewhere Specified

243   Millwork, Wood Kitchen Cabinets, Veneers, Plywood and Structural Wood Members Not Elsewhere Specified

244 Wood Boxes, Pallets and Containers Not Elsewhere Specified

245 Mobile Homes, Prefabricated Wood Buildings and Components

249 Wood Preserving; Particleboard; Wood Products Not Elsewhere Specified

250 *Furniture and Fixtures*

251 Wood and Metal Household Furniture; Mattresses and Bedsprings; Household Furniture Not Elsewhere Specified

252 Wood and Metal Office Furniture

253 Public Building and Related Furniture

254 Wood and Metal Partitions, Office and Store Fixtures

259 Drapery Hardware, Window Blinds and Shades; Furniture and Fittings Not Elsewhere Specified

260 *Paper and Allied Products*

261 Pulp Mills

262 Paper Mills

263 Paperboard Mills

264 Pulp, Paper, Paperboard and Cardboard Products Not Elsewhere Specified

265 Paperboard, Corrugated and Solid Fibre Boxes; Sanitary Food Containers and Fibre Containers

266 Building Paper and Building Board Mills

270 *Printing, Publishing and Allied Industries*

271 Newspaper Publishing and Printing

272 Periodical Publishing and Printing

273 Book Publishing and Printing

274 Miscellaneous Publishing

275 Commercial Printing; Engraving and Plate Printing

276 Continuous and Carbonised Stationery

277 Greeting Cards Publishing

278 Pads and Loose Leaf Binders; Bookbinding and Related Works

279 Typesetting, Photoengraving, Electrotyping and Stereotyping; Lithographic Platemaking and Related Services

280 *Chemical and Allied Products*

281 Alkalies, Chlorine, Industrial Gases, Inorganic Pigments and Industrial Inorganic Chemicals Not Elsewhere Specified

282 Plastic Materials, Synthetic Resins, Cellulosic Man Made Fibres and Synthetic Organic Fibres

283   Biological Products, Medicinal Chemicals, Botanical Products and Pharmaceutical Preparations

284   Detergents, Speciality Cleaners, Polishers, Surface Active and Finishing Agents, Sulphonated Oils; Perfumes, Cosmetics and Other Toilet Preparations

285   Paints, Varnishes, Lacquers, Enamels, and Allied Products

286   Gum and Wood Chemicals; Cyclic Organic Crudes, Organic Dyes and Pigments; Industrial Organic Chemicals Not Elsewhere Specified

287   Fertilisers, Pesticides and Agricultural Chemicals Not Elsewhere Specified

289   Chemicals and Chemical Preparations Not Elsewhere Specified

290   *Petroleum Refining and Related Industries*

291   Petroleum Refining

295   Asphalt Paving Mixtures, Blocks, Felts and Coatings

299   Products of Petroleum and Coal Not Elsewhere Specified

300   *Rubber and Miscellaneous Plastic Products*

301   Tyres and Inner Tubes

302   Rubber and Plastic Footwear

303   Reclaimed Rubber

304   Rubber and Plastic Hose and Belting

306   Fabricated Rubber Products Not Elsewhere Specified

307   Miscellaneous Plastic Products

310   *Leather and Leather Product Manufacturers*

311   Leather Tanning and Finishing

313   Leather Boot, Shoe Soles, Inner Soles

314   Leather Footwear, Excluding Athletic Footwear

315   Leather Gloves and Mittens

316   Leather Luggage

317   Personal Leather Goods

319   Leather Goods Not Elsewhere Specified

320   *Stone, Clay, Glass and Concrete Products*

321   Flat Glass

322   Pressed and Blown Glass and Glassware Not Elsewhere Specified

323   Glass Products Made of Purchased Glass

324   Cement, Hydraulic

325   Structural Clay Products and Clay Refractories

326   Pottery Products Including Vitreous China, Earthenware and Porcelain

327 Concrete and Concrete Products; Lime and Gypsum Products

328 Cut Stone and Stone Products

329 Non-Clay Refractories and Non-Metallic Mineral Products Not Elsewhere Specified

330 *Primary Metal Industries*

331 Blast Furnaces, Rolling Mills, Steel and Electro-Metallurgical Products

332 Iron and Steel Foundries

333 Primary Smelting and Refining of Non-Ferrous Metals

334 Secondary Smelting and Refining of Non-Ferrous Metals

335 Rolling, Drawing and Extruding of Non-Ferrous Metals; Drawing and Insulating of Non-Ferrous Wire

336 Non-Ferrous Foundries

339 Metal Heat Treating and Primary Metal Products Not Elsewhere Specified

340 *Fabricated Metal Products, Excluding Machinery and Transportation Equipment*

341 Metal Cans, Shipping Barrels, Drums, Kegs and Buckets

342 Cutlery and Hardware Not Elsewhere Specified

343 Enamelled Iron and Metal Sanitary Ware; Brass Plumbing Fixtures, Fittings and Trim; Heating Equipment, Except Electric and Warm Air Furnaces

344 Metal Work; Fabricated Metal Work; Prefabricated Metal Buildings and Components

345 Screw Machine Products; Bolts, Nuts, Screws, Rivets and Washers

346 Metal Forgings, Stampings, Crowns and Closures

347 Electroplating, Plating, Polishing, Anodising, Colouring, Coating, Engraving and Allied Metal Services

348 Ammunition, Small Arms, Ordnance and Accessories

349 Fabricated Metal Products Not Elsewhere Specified

350 *Machinery Manufacturing, Excluding Electrical Machinery*

351 Steam, Gas and Hydraulic Turbines and Turbine Generator Set Units; Internal Combustion Engines Not Elsewhere Specified

352 Farm and Garden Machinery and Equipment

353 Other Industrial and Commercial Machinery and Equipment

354 Machine Tools and Accessories; Special Dies, Industrial Moulds and Jigs; Power Driven Hand Tools; Metalworking Machinery Not Elsewhere Specified

355 Special Industrial Machinery Not Elsewhere Specified

356   General Industrial Machinery and Equipment Not Elsewhere Specified

357   Office Machines Including Electronic Computing Equipment

358   Air Conditioning, Warm Air Heating, Commercial and Industrial Refrigeration Equipment; Service Industry Machines Not Elsewhere Specified

359   Carburettors, Pistons, Piston Rings, Valves, Non-Electrical Machinery Not Elsewhere Specified

360   *Electrical, Electronic Machinery, Equipment and Supplies*

361   Power, Distribution and Speciality Transformers, Switchgear and Switchboard Apparatus

362   Electrical Industrial Apparatus Not Elsewhere Specified

363   Household Appliances Not Elsewhere Specified

364   Lighting Equipment and Fixtures

365   Radio and Television Receivers (Excluding Communication Types); Pre-Recorded Records and Magnetic Tapes

366   Telephone and Telegraphic Apparatus; Radio and Television Transmitting, Signalling and Detection Equipment and Apparatus

367   Radio and Television (Receiving Types) Electronic Tubes; Electronic Components Not Elsewhere Specified

369   Batteries, Electrical Machinery, Equipment and Supplies Not Elsewhere Specified

370   *Transportation Equipment Manufacture*

371   Road Transport Bodies, Parts and Accessories; Truck Trailers

372   Aircraft and Aircraft Engines, Parts and Auxiliary Equipment Not Elsewhere Specified

373   Ship and Boat Building and Repairing

374   Railway Equipment

375   Motorcycles, Bicycles, and Parts

376   Guided Missile and Space Vehicles, Propulsion Units, Parts and Auxiliary Equipment Not Elsewhere Specified

379   Transportation Equipment Not Elsewhere Specified

380   *Measuring, Photographic, Medical Instruments, Watches and Clocks*

381   Engineering, Laboratory, Scientific and Research instruments and Associated Equipment

382   Measuring and Controlling Devices

383   Optical Instruments and Lenses

384   Surgical, Medical and Dental Equipment, Appliances and Supplies

385   Ophthalmic Goods

386   Photographic Equipment and Supplies

387   Watches, Clocks, Clockwork Operated Devices and Parts

390   *Miscellaneous Manufacturing Industries*

391   Jewellery and Precious Metal Products

393   Musical Instruments

394   Dolls, Children's Games and Toys (Excluding Cycles); Sporting and Athletic Goods Not Elsewhere Specified

395   Pens, Pencils, Crayons, Artists' Materials, Marking Devices, Carbon Paper and Inked Ribbons

396   Costume Jewellery and Novelties (Excluding Precious Metals); Feathers, Plumes, Artificial Trees and Flowers; Buttons and Sewing Notions

399   Manufacturing Industries Not Elsewhere Specified

400   Transportation and Communications

400   *Railway Transportation*

401   Railways; Switching and Terminal Establishments

404   Railway Express Service

410   *Local Public Transport and Intercity Buses*

411   Local and Suburban Passenger Transportation Not Elsewhere Specified

412   Taxicabs

413   Intercity and Rural Road Passenger Transportation

414   Passenger Transportation Charter Service

415   School Buses

417   Bus Terminal Operations; Maintenance Facilities for Motor Vehicle Passenger Transportation

420   *Road Freight Transportation and Warehousing*

421   Road Haulage and Local Storage

422   Warehousing and Storage

423   Freight Trucking Terminal Operation

430   *Postal Services*

431   Postal Service

440   *Transportation By Water*

441   Deep Sea Foreign Transportation

442   Transportation To and Between Non-Contiguous Territories; Coastal and Domestic Transportation

444   Inland Water Transport

445   Ferries, Lighterage, Towing and Tugboat Services; Local Water Transportation Services Not Elsewhere Specified

446   Marine Cargo Handling; Canal Operation; Water Transportation Services Not Elsewhere Specified

450   *Air Transport*

451   Air Transportation, Certified Carriers

452   Air Transportation, Non-Certified Carriers

458   Airports, Airfields and Terminal Services

460   *Pipe Lines, Excluding Natural Gas*

461   Petroleum Pipe Lines; Pipe Lines Not elsewhere Specified

470   *Transportation Services*

471   Freight Forwarding

472   Arrangement of Passenger, Freight and Cargo Transportation

474   Rental of Railway Carriages

478   Services Incidental to Transportation Not Elsewhere Specified

480   *Communication*

481   Telephone Communication (Wire or Radio)

482   Telegraph Communication (Wire or Radio)

483   Radio and Television Broadcasting

489   Communication Services Not Elsewhere Specified

490   *Electrical, Gas and Sanitary Services*

491   Electric Companies and Systems

492   Natural Gas Transmission and Distribution; Mixed, Manufactured or Liquified Gas Production and Distribution

493   Combined Utilities

494   Water Supply

495   Sewerage, Refuse and Other Sanitary Services

496   Steam Supply

497   Irrigation Systems

500   **Wholesale**

500   *Wholesale Trade – Durable Goods*

501   Motor Vehicles; Automotive Parts and Supplies

502   Furniture and Home Furnishings

503   Construction Materials

504   Sports, Recreational, Toys, Hobby Goods and Supplies; Photographic Equipment and Supplies

505   Metal Service Centres and Offices; Coal and Other Minerals and Ores

506 Electrical Apparatus, Appliances and Equipment, Wiring Supplies and Construction Material; Electronic Parts and Equipment

507 Hardware; Equipment and Supplies for Plumbing, Heating, Air Conditioning and Refrigeration

508 Machines and Equipment – Commercial, Construction, Mining, Farm, Garden, Industrial; Equipment and Supplies – Industrial, Professional, Service Establishment, Transportation (Except Motor Vehicles)

509 Scrap and Waste Materials; Jewellery, Watches, Diamonds and Other Precious Stones; Durable Goods Not Elsewhere Specified

510 *Wholesale Trade – Non-Durable Goods*

511 Paper and Other Stationery Supplies

512 Drugs, Drug Proprietaries and Pharmaceutical Sundries

513 Piece Goods, Notions, Footwear, Clothing and Accessories

514 Groceries, Meat, Dairy, Poultry Products, Fish and Seafoods; Confectionery

515 Cotton, Grain, Livestock; Farm-Product Raw Materials Not Elsewhere Specified

516 Chemicals and Allied Products

517 Petroleum and Petroleum Products

518 Beer, Ale, Wine and Distilled Alcoholic Beverages

519 Non-Durable Goods Not Elsewhere Specified

520 Retail

520 *Building Materials, Garden Supply, Mobile Home Dealers*

521 Timber and Other Building Materials Dealers

523 Paint, Glass and Wallpaper Shops

525 Hardware Shops

526 Retail Nurseries, Lawn and Garden Supply Shops

527 Mobile Home Dealers

530 *General Merchandise Retailers*

531 Department Stores

533 Cash and Carry Stores

539 Miscellaneous General Merchandise Shops

540 *Food Retailers*

541 Grocers

542 Frozen Meat Stores; Meat, Fish and Seafood Markets

543 Fruit and Vegetable Shops and Markets

544 Nut and Sugar Confectionery Shops

545   Dairy Products Shops

546   Retail Bakeries, Baking and/or Selling

549   Miscellaneous Food Shops

550   *Motor Vehicle Dealers and Petrol Stations*

551   Motor Vehicle Dealers (New and Used)

552   Motor Vehicle Dealers (Used Only)

553   Auto and Home Supply Shops

554   Petrol Service Stations

555   Boat Dealers

556   Recreational, Utility Trailer and Caravan Dealer

557   Motorcycle Dealers

559   Automotive Dealers Not Elsewhere Specified

560   *Clothing and Accessory Retailers*

561   Men's and Boys' Clothing and Furnishings Shops

562   Women's Ready-to-Wear Shops

563   Women's Accessory and Speciality Shops

564   Children's and Babies' Wear Shops

565   Family Clothing Shops

566   Shoe Shops

568   Furriers and Fur Shops

569   Miscellaneous Apparel and Accessory Shops

570   *Furniture, Home Furnishings and Equipment Retailers*

571   Furniture, Floor Covering and Home Furnishing Shops

572   Household Appliance Shops

573   Radio, Television and Music Shops

580   *Eating and Drinking Places*

581   Eating and Drinking Places (Alcoholic Beverages)

590   *Miscellaneous Retail Trade*

591   Pharmacies and Proprietary Shops

592   Off-Licences

593   Used Merchandise Shops

594   Specialty Retail Shops Not Elsewhere Specified

596   Mail Order Houses; Automatic Merchandising Machine Operators; Direct Selling Establishments

598   Fuel, Fuel Oil, Liquified Petroleum Gas (Bottled Gas) and Ice Dealers

599   Florists, Tobacconists, Newsagents and News Stands; Miscellaneous Retail Shops Not Elsewhere Specified

600   Finance, Insurance and Real estate

600   Banking

601   Banks, Discount Houses and Licensed Deposit Takers

602   State Banks and National Banks

605   Foreign Exchange Establishments, Foreign Banks; Savings Banks

610   Credit Agencies Other Than Banks

611   Financial Institutions

615   Short-Term and Miscellaneous Business Credit Institutions

616   Mortgage Bankers, Loan Correspondents and Loan Brokers

620   Security, Commodity Brokers, Dealers, Exchanges and Allied Services

621   Stock Brokers, Dealers and Flotation Companies

622   Commodity Contracts Brokers and Dealers

623   Security and Commodity Exchanges

628   Services Allied with the Exchange of Securities or Commodities

630   Insurance

631   Life Insurance

632   Accident and Health Insurance; Hospital and Medical Service Plans

633   Fire, Marine and Casualty Insurance

635   Surety Companies

636   Title Insurance

637   Pension, Health and Welfare Funds

639   Insurance Carriers Not Elsewhere Specified

640   Insurance Agents, Brokers and Service

641   Insurance Agents, Brokers and Service

650   Real Estate

651   Operators of Non-Residential Buildings, Dwellings and Residential Mobile Home Sites; Lessors of Railway Property and Real Property Not Elsewhere Specified

653   Property Agents, Brokers and Managers

654   House and Estate Agents

655   Real Estate (including Cemetery) Subdividers and Developers

660   Combination of Real Estate, Insurance, Loans, Law Offices

661   Combination of Real Estate, Insurance, Loans, Law Offices

670   Holding and Other Investment Offices

671   Holding Companies

672   Management Investment Companies, Unit Investment Trusts, Face-Amount Certificate Companies

673   Trusts

679   Oil Royalty Companies; Commodity Trading Companies; Patent Owners and Lessors; Investors Not Elsewhere Specified

700   Services

700   *Hotels, Guest Houses, Camps and Other Lodgings*

701   Hotels, Motels and Tourist Courts

702   Guest Houses and Boarding Houses

703   Sporting and Recreational Camps; Trailer Parks, Camp and Caravan Sites

704   Organisation Hotels and Lodging Houses on Membership Basis

720   *Personal Services*

721   Laundry, Dry Cleaning and Garment Services

722   Photographic Studios, Portrait

723   Beauty Shops

724   Hairdressers

725   Shoe Repair Shops

726   Funeral Service and Crematoria

729   Miscellaneous Personal Services

730   *Business Services*

731   Advertising and Advertising Representatives

732   Consumer Credit Reporting Agencies, and Adjustment and Collection Agencies

733   Direct Mail; Reproduction and Stenographic Services; Commercial Photography, Art and Graphics

734   Window and Building Cleaning; Disinfecting, Exterminating and Maintenance Services

735   News Syndicates

736   Personnel Supply Services

737   Computer Software Services; Data Processing Services; Computer Related Services Not Elsewhere Specified

739   Research and Development, and Commercial Testing Laboratories; Detective Agencies and Protective Services; Business Services Not Elsewhere Specified

750   *Automotive Repair, Services and Garages*

751   Car, Truck, Utility Trailer and Recreational Vehicle Rental; Car and Truck Leasing

752   Car Parks

753 Automotive Repair and Paint Shops

754 Car Washes and Automotive Services, Except Repair

760 *Miscellaneous Repair Services*

762 Electrical and Electronic Repair and Service Shops

763 Watch, Clock and Jewellery Repair

764 Reupholstery and Furniture Repair

769 Repair Shops and Related Services Not Elsewhere Specified

780 *Motion Pictures*

781 Motion Picture and Tape Production, and Allied Services

782 Motion Picture Film and Tape Distribution, and Allied Services

783 Cinemas and Theatres

790 *Amusement and Recreation Services, Excluding Cinemas*

791 Dance Halls, Studios and Schools

792 Theatrical Producers and Miscellaneous Theatrical Services; Bands, Orchestras, Actors and Other Entertainers

793 Billiard and Pool Establishments; Bowling Alleys

794 Professional Sports Clubs and Promoters; Racing and Track Operation

799 Amusement and Recreational Services and Clubs Not Elsewhere Specified

800 *Health Services*

801 Doctors

802 Dentists

803 Osteopaths

804 Chiropodists, Opticians and Health Practitioners Not Elsewhere Specified

805 Nursing and Personal Care Facilities Not Elsewhere Specified

806 Hospitals

807 Medical and Dental Laboratories

808 Outpatient Care Facilities

809 Health and Allied Services Not Elsewhere Specified

810 *Legal Services*

811 Legal Services

820 *Educational Services*

821 Elementary and Secondary Schools

822 Colleges, Universities, Professional Schools, Junior Colleges and Technical Institutes

823 Libraries and Information Centres

824	Correspondence and Vocational Schools (Except Vocational High Schools) Not Elsewhere Specified
829	Schools and Educational Services Not Elsewhere Specified
830	*Social Services*
832	Individual and Family Social Services
833	Job Training and Vocational Rehabilitation Services
835	Child Day Care Services
836	Residential Care
839	Social Services, Not Elsewhere Specified
840	*Museums, Art Galleries, Botanical and Zoological Gardens*
841	Museums and Art Galleries
842	Arboreta, Botanical, and Zoological Gardens
860	*Membership Organisations*
861	Business Associations
862	Professional Membership Organisations
863	Trade Unions and Similar Trade Organisations
864	Civic, Social and Fraternal Associations
865	Political Organisations
866	Religious Organisations
869	Non-Profit Membership Organisations Not Elsewhere Specified
880	*Private Households*
881	Private Households
890	*Miscellaneous Services*
891	Engineering, Architectural and Surveying Services
892	Non-Commercial Educational, Scientific and Research Organisations
893	Accounting, Auditing and Book-Keeping Services
899	Services, Not Elsewhere Specified

910	**Public Administration**
910	*Executive, Legislative, General Government, Excluding Finance*
911	Executive Offices
912	Legislative Bodies
920	*Justice, Public Order and Safety*
921	Courts
922	Police, Enforcement, Correctional Institutions and Fire Protection
930	*Public Finance, Taxation, and Monetary Policy*

931 Public Finance, Taxation, and Monetary Policy
950 *Administration of Environmental Quality and Housing Programmes*
951 Air, Water Resource and Solid Waste Management
970 *National Security and International Affairs*
971 National Security
972 International Affairs
990 *Unclassified Establishments*
999 Unclassified Establishments

Appendix 3: Postcode Areas of the United Kingdom

Source: Royal Mail.

AB	Aberdeen	DN	Doncaster, South Yorkshire
AL	St Albans, Hertfordshire	DT	Dorchester, Dorset
B	Birmingham	DY	Dudley, West Midlands
BA	Bath	E	London E
BB	Blackburn	EC	London EC
BD	Bradford, West Yorkshire	EH	Edinburgh
BH	Bournemouth	EN	Enfield, Middlesex
BL	Bolton	EX	Exeter
BN	Brighton	FK	Falkirk
BR	Bromley	FY	Blackpool
BS	Bristol	G	Glasgow
BT	Belfast	GL	Gloucester
CA	Carlisle	GU	Guildford, Surrey
CB	Cambridge	HA	Harrow, Middlesex
CF	Cardiff	HD	Huddersfield
CH	Chester	HG	Harrogate, North Yorkshire
CM	Chelmsford	HP	Hemel Hempstead, Herts.
CO	Colchester	HR	Hereford
CR	Croydon	HU	Hull
CT	Canterbury, Kent	HX	Halifax, West Yorkshire
CV	Coventry	IG	Ilford, Essex
CW	Crewe	IP	Ipswich
DA	Dartford	IV	Inverness
DD	Dundee	KA	Kilmarnock, Ayrshire
DE	Derby	KT	Kingston-upon-Thames, Surrey
DG	Dumfries		
DH	Durham	KW	Kirkwall, Orkney
DL	Darlington	KY	Kirkcaldy, Fife

L	Liverpool	SG	Stevenage, Hertfordshire
LA	Lancaster	SK	Stockport, Cheshire
LD	Llandrindod Wells, Powys	SL	Slough
LE	Leicester	SM	Sutton, Surrey
LL	Llandudno, Gwynedd	SN	Swindon
LN	Lincoln	SO	Southampton
LS	Leeds	SP	Salisbury
LU	Luton	SR	Sunderland
M	Manchester	SS	Southend-on-Sea
ME	Medway	ST	Stoke-on-Trent
MK	Milton Keynes	SW	London SW
ML	Motherwell, Lanarkshire	SY	Shrewsbury
N	London N	TA	Taunton
NE	Newcastle-upon-Tyne	TD	Galashiels, Selkirkshire
NG	Nottingham	TF	Telford, Shropshire
NN	Northampton	TN	Tonbridge, Kent
NP	Newport, Gwent	TQ	Torquay
NR	Norwich	TR	Truro, Cornwall
NW	London NW	TS	Cleveland
OL	Oldham	TW	Twickenham
OX	Oxford	UB	Southall, Middlesex
PA	Paisley, Renfrewshire	W	London W
PE	Peterborough	WA	Warrington
PH	Perth	WC	London WC
PL	Plymouth	WD	Watford
PO	Portsmouth	WF	Wakefield, West Yorkshire
PR	Preston	WN	Wigan, Lancashire
RG	Reading	WR	Worcester
RH	Redhill	WS	Walsall
RM	Romford	WV	Wolverhampton
S	Sheffield	YO	York
SA	Swansea	ZE	Lerwick, Shetland
SE	London SE		

There are 120 postcode areas. The Isle of Man and the Channel Islands are separate Postal Authorities.

Index

ACORN household classification 56–7
advantages *see* features, advantages, benefits
Ansoff matrix 130–1, 147–8
attributes 85

beer market segmentation 8
benefits 76, 90–3
  company 91
  differential 91–2
  listing 76, 92–3
  standard 91
bolt-on segmentation 13
  see also segmentation archetypes
Boston Consulting Group 104–5, 143
Boston matrix 104–5
Bottoms Up segmentation 4–6
business classification *see* Standard Industrial Classification
business market segmentation, standard approaches 49–54
  demographic 49–53
  geographic 54
  psychographic 54
buyers and specifiers 44–5

'cash cows' 104, 105, 135
'cash dogs' 136
channels *see* where it is bought
Chief Executive, role of 158–9, 162–3, 167
clustering 95–8
  example, manual 96–8
  routines, optional 95–6
  segment size, minimum level 94
  segments, manageable number 94
company competitiveness 119–23
  critical success factors (CSF) 119–21
  definition 119
  portfolio matrix, position on 123
  scoring, company and competitors 121–3

weighting factors 121
company size 159–62, 165
competitive strategies 137, 140, 142–5
consumer market segmentation, standard approaches 54–9
  demographic 54–6
  geodemographic 56–7
  geographic 56
  psychographic 57–9
corporate/company objectives 128–30, 132
corporate planning, integration with segmentation 166
corporate strategies 130, 132
critical purchase influences (CPI) 69, 85–7, 88–9
  attaching, with values, to micro-segments 88–9
  market CPIs 87
  splitting into buying criteria or attitude 87
critical success factors (CSF) 119–21

definitions, full list 17, 20–4
demographic segmentation
  business 49–53
  consumer 54–6
directional policy matrix (DPM) 103, 107, 125
diversity of companies 159–62, 165
'dogs' 104, 105, 136–7

experience effect 142–4

features, advantages, benefits 60, 90–3
features of products/services *see* what is bought
Fertiliser Manufacturers Association, the (UK) 187
final users in market maps *see* market map construction

gap analysis, needs 78–80
  car manufacturing 78–9
  photocopiers 79–80
gap analysis, revenue 145–50
General Electric, GE/McKinsey
    matrix 105–6
geodemographic segmentation 56–7
geographic segmentation
  business 54
  consumer 56
Goldthorpe, J. H. *et al.* 229
Gubar, G. and Wells, W. D. 231

Haley, R. 6
how it is bought 63

ICIF segmentation
  process, key stages 191–2
  seven segment portfolio 194
  seven segment strategy (1990–93) 208
  seven segment summary 192–3
  traditional 191

Jenkins M. and McDonald M. H. B. 12
junctions (on market maps) 33–4
  coding company/customer types 35,
    36, 40, 41
  market leverage points 38, 39–42
  which to segment 38–9

lapsed users, as preliminary segments 46
learning curve *see* experience effect
leverage points *see* market leverage
    points
Lidstone, J. 81
life cycles, human 231–2
life cycles, segments and products 134–5
line management support 164–5

male psychographic segments 57–8
management information for
    segments 169
market, defining 1–2, 4
  example 2–4
market leverage points 38, 39–42, 46–7
  coding channels/users, leverage and
    non-leverage 40, 42
  groups to segment, identifying 46–7
  junctions to segment, identifying 38–9

market map construction 27–38, 40,
    41–2
  coding company/customer types 35,
    36, 40, 41
  company/customer types at
    junctions 34, 35
  contractors 28–9, 30
  final users 27, 28–9
  influencers 32–3, 34
  junctions 33–4
  leverage points *see* market leverage
    points
  market share 32
  products incorporated into other
    products 30
  purchasing departments 29, 31
  purchasing procedures 30, 31
  starting point, organisational level 28
  table form 35, 36–8
  volume/value 32
market research notes
  attributes, uncovering 85
  CPI values, determining 88–9
  final user requirements 29
  needs, understanding 84
  sample frame, identifying 42
  what, where, when and how, collecting
    data 69
  who buys, collecting descriptive
    information 45
market segment *see* segment
Market Segment Master, The 94
market segmentation *see* segmentation
market share and return on
    investment 1
marketing objectives 127–30, 133, 138–9
  Ansoff matrix 130–1, 147–8
  and corporate/company
    objectives 128–30, 132–3
  setting 130–1, 134–7
  see also competitive strategies, *and* gap
    analysis, revenue
marketing planning, integration with
    segmentation 166
marketing strategies 132–3, 135–7,
    138–9, 150–2
McDonald, M. H. B. 3, 12, 106, 112,
    132, 134, 148, 152
McKinsey, GE/McKinsey matrix 105–6

micro-segments
  attributes, accounting for different   85
  clustering into market segments   95–6
  clustering, manual example   96–8
  CPIs and their values, attaching   88–9
  developing   66–8
  labelling   68, 75
  profile building   69,75
  protecting those with potential   72,
    94–5
  reduction   69–73; purchase category
    importance   69–70; repeated
    items   70–1; superfluous
    items   71–2;
    unattractiveness   72–3
  unmet needs, accounting for   84
  volumes/values, attaching   73–4
mission statement   132, 168–9
Monk, D.   212
MOSAIC profiling   59

needs, uncovering real   76–7
needs, uncovering unmet   77–84
  needs cascade   80–2
  needs gap analysis   78–80
  perceptual mapping   82–4
needs, unmet, including in the
    process   84

occupational classification   229–30,
  233–4
off-licence segmentation   4–6
organisational segmentation   12–13
  see also segmentation archetypes
organisational structure around
    segments   167–8
  see also segmentation archetypes,
    strategic segmentation

perceptual mapping   82–4
  soap market   82–3
  tabloid newspapers   83–4
'personalising' segments   170–1
planning for segmentation   164
Population, Censuses and Surveys, Office
  of (UK)   233
Porter, M. E.   110, 140, 143
  five-forces model   110

portfolio analysis   103–7
  time horizon   108
portfolio matrix
  company position   123, 125; *see also*
    company competitiveness
  four-box   104–5, 106–7
  nine-box   105–6
  segment position   114–17, 123–5; *see*
    also segment attractiveness
  segment size at intersections   124
postcode areas (UK)   267–8
preliminary segments   44–6
  car market example   45
  how many   47–8
  labelling   45, 48
  lapsed users   46
  profiles, building   48–9
  prospects (potential users)   46
price   65, 76–7, 87–8
products, level of descriptive detail   61
prospects (potential users), as preliminary
    segments   46
psychographic segmentation
  business   54
  consumer   57–9
purchase frequency   *see* when it is
    bought
purchase methods   *see* how it is bought
purchase organisation   *see* how it is
    bought

'question marks'   104, 105, 136–7

Registrar-General   233
return on investment and market
    share   1
Royal Mail (UK postcode areas)   267

sagacity segmentation model   55–6
sales-based segmentation   12
  see also segmentation archetypes
SBUs   *see* strategic business units
Schnaars S. P. and Schiffman L. G.   99
segment attractiveness   109–14
  definition   109
  factor parameters   113, 114
  factor weighting   112–13
  factors   109–12
  scoring segments   113–14

unexpected results, possible
    reasons 118
segment checklist, criteria, rules 15,
    100–2
segmentation, advantages 15–16
segmentation archetypes 11–14
    bolt on 13
    organisational 12–13
    sales-based 12
    strategic 13–14
segmentation case histories 4–8
    beer market 8
    national off-licence chain 4–6
    toothpaste 6–7
segmentation definition and
    purpose 10–11
segmentation, ICIF *see* ICIF
    segmentation
segmentation, integration with marketing
    planning and corporate
    planning 166
segmentation, junctions to include 38–9
segmentation, organisational levels
    for 14, 28
segmentation process, for leverage and
    non-leverage groups 46–7
segmentation process summary 16–17,
    18–19
segmentation team 14–15, 108, 166–7
segments, manageable number 94
segments, prioritising and selecting,
    summary 19
    see also company competitiveness, *and*
        segment attractiveness
senior management, role of 158–9,
    162–3
services, level of descriptive detail 61
Shell, A. 171
social classes, Registrar-General's 233–4
social grades
    and occupations 212–23
    by occupations under
        industries 223–9
    summary 55

sodium tri-poly phosphate
    segmentation 6–7
specifiers and buyers 44–5
Standard Industrial Classification
    (SIC) 49–53, 235–66
    segmentation, concerns as basis
        for 9–10
    UK detail 235–49
    UK summary 49–51
    USA detail 250–66
    USA summary 51–3
'stars' 104, 105, 136
strategic business units (SBUs) 27–8, 90
    extending the process to all 90
strategic segmentation 13–14
    see also segmentation archetypes

tactical support for segments 170
television regions (UK) 56
Thornton, J. 6
time horizon *see* portfolio analysis
toothpaste segmentation 6–7

Wells, W. D. 58
what is bought 60–2
    features to include 61–2
what, where, when and how lists 66–7
    complexity, reducing 63–4
    correlated variables, combining 67
    ranking by importance 69–70, 85–6
when it is bought 63
where it is bought 62–3
who buys 44–9
why is it bought 76–88
    attributes 85
    critical purchase influences (CPI) 69,
        85–7, 88–9
    features, advantages and
        benefits 90–3
    needs, real and unmet 76–84
    price, role of 87–8
    ranking requirements 85–6

'wildcat' *see* 'question mark'